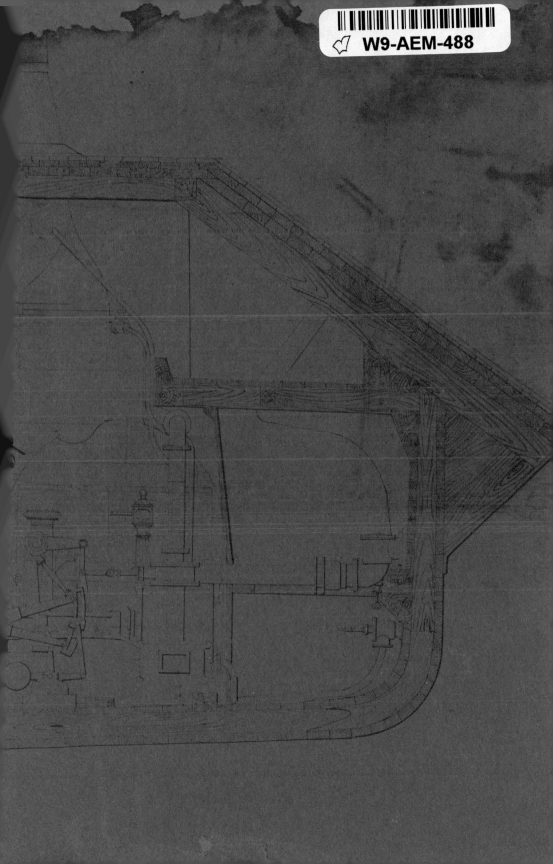

IRON
AFLOAT

IRON
AFLOAT

IRON AFLOAT

The Story of the
Confederate Armorclads

WILLIAM N. STILL JR.

Vanderbilt University Press
1971

Copyright © 1971
Vanderbilt University Press

International Standard Book Number 0-8265-0115-9

Library of Congress Catalogue
Card Number 78–124115

Composed by Service Typographers, Inc.
Indianapolis, Indiana

Printed and bound in the United States of America

Copyright © 1971
Vanderbilt University Press

International Standard Book Number 0–8265–1161–9

Library of Congress Catalogue
Card number 78–124116

12-17-71

Composed by Service Typographers, Inc.
Indianapolis, Indiana

Printed and bound in the United States of America

FOR MILDRED

FOR MILDRED

Acknowledgments

I AM indebted to many individuals and institutions for aid in the preparation of this manuscript. I wish especially to express my appreciation to Professor Robert E. Johnson of the University of Alabama for his encouragement and help; my former colleagues Thomas H. Baker and Charles Edmondson for reading the manuscript and making valuable suggestions; Mrs. Richard W. Lucht of East Carolina University for invaluable editorial assistance; William E. Geoghegan, Museum Specialist of the Smithsonian Institution, for suggestions concerning the technical aspects of Confederate ships and shipbuilding, as well as providing a number of drawings of Confederate ironclads. I also wish to express my gratitude to the Smithsonian Institution for allowing me to include several of these drawings in the book. My colleague John C. Atkeson drew the maps and reproduced many of the drawings. I am most grateful to him for this. Much of the research was done through the generous financial assistance of Mississippi State College for Women. My wife Mildred accompanied me on many research trips and aided me in innumerable ways in completing the manuscript. Without her endeavors, encouragement, and understanding this volume would not have been possible.

William N. Still Jr.

Contents

List of Illustrations

IRON
AFLOAT

Prologue

As THE capital and heart of a nation at war, the city of Richmond resembled an armed camp in 1861. Soldiers thronged the walks along Main and Bank streets. More were arriving daily from the Carolinas and the Gulf states to mingle with Virginians, Kentuckians, and Tennesseans. Bivouacs were established in and about the city—the Central Fair Grounds, Richmond College, as well as outlying areas.

Business was still good that first summer of the war. Military equipment, uniforms, and books such as *The Troop's Manual* and *Hardee's Infantry Tactics* were in great demand. Some items, however, particularly those that were imported from Europe before the war, were beginning to disappear from the shelves.

The city was crowded not only with men in uniform but civilians as well. Jefferson Davis's provisional government attracted scores of would-be bureaucrats and office-holders, while the steady influx of travelers and refugees from border states, coastal areas, and the North further swelled the population. By July the normal population of 40,000 had nearly tripled.

Hotel accommodations were simply not available. The Exchange, the American, and the elegant Spotswood, where the President had a suite, were full: even parlors, halls, and billiard rooms were occupied in the Spotswood.

In the center of the city stood Capitol Square, "a large, iron-fenced space, beautifully undulating and with walks winding under grand old trees." Around the green hill of the square—dominated by the Grecian-columned state capitol designed by Thomas Jefferson—the new government had established its offices and bureaus. The old United States Customs House was the new Treasury Building. The Treasury Department occupied the first floor, the President and State Department the second and third. Nearby was the Mechanics Institute, an ungainly pile of bricks formerly used as a library and lecture hall. Here other departments, including War and Navy, were housed.

On July 11, carpenters were still converting the Institute into a government building. Despite the hammering and other somewhat chaotic activities, both the military and naval departments were hard at work. News of a battle was expected hourly. Union General Irving McDowell had crossed with an army into Virginia, and Confederate forces under Generals P. G. T. Beauregard and Joseph E. Johnston were watching and waiting. President Jefferson Davis had just received a communication from Beauregard, darkly pessimistic because of the strength of the forces under his command. Five days later McDowell moved on Manassas.

An important conference was scheduled for July 11 in the offices of the Navy Department. Secretary of the Navy Stephen R. Mallory had called in three members of his staff for a final decision on the *Merrimack,* a warship partially destroyed and burned when Union forces evacuated the navy yard in Norfolk a few weeks before. At the end of the meeting, Mallory wrote out an order to Flag Officer French Forrest, commandant of the Gosport Navy Yard, Norfolk, and handed it to one of the officers present. The order read, "You will proceed with all practicable dispatch to make the changes in the *Merrimac* . . . according to the design and plans of the constructor and engineer, Messrs. Porter and Williamson." This order initiated the construction of ironclad vessels-of-war within the Confederacy.[1]

1. John Mercer Brooke, "The *Virginia* or *Merrimac:* Her Real Projector," *Southern Historical Society Papers,* XIX (1891), 12–13; John W. H. Porter, A Record of Events in Norfolk County, Virginia (Portsmouth, Virginia, 1892), 334.

1

Mallory and the Origin of the Confederate Ironclad Program

THE CONFEDERATE naval secretary's decision to build an armored warship was not particularly surprising. The American Civil War had become a testing ground for new developments in military technology, including ironclads. European maritime powers were well aware of the significance of this technological revolution in naval warfare. By the beginning of the Civil War, England and France possessed ironclads, and other European nations were considering adding one or more to their fleets. In the United States the importance of the ironclad had been recognized for a number of years. As early as 1842 Congress had made an appropriation for an armored steam vessel. Designed by Robert L. Stevens and laid down at Hoboken, New Jersey, the "Stevens battery" was modified a number of times during construction, abandoned for several years, and was still on the stocks when the Civil War broke out.[1]

Although both the Union and Confederate governments would emphasize the construction of armored vessels during the war, it would be the Confederates who took the first step. It was only natural that the South, lacking both a navy and the potential to keep pace with their opponents in building vessels-of-war, would experiment with new types of ships. Of these, the most successful was the ironclad.

This development, however, was not forseen when the naval committee of the provisional congress met in early February, 1861. At that time the Confederate Congress was concerned primarily with creating a small naval auxiliary force to co-operate with the army. Although President Davis was not "against the navy," as some contemporaries have implied, he certainly had no understanding of the importance of sea power and consistently ignored naval policy. John Newland Maffitt, one of the first naval officers to

---

1. For the Stevens battery, see Archibald D. Turnball, *John Stevens: An American Record* (New York: 1928); James P. Baxter, III, *The Introduction of the Ironclad Warship,* 48–52, 211–219. The standard monograph on the development of the armored warship is Baxter, *Ironclad Warship.*

resign his commission to go South, wrote in his journal after an interview with Davis that he "was not impressed with the necessity of building ships."[2] Nevertheless, a Navy Department was formally established, and on February 21, 1861, Mallory was appointed as secretary of the Confederate States Navy.

The naval secretary was born on the island of Trinidad in 1813, the son of a civil engineer from Reading, Connecticut, and of an Irish mother. After spending most of his boyhood years in Key West, Florida, he served as inspector and collector of customs, studied law, fought as a volunteer in the Seminole War, and became a United States Senator from Florida in 1851. Although not in favor of secession, he resigned his seat and followed his state in 1861.

Mallory was as well qualified as most appointees to Confederate Cabinet positions. He had a certain amount of administrative ability, and as chairman of the United States Naval Affairs Committee, he had gained a limited knowledge of naval affairs. In spite of the fact that he remained in the cabinet throughout the war, he was unpopular with the press, the public, and a large number of naval officers. In view of the many naval disasters during the war, this unpopularity is understandable.[3]

There was no chief of naval operations or its equivalent in the Confederate States Navy and no Gustavus Fox to consult on technical, tactical, and strategic matters.[4] Davis allowed Mallory to run the department without interference. The naval secretary, however, leaned heavily upon various officers and key members of his staff for advice. In many cases the counsel was sound—as in the decisions to build ironclads and to utilize mine warfare—but in other cases conflicting recommendations produced confusion and divided responsibility.

Although Mallory unquestionably had a keen mind, his physical appearance was unimpressive. With his round face and ruddy complexion, he certainly was not handsome, and one newspaper reporter portrayed him as a "stumpy, 'roly-poly' little fellow . . . for all the world like one of the squat 'gentleman farmers' you find in the south of England." According to John B. Jones, a secretary in the War Department, the naval secretary was fond

2. Emma M. Maffitt, *The Life and Services of John Newland Maffitt*, 221.
3. The standard biography of Mallory is Joseph T. Durkin, *Stephen R. Mallory: Confederate Navy Chief*. See also Philip Melvin, "Stephen Russell Mallory, Naval Statesman," *Journal of Southern History*, X (1944), 137–160.
4. Gustavus Fox was Union Secretary of the Navy Gideon Welles' assistant secretary. Fox was a regular officer in the navy for many years before resigning to become a businessman. His knowledge of naval affairs was extremely valuable to Welles.

of good living. Jones recorded in his diary on one occasion, "I saw a note of invitation to-day from Secretary Mallory to Secretary Seddon, inviting him to his house at 5 P.M. to partake of 'pea-soup' with Secretary Trenholm. His 'pea-soup' will be oysters and champagne, and every other delicacy relished by epicures. Mr. Mallory's red face, and his plethoric body, indicate the highest living."

When Mallory was appointed to the Confederate cabinet, he found that he was a naval secretary without a navy. Of the ninety ships in the United States Navy at the time of President Lincoln's inauguration, only one fell into the hands of Southerners, and that was the *Fulton,* an old side-wheeler built in 1837 and laid up at Pensacola. To this the South added four captured revenue cutters, three commandeered slavers, and, by purchase, two small privately-owned steamers. Thus, by February 1861 the Confederate States Navy had a nucleus of ten vessels carrying fifteen guns. Further expansion came with the subsequent incorporation of several state navies and the seizure of the Norfolk navy yard.[5] Naval officers from Southern states in command of United States naval vessels to a man refused to turn their vessels over to Confederate authorities when their states seceded. John N. Maffitt, commanding the *Crusader* in Mobile Bay, was ordered to surrender her to the Alabama navy. He replied, "I may be overpowered . . . but, in that event, what will be left of the *Crusader* will not be worth taking."[6]

The lack of ships was not yet the most pressing problem to Mallory, nor would it be until the Fort Sumter crisis and the actual outbreak of hostilities. For the moment, he was more concerned with organizing his department and finding assignments for the officers who were leaving the United States Navy to follow their states.

The organization of the Confederate Navy Department was similar to that of the United States Navy since 1842. Under the secretary (a political appointee by the President) there were four bureaus: Order and Detail, Provisions and Clothing, Medicine and Surgery, and Ordnance and Hydrography. Mallory appointed the bureau heads.[7]

The Bureau of Orders and Detail—the equivalent of the present Bureau

5. J. Thomas Scharf, *History of the Confederate States Navy,* 24–25; James R. Soley, "The Union and Confederate Navies," in Robert U. Johnson and Clarence C. Buel (eds.), *Battles and Leaders of the Civil War,* 4 vols., I, 624–25; hereinafter cited as *Battles and Leaders.*

6. Maffitt, *John Newland Maffitt,* 216.

7. There were five in the United States Navy. They were the same except there was no Bureau of Orders and Detail in the U. S. Navy, and the Confederate Navy did not have a Bureau of Yards and Docks, or a Bureau of Construction, Equipment and Repair.

of Personnel—handled all matters concerning naval personnel, both officers and enlisted men. It filled ship complements, assigned officers to ship and shore duty, determined ranks and promotions, administered courts martial and courts of inquiry, and directed the recruiting service. Lawrence Rousseau of Louisiana, the oldest of the captains who resigned from the United States Navy, was the first officer appointed to head this office.

Three officers were in charge of the Bureau of Ordnance and Hydrography during the war. Duncan M. Ingraham was the first, but shortly after Virginia entered the Confederacy he relinquished his duties to George Minor who was subsequently replaced by John M. Brooke in March 1863. The accomplishments of this office were impressive. Under the capable leadership of Minor and Brooke, facilities for the manufacture of guns, powder, and ordnance stores such as shot, shell, fuses, and caps, were established, and by late 1862 the navy was able to arm its vessels adequately. In fact, Tredegar, the Bellona Iron Works in Richmond, and the Selma, Alabama, Naval Works produced enough guns to supply the army, too. Selma alone cast nearly two hundred guns between July 1863 and December 1864.[8]

In the United States Navy all naval yards came under the Bureau of Yards and Docks, and ship construction was the responsibility of the Bureau of Construction, Equipment, and Repair. The senior naval officer in charge of the latter bureau was responsible for initiating the navy's shipbuilding program as envisioned by the secretary of the navy and approved by Congress. In the Confederate Navy Department there was no bureau of construction, equipment, and repair, bureau of docks, or their equivalent. Instead, the Confederate naval secretary directly controlled the navy's shipbuilding program throughout the war. In 1862 semiautonomous positions were created to handle specific aspects of the program; William P. Williamson was appointed engineer-in-chief, and John L. Porter was appointed chief naval constructor. These positions were basically administrative, with Mallory continuing to initiate ship construction. The details of construction and the supervision of the program in the various private and public yards were left to Porter and to the constructors under him.

Mallory followed three plans in his shipbuilding program: construction of ships in navy yards under direct supervision of the department; authorization of departmental agents to supervise the building of vessels; contract with private yards for Confederate vessels. A large majority of the vessels constructed, or at least laid down, in the Confederacy were built by contract.

8. William N. Still, Jr., "Selma and the Confederate States Navy," *Alabama Review*, XIV (1962), 29.

This does not reflect necessity as some writers have emphasized, but was the prevailing economic philosophy of the Confederacy. The Confederate government was not generally interested in developing shipbuilding or other industries of its own. On the contrary, it tried several means of encouraging private industry, including bonuses, subsidization of new industries, and advancing money. The government did attempt to regulate profits, labor, and transportation in private industry including shipbuilding. In a few instances ships under construction were taken over completely by the department, but in most cases naval officers were ordered to assist the contractors in fulfilling their obligations.[9]

The provisional congress not only provided for a navy of sorts in February 1861 but immediately sent telegrams to officers from Southern states appealing for their services. Commander Raphael Semmes, Captain Victor Randolph, and others submitted resignations to Union Secretary of the Navy Gideon Welles and left for the South. Others waited, however, hoping that the Union would be preserved. Still, the supply of commissioned officers surpassed the demand, since the embryonic Confederate Navy possessed only a few small vessels. The acquisition of more ships would, of course, create additional billets.

On March 15, four days after the adoption of the provisional constitution, Congress authorized the construction or purchase of ten gunboats for coastal defense. Two days later three naval officers were sent to New Orleans to obtain the authorized vessels. The *Sumter* and *McRae* were the first steamers fitted out under this act, and by July the others were either in conversion or under construction.[10]

In March the department obtained its first yard at Pensacola when Congress formally instructed the states to relinquish to the Confederate government the forts, arsenals, navy yards, and other property once belonging to the United States. Yet this yard was of little immediate consequence to the navy since its prewar status was that of a repair station.

At 4:30 A.M., April 12, a mortar shell burst over Fort Sumter in Charleston harbor—the opening shot of the Civil War. Within a week Lincoln had called for 75,000 militia from the states and proclaimed a blockade of Southern ports; thus the creation of a full-fledged Confederate Navy became a matter of urgent necessity. Fortunately, Virginia's entry into the Confederacy provided the Navy Department with the seized Gosport Navy

9. William N. Still, Jr., "Facilities for the Construction of War Vessels in the Confederacy," *Journal of Southern History*, XXXI (1965), 290–291.

10. *Official Records of the Union and Confederate Navies in the War of the Rebellion*, Ser. II, Vol. II, 76, hereinafter cited as *Official Records, Navies*.

Yard at Norfolk, one of the best equipped in the United States. The Confederates thereby obtained a number of miscellaneous naval craft and more than a thousand guns of all caliber, including fifty-two Dahlgrens, but the only important capital ship in the yard was the frigate *Merrimack,* a 3200-ton screw steamer built in Boston seven years before the war. On April 20 when the yard was evacuated and partially destroyed by Union forces, nine vessels were set afire, and four of these, including the *Merrimack,* were also scuttled.

By May the organization of the Navy Department was well underway. Most of the available officers were already assigned to some sort of work, but there were still few commissioned ships-of-war. Attempts to purchase suitable vessels were not very successful. Mallory emphasized the difficulties in this when he reported on April 26 that

Steam vessels which can be most advantageously employed . . . have been actively sought for, but they are very rarely found. . . . Side-wheel steamers, from the exposure of their machinery to shot and shell . . . and [the fact] that they cannot carry to sea sufficient coal for any but short cruises, are regarded as unfit for cruising men of war.[11]

Naval officers were sent to seaports throughout the Confederacy, along the eastern seaboard of the United States, and even to Canada, but only a few ships in the South were obtained. On May 9, Lieutenant James D. Bulloch, CSN, was ordered to England to purchase or have built six steamers. The next day the Secretary of the Navy wrote to the chairman of the House Committee on Naval Affairs:

I regard the possession of an iron-armored ship as a matter of the first necessity. . . . If we . . . follow their [the United States Navy] . . . example and build wooden ships, we shall have to construct several at one time; for one or two ships would fall an easy prey to her comparatively numerous steam frigates. But inequality of numbers may be compensated by invulnerability; and thus not only does economy but naval success dictate the wisdom and expediency of fighting with iron against wood, without regard to first cost.[12]

This letter concluded with the recommendation that funds be appropriated to purchase ironclad vessels in Europe.

The significance of this communication is obvious. For the first time Mallory strongly urged the Confederate government to emphasize armored ships in its naval program. He also outlined several important points to the committee:

11. *Ibid.,* 52.
12. *Ibid.,* 67–69.

—that the South did not yet have the facilities to build an ironclad frigate "able to traverse the entire coast of the United States . . . and encounter with a fair prospect of success . . . [the Union] navy."

—that the South could not possibly challenge the Union Navy by constructing wooden vessels—again, shipbuilding facilities were not available.

—therefore, armored ships should be purchased in Europe. Congress evidently agreed with the logic and urgency of this proposal, for that same day $2,000,000 was allotted for this purpose.

It is not clear when Mallory originally gave serious consideration to the acquisition of armored vessels. In all probability, he was referring to ironclads when he wrote on April 26: "I propose to adopt a class of vessels hitherto unknown to naval service. The perfection of a warship would doubtless be a combination of the greatest known ocean speed with the greatest known floating battery and power of resistance. . . ."[13]

In any case, there is considerable evidence that a number of individuals, including naval officers, had already encouraged him to purchase or build ironclads. On February 2 Congressman William P. Chilton of Alabama introduced a resolution "that the Committee on Naval Affairs be instructed to inquire into the propriety of constructing by this Government of two iron-plated frigates and such iron-plated gunboats as may be necessary to protect the commerce and provide the safety of this Confederacy." E. C. Murray, builder of the ironclad *Louisiana,* later testified before a congressional committee that he went to Montgomery and submitted a plan for an armored vessel to the Navy Department in April. On May 6, Lieutenant John M. Brooke, formerly of the U.S. Navy and at that time a member of General Robert E. Lee's staff (Lee was in command of Virginia's military forces, including her navy, before they became a part of the Confederate service), wrote a letter to Mallory urging the purchase of an iron-plated ship in Europe. Jones recorded in his diary shortly after this, "I have heard [Mallory] . . . soundly abused for not accepting some propositions . . . to build ironclad steam rams. . . ."[14]

The secretary had already appraised the possibility of constructing an ironclad steamer in the Confederacy, but the initial investigations were disappointing. On May 4 a telegram was sent to Captain Lawrence Rousseau at New Orleans ordering him to determine the availability of wrought-iron

13. *Ibid.,* 51

14. John B. Jones, *A Rebel War Clerk's Diary at the Confederate State Capital,* 21. See also *Journal of the Congress of the Confederate States of America, 1861–65,* 7 vols., I, 90; *Official Records, Navies,* Ser. II, I, 757; George M. Brooke, Jr., "John Mercer Brooke," II, 760.

plates "of any given thickness from two and one-half to five inches. . . ."
Rousseau replied that none could be rolled of that size and thickness. Later
that month, Captain Duncan N. Ingraham was directed to ascertain whether
plates could be manufactured by iron works in Tennessee, Kentucky, or
Georgia. His report was no more encouraging than Rousseau's. The few
iron works in the Confederacy were already under contract with the government and were quite reluctant to undertake expensive conversion of
machinery in order to roll heavy iron plate. The one exception to this was
Tredegar Iron Works in Richmond, which did have the facilities to roll one-
to two-inch plate.

During most of May and June, Mallory unsuccessfully attempted to
procure vessels in Europe, but it was soon evident that no existing ships
could be purchased. The naval agents then sought to locate contractors to
construct the vessels, and eventually they signed contracts for the building
of several armored ships.[15]

In May Congress voted to transfer the capital of the Confederacy from
Montgomery, where it had been meeting since February, to Richmond. The
President arrived in the new capital on May 29, followed in a few days by
his cabinet, Congress, and the remainder of the government. On June 3 the
secretary of the navy and various members of his department arrived and
immediately began work. Late that night the tired Mallory conferred with
Lieutenant Brooke and discussed, among other things, the possibility of
building an ironclad within the Confederacy. Four days later Brooke wrote
his wife that "Mallory wants me to make some calculations in regard to
floating batteries which I shall do today."[16] In later testimony before the
Joint Committee of Congress to Investigate the Navy Department, Brooke
stated,

The Secretary and myself had conversed upon the subject of protecting
ships with ironclading [sic] very frequently, and at last I proposed to him
a plan. That was about early in June, 1861, just after the Secretary came
here from Montgomery.[17]

Brooke was undoubtedly one of the most capable Southern naval officers to follow his state at the outbreak of war. While head of the Bureau of
Ordnance and Hydrography he would later develop the standard gun used

15. For a description of various attempts to obtain these ironclads in Europe see
Herbert H. Todd, *The Building of the Confederate States Navy in Europe;* James D.
Bulloch, *The Secret Service of the Confederate States in Europe,* 2 vols.
16. Quoted in Brooke, "John Mercer Brooke," II, 763.
17. *Official Records, Navies,* Ser. II, I, 783.

by the C.S. Navy. Mallory, fully cognizant of his expertise and versatility, leaned heavily upon his advice. Indeed, there is evidence that Brooke's influence with the naval secretary was not altogether limited to technical matters. During the first year and a half of the war the secretary constantly sought his advice on policy in regard to ironclads.[18]

Early in June Brooke completed "outline drawings—body, sheer, and deck plans" of an ironclad and submitted them to Mallory. The secretary approved and assigned a naval constructor or draftsman to work up the details. When the individual chosen proved to be totally unfit for the work, however, constructor John L. Porter was ordered to report to the Navy Department in Richmond. On June 23, Brooke, constructor Porter, and chief engineer William P. Williamson met with the secretary. Porter brought with him a model of an ironclad ship.

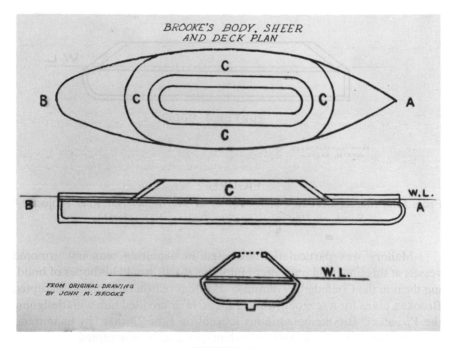

FIGURE 1

From John Mercer Brooke, "The *Virginia* or *Merrimac:* Her Real Projector," *Southern Historical Society Papers,* XIX (1891).

18. Brooke, "John Mercer Brooke," II, 790, 849; Brooke to Warley, January 4, 1863, folder on design of Confederate vessels, Confederate Subject and Area Files, in Record Group 45 (War Records Branch, The National Archives).

During this meeting, both Porter's model and Brooke's drawings were examined. Both featured an inclined casemate or shield, the armored box-like structure above the main deck which housed the guns, but there the similarities ended. Porter's model, as he wrote later, "was intended for harbor defense only, and was of light draft. . . ." Brooke's plans envisioned a ship capable of going to sea. The really significant and unique difference between the two was Brooke's plan for submerging the ends (bow and stern) of the vessel. He later obtained a Confederate patent on this, and Porter never contested it. Each, however, claimed as his own the idea of submerging the eaves of the casemate. According to Brooke, the object of submerging the ends and sides was to gain buoyancy and, surprisingly, speed.[19]

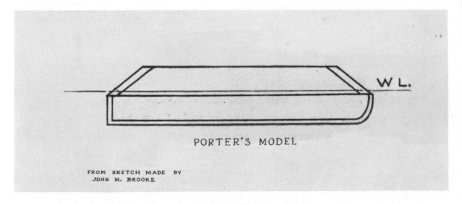

FIGURE 2

From John Mercer Brooke, "The *Virginia* or *Merrimac:* Her Real Projector," *Southern Historical Society Papers,* XIX (1891).

Mallory was particularly interested in acquiring seagoing armored vessels at this time, and only after Hampton Roads would his hopes of building them in the Confederacy diminish. For that reason he probably accepted Brooke's plans for a seagoing ironclad, and later credited him with designing the *Virginia.*[20] Brooke noted in his journal on June 23 that "by unanimous consent" the principle of extended submerged ends was accepted.

19. *Official Records, Navies,* Ser. II, I, 784; see also Brooke, "John Mercer Brooke," II, 842, 771–72. See figures one and two.

20. *Official Records, Navies,* Ser. II, II, 174. In this report Mallory stated that the submerged ends of the ship and the eaves of the casemate were the novel and distinctive features of the *Virginia.*

Although Porter's claim that he designed the *Virginia* is apparently not valid, he did provide the plans and drawings for most of the other armored vessels, and later, as chief naval constructor, he would supervise the entire Confederate shipbuilding program. In the fall of 1861, Porter confided to a friend:

I never was so busy in all my life. I have all the work in the [Gosport] navy yard to direct, and all the duties of the Bureau of Construction. . . . I have all the planning of the various gun boats to do which are being built all over the South. . . . The Secretary refers most of the matter concerning the building of vessels, buying materials, etc. to me. . . .[21]

On June 24, Brooke and Williamson went to Norfolk to find machinery for the proposed ironclad, while Porter completed the necessary drawings. After an exhaustive search revealed no usable engines and boilers, Williamson suggested examining the engines of the partially destroyed *Merrimack*— lying in drydock after being raised from the floor of the anchorage. It was probably during this examination that the chief engineer advocated converting the frigate into an armorclad. Upon their return to Richmond, the two naval officers discussed this possibility with Porter. He agreed that the idea was feasible, and it was then presented to Mallory who quickly gave his approval. On June 28 Brooke noted in his journal, "my plan for a floating battery will be applied to the *Merrimac*. . . ." Between June 28 and July 11, Porter and his assistants prepared the detailed drawings and plans which had to precede the actual work of rebuilding the burned hulk into an ironclad. The final conference, held on July 11, resulted in Mallory's order to Commodore Forrest to begin work immediately on the conversion. Immediately thereafter the naval secretary began thinking in terms of building additional armored vessels, particularly in the West.

Early in the summer of 1861 there appeared disturbing intelligence reports of gunboat construction and other activities in cities along the upper Mississippi and Ohio rivers. Confederate and various state governments became increasingly concerned over the threat of invasion. The Tennessee State Legislature manifested this in a joint resolution of June 24, 1861, emphasizing the lack of defense along the western rivers and asking the Confederate government for an appropriation of $250,000 to remedy this deficiency. Simultaneously the New Orleans *Picayune* and other newspapers were urging the building of a navy on the Mississippi. On July 30, Mallory conferred with a group of his officers about the possible creation of a western

21. John Porter to the Rev. Moore, November 4, 1861, in Miscellaneous Letters File, Confederate Museum, Richmond.

armored fleet capable of opposing an invasion, and going to sea if necessary. Shortly thereafter, John T. Shirley, a prominent Memphis constructor who was concerned over river defenses, proposed to build ironclad gunboats for river service. The proposal with the endorsement of General Leonidas K. Polk, in command of Confederate forces in Tennessee and Kentucky, was carried to the Confederate House of Representatives by David M. Currin, a member of the House Naval Affairs Committee from Memphis. The chairman, of the Committee on Naval Affairs on August 23, 1861, requested additional appropriations for the navy. Representative Currin voiced his support for such action and requested $160,000 "for the construction, equipment, and armament of two ironclad gunboats, for the defense of the Mississippi River and the city of Memphis." The bill and amendment were passed, forwarded to the President, and signed into law the following day. Shirley then received a contract to build the two vessels.[22]

The bill which provided that ironclads be constructed at Memphis also included an appropriation of $800,000 "for floating defenses of New Orleans." Two days after Davis signed the bill, two brothers, Asa and Nelson Tift, arrived in Richmond and conferred with Mallory, an old friend. Although the Tifts had no experience in shipbuilding—Nelson was a Georgia planter, and Asa had been an editor, merchant, president of a railroad, legislator, and owner of a boat repair yard in Key West—they brought with them the model of an ironclad warship designed by Nelson. The projected craft would have neither curves or rounded ends, so that as Nelson said, even house carpenters could build it. Later the Tifts offered to arrange the construction of one or more "such vessels" without compensation except for traveling expense. Mallory accepted their proposal, and on September 1 wrote in his diary, "I have concluded to build a large ship at New Orleans upon Nelson Tift's plan and will push it."[23]

By the end of August, the Confederate naval secretary had authorized the construction of three powerful armored vessels in the West; two weeks later he was negotiating for the building of a fourth. On September 18, E. C. Murray, a Kentuckian and an experienced ship and boat builder, contracted for an ironclad at New Orleans.

It was now clear that Mallory was beginning to concentrate on building

22. *Journal of the Congress of the Confederate States,* I, 396. Currin had earlier introduced a bill to build two ironclads by Shirley's design and it had been referred to the Committee on Naval Affairs. A contract was signed with Shirley on the day that Davis signed the bill.

23. Stephen R. Mallory Diary (Typescript in Southern Historical Collection, University of North Carolina Library, Chapel Hill), 13–14.

armored warships within the Confederacy. While not neglecting other types of vessels, the secretary declared throughout the war that he would "put his faith" in a few powerful ironclads. This policy was indicated in his report to the President:

The judgment of naval men and of other experts in naval construction have . . . been consulted [and] . . . it is believed, enable us with a small number of vessels comparatively to keep our waters free from the enemy and ultimately to contest with them the possession of his own. The two ironclad frigates at New Orleans, the two plated ships at Memphis . . . and the *Virginia* are vessels of this character.[24]

The five ironclads mentioned in this report were all unusually large in contrast to the later "home water" armored vessels and were designed to operate on the open sea as well as inland waters.

By October 1861, construction was well under way, but even as the builders struggled with problems that threatened to delay completion, the first ironclad of the Confederate States Navy attacked an enemy force.

24. *Official Records, Navies*, Ser. II, II, 152.

2

The *Virginia*

THE GOSPORT Navy Yard lay above the cities of Norfolk and Portsmouth on the Portsmouth side of Elizabeth River. For building or repairing ships, the yard contained a dry dock, two large ship houses and a third under construction, sail lofts, rigger's lofts, gunner's lofts, sawmills, timber sheds, spar houses, carpenter shops, foundries, machine shops, boiler shops, and an ordnance store and laboratory.[1]

Captain French Forrest, a "blusterer of the real old-tar school," was the yard commandant. With his immaculate dress, stern countenance, and flowing white hair, he was one of those elderly officers who had resigned their commissions and came south, bringing with them, as Raphael Semmes said, "nothing but their patriotism and their grey hairs." Throughout the war, Forrest constantly sought an active command, and when the secretary wisely denied this—except for a brief period as commanding officer of the James River Squadron—he became embittered toward Mallory.[2] Nor did he approve of the secretary's order to rebuild the recently raised frigate *Merrimack* as an armored ship.

Forrest, however, had only administrative control. The actual conversion of the burnt hulk into an ironclad man-of-war was divided among the three men who had persuaded Mallory that the idea was feasible. Porter would be in charge of the construction, Williamson would overhaul the machinery, and Brooke would remain in Richmond to supervise the preparation of the armor and armament. This division of responsibility resulted in discord, especially between Porter and Brooke. The latter, as a liaison officer, made frequent "visits of inspection" to the drydock where the conversion was taking place. Also, he frequently suggested various alterations and improvements to the secretary and Porter. Although his ideas were usually quite sound, they irritated the constructor, who was probably still smarting

---

1. Richard S. West, Jr., *Mr. Lincoln's Navy*, 30–31.
2. Mallory to Forrest, June 18, 1864, quoted in Charleston *Daily Courier,* July 1, 1864; Simple to Jones, June 16, 1864, in Area file, Confederate Subject and Area Files, National Archives Record Group 45.

from Mallory's preference for Brooke's design.[3] The fact that there were a number of serious weaknesses in the vessel when it finally became operational deepened the animosity between the two.

Mallory was mistaken, as he later recognized, in dividing the responsibility. Much of the trouble between Brooke and Porter could have been avoided if one individual had been given undisputed command of the project. The practice in the United States Navy was to appoint a line officer to supervise such a project, with a naval constructor in charge of actual construction. Only after his troubles in New Orleans and Norfolk did the secretary begin to follow this policy.[4]

The work of cutting away the burnt part of the ship was well under way by the middle of July, despite the absence of funds. On July 18 the naval secretary applied for the requisite money, stating that rebuilding the *Merrimack* as a frigate would require at least $450,000, whereas only $172,-523 would be needed to make her into an ironclad.[5] Obviously ex-Senator Mallory understood the parsimonious nature of a congress. Congress quickly voted the lower figure; and by the end of the month the burned timber had been cleared away, the shield deck had been finished, and construction of the casement or shield was begun.

Meanwhile the problem of obtaining armor continued to occupy Brooke in Richmond. On July 24 Joseph R. Anderson, president of the Tredegar Iron Works, contracted with the Navy Department to produce the "iron work necessary for fitting up the *Merrimac.* . . ." The contract specified rolling iron plates, one inch thick, eight feet long, and of various widths. Tredegar had adequate facilities, and within a week, the first plates were ready for transportation to Norfolk.[6]

3. *Official Records, Navies,* Ser. II, I, 783–784; letter of Porter in Richmond *Examiner,* April 3, 1862; Brooke to Catesby ap R. Jones, July 14, 1874, construction at Norfolk file, Confederate Subject and Area Files, National Archives Record Group 45; Brooke, "The *Virginia* or *Merrimac:* Her Real Projector," 14–15. A majority of Brooke's suggestions were adopted (a. substitution of two-inch plate for one-inch; b. the removal of the overhead of inner planking of the shield, and the application of four inches of oak outside under the iron; c. "The third proposition made by me [Brooke] was to pierce the shield for bow and quarter ports, for you [Porter] had omitted them, leaving four points of approach without fire. . . ." d. changing the wheel ropes from "beneath the plates outside, where they were liable to be jammed by a shot. . . ."). Quotations and suggestions from S. B. Besse, *C. S. Ironclad Virginia, with data and References for a Scale Model,* 17–20.

4. For New Orleans see Chapter III.

5. *Official Records, Navies,* Ser. II, II, 77–79.

6. A clause in the contract called for a naval officer (Brooke) to supervise and inspect the work. Contract quoted in a letter to Mallory from Anderson, July 24, 1861,

They never reached the *Virginia,* however; for tests conducted on Jamestown Island resulted in the decision to armor her with two layers of two-inch plate rather than one-inch.[7] Informed of the test results, Porter noted that the ship could carry additional armor. On September 15, Tredegar was ordered to stop work on one-inch plate and to change over to two-inch plate.[8] Such action was necessary, but it resulted in unfortunate delays. Time was required, of course, to alter the machinery so that two-inch plate could be rolled. Also, the original contract called for the iron to be "punched" for bolts and ready for use, but cold iron two inches thick could not be punched with the tools then available. The only alternative was to drill the plates, and this was slower and more expensive than punching.

From October until February 1862 Tredegar concentrated largely on the *Virginia's* armor: "We are now pressed almost beyond endurance for the heavy iron work to complete one of the war vessels *now ready for operations.* When that is completed we expect to commence on another vessel which will keep us till the end of the year," wrote one of the foundry's owners to a disgruntled railroad customer in October. "It is a most fortunate thing that we could render this assistance to our little Navy. . . ."[9]

As the plates rolled off the lines ready for shipment, the Navy Department requested rail transportation to Norfolk. At this juncture a new difficulty arose. The Army Quartermaster Bureau was responsible for rail shipping, and already it was overwhelmed by the growing logistic problems of the war. There was a serious shortage of engines and cars, and rails were beginning to wear because of heavy traffic in troops and supplies. Early in October, the Richmond and Petersburg Railroad Company was asked to provide transportation for "some 70 to 100 tons of the [*Virginia's*] iron now ready to ship." The railroad could not comply immediately, for flatcars were unavailable.[10] The impact of this was reflected by Porter's estimate that only two of the necessary 1,000 tons of armor plate had reached him in October. Faced with urgent appeals from both the constructor and Mallory, who made several trips to the rolling mill to "encourage the work," Tredegar's president

1861–1862 letterbook, Tredegar Rolling Mill and Foundry Collection, 1861–65 (Virginia State Library, Richmond, Virginia).

7. For these tests see page 97.

8. Anderson to D. N. Ingraham, September 15, 1861, 1861–1862 letterbook, Tredegar Rolling Mill and Foundry Collection.

9. Quoted in Charles B. Dew, *Ironmaker to the Confederacy: Joseph R. Anderson and the Tredegar Iron Works,* 117.

10. Anderson to Forrest, November 5, 7, 9, 19, 22, 23, 1861, 1861–1862 letterbook, Tredegar Rolling Mill and Foundry Collection.

replied that he was forwarding the bow and stern iron as "rapidly as we can get it transported."[11] In order to expedite the shipments, the company began routing some of the plates over the Richmond and Danville Railroad to Burkeville and from there over the Southside Railroad to Petersburg. This eased but did not solve the problem. "We have iron for the Navy Yard that has been lying on the bank for 4 weeks," a member of the company wrote in mid-November. Two weeks later the worried Navy Department arranged for the Petersburg Railroad to carry it to Weldon, North Carolina, where it was transferred to the Seaboard and Roanoke and taken to Norfolk. Although this greatly increased the number of flatcars available to transport the iron, Christmas found the vessel still without her stern armor.[12]

In November, Lieutenant Catesby ap R. Jones was ordered to the *Virginia* as executive officer with instructions to expedite construction, secure and mount the ship's ordnance, assemble a crew, and prepare the ship for sea.[13] It was customary for the executive officer to take charge of outfitting a newly commissioned ship for sea, but this was somewhat premature in November. In all probability, the frequency of delays in construction and the mounting friction between Porter and Brooke prompted Mallory to send Jones so early.

Jones was no newcomer to the vessel, having served as one of her officers before the war. His competency was beyond question. In fact, Admiral David Dixon Porter later remarked that he regretted the loss of only two officers to the Union service, Jones and Brooke. Significantly, both were recognized ordnance experts, and the Confederate success in this area may be attributed largely to them. It is ironic that Jones's knowledge of guns and gunnery prevented his getting what he desired most, command of a warship.[14]

11. Voucher to pay Anderson, November 2, 1861, construction at Norfolk file, Confederate Subject and Area Files, National Archives Record Group 45; Anderson to Forrest, November 7, 1861, 1861–1862 letterbook, Tredegar Rolling Mill and Foundry Collection; Brooke, "John Mercer Brooke," II, 796. Forrest was frequently sending officers to follow the rails until the cars of iron were located, and to expedite their movement immediately. Forrest to Webb, November 21, 1861, French Forrest Papers (Southern Historical Collection, University of North Carolina Library, Chapel Hill).

12. Catesby ap R. Jones, executive officer of the *Virginia,* blamed Tredegar for the plates delay. See Jones to Brooke, n.d. quoted in Brooke, "John Mercer Brooke," II, 808.

13. *Official Records, Navies,* Ser. I, VI, 742; Mallory to Jones, November 11, 1861, Catesby ap R. Jones folder, BZ File (Naval History Division, Department of the Navy, National Archives Building).

14. He did command the gunboat *Chattachoochee* for a brief period while she was fitting out, but from the summer of 1863 until the end of the war he was in charge

Although Jones was responsible for testing and mounting, Brooke actually selected the *Virginia's* battery. Six 9-inch Dahlgren smoothbores, the standard weapon in the U.S. Navy, were to be her broadside guns, while the four bow and stern chasers were to be powerful rifled cannon of a new pattern. Designed by Brooke, these rifles were cast by Tredegar in the fall of 1861. On November 2, he recorded in his journal, "by order of the Secretary I designed two rifled cannon of 7-inch calibre for the *Merrimac*—one of them has been cast and is now nearly bored."[15] Mallory had ordered these two guns on September 21, and their success resulted in the ordering of additional Brooke guns. Two 7-inch and two 6.4-inch Brookes went on board the *Virginia* in addition to the six 9-inch Dahlgrens. The guns were first mounted on temporary carriages and tested in a battery at the Norfolk naval hospital before being hoisted onto the ironclad's gundeck.[16]

Shipping a crew proved to be a problem for Jones, as it would continue to be for the entire navy. The cause of the difficulty was that nearly all of the South's experienced seamen were in the army, which was increasingly reluctant to part with its men. Captain Franklin Buchanan, head of the Office of Orders and Detail, established recruiting offices in Richmond and Norfolk, but there were few enlistments. As late as February 10, Buchanan wrote, "The *Merrimack* has not yet received her crew, notwithstanding all my efforts to procure them from the Army."[17] Eventually two hundred volunteers were recruited from General John B. Magruder's command at Yorktown to fill out her crew.

Conversion should have been completed by the end of November 1861, but she was far from ready at the end of the year. In January 1862, the shipyard workers began working seven days a week trying to complete the vessel. On January 11, blacksmiths, machinists, and bolt-drivers agreed to work until eight o'clock every night without extra pay. In spite of this patriotic zeal, Jones was far from satisfied. He informed Brooke on January 24 that "somebody ought to be hung."[18] His irritation was largely justified, for

---

of the Naval Ordnance Works at Selma, Alabama. He applied for command of the *Tennessee* but was turned down.

15. Quoted in Brooke, "John Mercer Brooke," II, 799.

16. Forrest to Jones, November 23, 1861, Forrest Papers. Jones was unable to test the 7-inch gun properly because of the lack of suitable ammunition. After the battle in Hampton Roads, Mallory wrote Jones a most complimentary letter concerning the *Virginia's* battery, its preparation, and efficiency. See letter of March 13, 1862, Jones Family Collection (Manuscripts Division, Library of Congress).

17. *Official Records, Navies,* Ser. I, VI, 766.

18. Quoted in Brooke, "John Mercer Brooke," II, 811.

although her armor was finished by January 27, the *Virginia* was not launched until seventeen days later. As the vessel approached completion, Jones' impatience grew. On February 20, three days after she was placed in commission, he wrote, "we are living aboard, and are as uncomfortable as possible—there has not been a dry spot aboard of her, leaks everywhere—mechanics are at work at a thousand things which should have been done months ago."[19]

He was particularly upset by the naval constructor's apparent miscalculation in the vessel's displacement which resulted in her riding too high in the water. "The water is now just above the eaves," he informed Brooke on February 25; but he added hopefully, "we have yet to take [on] our powder, and most of the shells, and 150 tons of coal which it is thought will bring it down a foot more. . . ." Ballast was added in an attempt to correct the mistake but this proved to be unsatisfactory.[20] Jones was extremely perturbed over this weakness as late as March 5, two days before she steamed toward the Union fleet in Hampton Roads:

The ship will be too light, or I should say, she is not sufficiently protected below the water. Our draft will be a foot less than was first intended, yet I was this morning ordered not to put any more ballast in fear of the bottom. The eaves of the roof will not be more than six inches immersed, which in smooth water would not be enough; a slight ripple would leave it bare except the one-inch iron that extends some feet below. We are least protected where we most need it. The constructor should have put on six inches where we now have one.[21]

Jones should have commanded the *Virginia,* and he evidently had some hopes of this. Mallory's failure to appoint him captain was, therefore, a severe disappointment. "Having had so much to do with her I was actually oppressed with the undue expectation and confess that I never entirely reconciled myself. . . ." he later told a fellow officer.[22] In fact the *Virginia* went into action without a captain.

19. *Ibid.,* 814. For the *Virginia's* launching see William R. Cline, "The Ironclad Ram *Virginia," Southern Historical Society Papers,* XXXII (1904), 244.

20. According to Porter, "Kentledge [pig] iron on her ends and in her spirit room" was supposed to bring the vessel down to the correct waterline, and did so; but the action on March 8 consumed coal and ammunition to such an extent that she drew much less water. Besse, *Ironclad Virginia,* 14.

21. Quoted in Brooke, "The *Virginia* or *Merrimac:* Her Real Projector," 31. Porter was aware of this mistake but defended it. See Besse, *Ironclad Virginia,* 14.

22. Jones to Johnston, May 10, 1864, Catesby ap R. Jones letterbooks, National Archives Record Group 45. Even before Jones was ordered to the *Virginia* as her executive officer he expressed more than just a passing interest in the vessel: "I consider

Why was the position of captain left vacant? Mallory undoubtedly wanted his most aggressive senior officer to command the vessel and unhesitatingly chose Captain Franklin Buchanan, at that time in charge of the Office of Orders and Detail. At least two men senior to Buchanan—French Forrest and Victor Randolph—had applied unsuccessfully for the command. The secretary strongly opposed the traditional system of determining command by seniority, and he evaded the issue by appointing Buchanan flag officer in command of naval defenses on the James River rather than just captain of the *Virginia*. In that way Buchanan could operate the ironclad without interference from a senior officer.

This seniority system did, however, keep Jones in the subordinate position of executive officer. Buchanan was evidently aware that he would command the *Virginia* sometime before he actually assumed this position, and he personally recommended Jones and the other officers to the ironclad. Nevertheless, there were a number of commanders and lieutenants senior to Jones in service, and as John Taylor Wood, later aide to Jefferson Davis but then a lieutenant on the *Virginia,* wrote, "Jones is not old enough, this is our system."[23]

Buchanan was detached from the Bureau of Orders and Detail on February 24 and assumed the responsibility of completing and outfitting the ironclad the following day. Previously he had made only one hurried trip to Norfolk to acquaint himself with his new command. On February 25 the vessel began taking on coal and ammunition. The ship's bunkers were quickly filled, but nearly two weeks would pass before an adequate supply of powder could be obtained. The army finally agreed to provide powder, and on March 7 the last consignment was stored in the magazines.

The transformed *Merrimack* was two hundred and sixty-two feet, nine inches from stem to stern. The sides of the armored superstructure, or casemate, which was 170 feet long at its base, were at an angle of approximately thirty-six degrees, and both of the casemate's ends were horizontally rounded. The upper deck of the casemate was an iron grating two inches thick in which there were three hatchways closed by pivoted shutters. Conical pilot houses of cast iron were superimposed on each end of the upper deck. The armor, rolled from railroad iron into plates, was attached in two layers, the

---

the *Merrimac* the most important naval affair the country has to deal with and consequently am deeply interested in her success." He wrote this to Lieutenant Robert Minor, September 1861, in the George W. and Robert Minor Papers (Virginia Historical Society, Richmond).

23. To his wife, March 26, 1862, in John Taylor Wood Papers (Duke University Library, Durham, North Carolina).

first course running horizontally, and the second vertically. Fourteen elliptical gun ports were cut into the casemate, four to a side and three to an end.

She had weaknesses as do most experimental ships, the most serious in the case of the *Virginia* being her power plant. Her engines were the same ones that had caused the Union Navy to send the frigate to the yard, and her speed was generally six miles an hour and eight at the maximum. The steerage was so poor that it took from thirty to forty minutes to turn 180 degrees. As one of her officers later recalled, she was as unmanageable as a "water-logged vessel."

The many people who witnessed the memorable events in Hampton Roads on Saturday March 8 and who left their impressions of them, unanimously agreed that the day was unusually beautiful for that time of year—clear and bright, the water calm with only small waves stirred up by a gentle breeze from the northwest.[24] At the navy yard, workmen, as usual, were swarming all over the *Virginia*. For weeks they had been working under tremendous pressure to complete the ironclad; that morning there was extra activity as the ship received last-minute alterations before getting under way for the first time. Most of the workmen assumed that Buchanan would only make a trial run down Elizabeth River in order to test both the machinery and the crew who were in the words of one officer, "strangers to one another and also to the ship."[25] With the exception of the flag officer, his executive officer, and flag lieutenant, no one suspected that "Old Buck" had determined to attack the Federal vessels off Newport News.

Shortly before 11:00 A.M., all workmen and other noncombatants were

24. The most useful accounts of the *Virginia's* engagements on March 8 and 9 are Robert W. Daly, *How the Merrimac Won;* E. B. Potter and Chester W. Nimitz (eds.), *Sea Power: A Naval History*, 262–272; William Tindall, "The True Story of the *Virginia*," *Virginia Magazine of History and Biography*, XXXI (1923), 1–38, 89–145. A large number of the *Virginia's* officers wrote accounts of the battles: John R. Eggleston, "Captain Eggleston's Narrative of the Battle of the *Merrimac*," *Southern Historical Society Papers*, XLI (1916), 166–178; Catesby ap R. Jones, "Services of the *Virginia*," *Southern Historical Society Papers*, XI (1883), 65–75; Virginius Newton, "The *Merrimac* or *Virginia*," *Southern Historical Society Papers*, XX (1892), 1–26; H. Aston Ramsay, "Wonderful Career of the *Merrimac*," *Confederate Veteran*, XXV (1907), 310–313; Arthur Sinclair, "How the *Merrimac* fought the *Monitor*," *Hearst's Magazine*, (1913), 884–894; John Taylor Wood, "The First Fight of Iron-Clads," *Battles and Leaders*, I, 692–711; Dinwiddie B. Phillips, "Notes On the *Monitor-Merrimac* Fight," *Battles and Leaders*, I, 718; H. Aston Ramsay, J. L. Worden, and S. D. Greene, *The Monitor and the Merrimac* (New York, 1912); Virginius Newton, *Merrimac or Virginia* (Richmond, 1907); E. V. White, *The First Iron Clad Naval Engagement in the World* (Privately Printed, 1906).

25. Wood, "The First Fight of Iron-Clads," 696.

ordered ashore. The tide was at halfflood—barely enough water to float the *Virginia's* twenty-two foot draft—but it would continue rising until early afternoon. At 11:00, Buchanan hoisted the red ensign of a flag officer and ordered the lines cast off. As the ironclad moved slowly into the river, thousands of citizens of Norfolk and Portsmouth lined the wharfs, landing, and river bank. This dramatic scene was described by a Confederate soldier on leave in Norfolk:

At 11:00 a gun was fired at the Navy Yard, which appeared to be the signal for something. In an instant the whole city was in an uproar, women, children, men on horseback and on foot running down towards the river from every conceivable direction shouting 'the *Merrimac* is going down. . . .[26]

It took the ponderous ironclad nearly two hours to steam from her docking point to Hampton Roads, a distance of some ten miles. Midway, near Craney Island, she would not answer her helm and had to be towed past the island into deeper water. Even though the crew and most of the officers were still "officially" ignorant of the vessel's objective, they now began to realize that this was no trial run. Shortly after 12:30 the *Virginia,* accompanied by the *Beaufort* and the *Raleigh* of Buchanan's squadron, reached the river's mouth near Sewell's Point. As the Confederates turned into the south channel of the James, they could see clearly the Federal ships anchored off Newport News. Buchanan evidently chose this moment to inform his crew of his intentions. The accounts of his exact words differ, but he told them briefly of his plan and ended with an appeal to duty.

The plan of attack had been worked out several days earlier. Upon the appointment of Buchanan to command the James River Squadron, Mallory had written, "The *Virginia* is a novelty in naval construction, is untried and her power unknown. . . . The Department will not give specific orders as to her attack upon the enemy." Although he refused to give "specific orders," he did suggest that "a dashing cruise on the Potomac as far as Washington, would be well worthwhile." Clearly his principal desire was for "action—prompt and successful action."[27]

More realistic, Buchanan envisioned a joint army-navy operation against Newport News in which the forces of General John B. Magruder would attack down the Yorktown Peninsula, while the naval squadron engaged Federal vessels off the city. "Prince John" initially agreed to this scheme, but by the end of February he had retreated, advising the War

26. James Keenan to Dear——, March 11, 1862, in Miscellaneous Confederate Soldier's Letters (Georgia Department of Archives and History, Atlanta).
27. Official Records, Navies, Ser. I, VI, 776–777.

Department: "I am . . . satisfied that no one ship can produce such an impression upon the troops at Newport News as to cause them to evacuate the fort. . . ." On February 25, he observed, "I think the roads are almost impassable for artillery. . . . I do not think the movement advisable."[28] On March 2, the flag officer was notified that the joint operation was canceled. Ironically, Buchanan sent Magruder the final plans of attack on that same day, declaring his intention "to be off Newport News early on Friday morning next unless some accident occurs to the *Virginia* to prevent it. . . . My plan is to destroy the Frigates first, if possible and then turn my attention to the battery on shore. . . ."[29] Now in the face of the army's refusal to co-operate, Buchanan decided to proceed as planned.

He had hoped originally to slip down to the river's entrance Thursday night and attack at first light, but unfavorable weather delayed the operation for twenty-four hours. Then the idea of moving down the river at night had to be abandoned because of opposition from the pilots. Catesby Jones later declared, "the pilots, of whom there were five, having been previously consulted . . . all preparations were made, including lights at obstructions . . . [but] the pilots claimed that they could not pilot the ship during the night."[30] The delay did enable Buchanan's flag lieutenant to make another reconnaissance, and his report was evidently optimistic. He wrote his wife after returning: "I have great hopes in our success. . . . I reconnoitered the enemy off Newport News and Old Point and was glad to be able to report that they were not in such force as I had been led to suppose."

Hampton Roads is the body of water where the James, Elizabeth, and Nansemond Rivers converge and flow into Chesapeake Bay. It is approximately six miles at its widest point and has been described as a sort of "natural naval amphitheater." Thousands of Union and Confederate soldiers as well as civilians therefore had the unique opportunity on March 8 and 9 to witness one of the most spectacular naval battles in American history. The north shore was held by Federal forces—Fortress Monroe on Old Point Comfort and Newport News to the west. Confederate troops were in control of the south bank.

Union naval forces in Hampton Roads were under the command of

28. *The War of the Rebellion: A Compilation of the Official Records of the Union and Confederate Armies* (Washington, 1880–1901), Ser. I, Vol. LI, pt. 2, 480.
29. Franklin Buchanan Letterbook 1861–63 (Southern Historical Collection, University of North Carolina Library, Chapel Hill); see also Robert Minor to wife, March 5, 1862, Minor Papers, and Jones, "Services of the *Virginia*," 67. For a detailed analysis of Buchanan's plan of operation see Daly, *How the Merrimac Won, Passim.*
30. Jones, "Services of the *Virginia*," 67–68.

Louis M. Goldsborough, flag officer, Atlantic Blockading Squadron. Of immense size (estimates run from 300 pounds up) and stubborn, he possessed "manners somewhat rough, so that he would almost frighten a subordinate out of his wits."[31] Many naval officers on both sides remembered Goldsborough for his classic remark when a group of middies set fire to his backyard privy while he was superintendent of the naval academy. He allegedly roared, "I'll hang them! yes, I'll hang them! So help me God, I will."

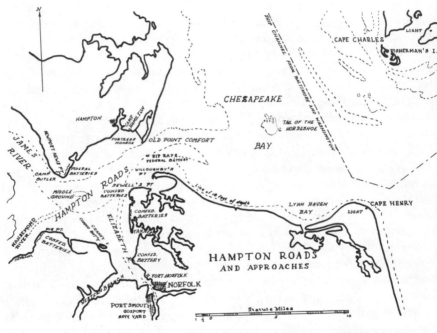

FIGURE 3

Goldsborough and the Union Navy Department had long known about the conversion of the *Merrimack* into an armored ship and had accurately surmised her objective. In October 1861, the flag officer first warned Secretary Welles about her. On October 17 he wrote, "I have received further minute reliable information with regard to the preparation of the *Merrimack* for an attack on Newport News and these roads. . . ." Henceforth information on the ironclad's progress flowed into the Union Navy Department and it was remarkably accurate in spite of Confederate endeavours to mislead the

31. S. R. Franklin, *Memories of a Rear Admiral* (New York, 1892), 143.

enemy by publishing false details in the newspapers. The senior naval officer in Hampton Roads reported to Goldsborough on February 22, "Night before last General [John E.] Wool sent me a dispatch he had received from Norfolk, informing him that the *Merrimack*, in conjunction with the *Yorktown* and *Jamestown*, would attack Newport News within the next five days; the attack will be at night."[32] Yet Buchanan still achieved tactical surprise. When the Confederate vessels were first sighted, Goldsborough was not present, the captain of the *Cumberland* was having lunch on another vessel, laundry was hanging on the riggings of several ships, and boats were at the booms of both the *Congress* and *Cumberland*.

Only a few of the fifty-odd vessels in the North Atlantic Blockading Squadron were in Hampton Roads that day. Nonetheless, the remaining flotilla was quite formidable—the fifty-gun screw frigates *Minnesota* and *Roanoke*, the forty-four-gun sailing frigates *St. Lawrence* and *Congress*, and the twenty-four-gun sailing sloop *Cumberland*. As the vessels nearest to Newport News, the *Cumberland* and the *Congress* would be attacked first.

At 12:45 A.M., the *Virginia, Beaufort,* and *Raleigh,* were first observed steaming out of Elizabeth River by lookouts on the *Congress* and *Cumberland*. The quartermaster of the *Congress* supposedly remarked to one of the deck officers, "I wish you would take the glass and have a look over there, Sir. I believe *that thing* is a-comin' down at last."[33] Both ships promptly beat to quarters and cleared for action.

The Union vessels had ample time to prepare for battle, because the slow-moving ironclad took slightly more than an hour to steam within firing range. Buchanan intended to ram the *Cumberland* first—she had a much heavier battery than the *Congress*—then turn on the *Congress*. Shortly after 2:00 the *Virginia* and *Congress* exchanged broadsides at 1,500 yards as the Confederate warship passed the starboard beam of the *Congress*. The *Cumberland* was anchored 800 yards from the shore lying athwart the river with her bow outward, an unfortunate position because she could not be swung to meet her opponent. The *Cumberland* opened fire as soon as her guns could be brought to bear; the *Virginia* replied and as the ironclad closed, the two vessels continued to exchange fire. The *Cumberland* definitely received the worst of it. Shots bounced off the ironclad's armor while shells from the *Virginia* penetrated the Union vessel's fragile hull and exploded among her crew. One shot alone wiped out a sixteen-man gun crew. After raking the

32. *Official Records, Navies,* Ser. I, VI, 661.
33. Quoted in Charles Lee Lewis, *Admiral Franklin Buchanan: Fearless Man of Action,* 184.

helpless wooden vessel for a few minutes, the *Virginia* rammed the *Cumberland's* starboard side, crushing her hull directly below the berth deck. Upon impact the ironclad fired one of her bow rifles into the stricken ship, killing ten men. The *Cumberland* began immediately to settle by the bow with a list to port. She nearly dragged the *Virginia* down too, for the ram had stuck in the victim's hull. However, the ram broke, and the ironclad was able to back clear.

Even with tons of water pouring into her broken hull the *Cumberland* refused to surrender. "Solid broadsides in quick succession were [fired] . . . into the *Merrimac* at a distance of not more than one hundred yards," a Union officer recalled in his memoirs.[34] The muzzle of one of the armorclad's broadside guns was broken off by a well-placed shot, and a few more men were killed and wounded, but much to the "rage and despair" of the *Cumberland's* gunners no serious damage was done. The *Virginia* continued to rake her adversary until about half past three when the Union vessel lurched forward quickly and with a roar, sank bow first with her stern high in the air. Her colors were still flying as she slipped beneath the surface.

Having disposed of the *Cumberland,* the victorious ironclad turned her attention to the *Congress* which had been exchanging shots with the two smaller Confederate vessels, *Beaufort* and *Raleigh*. With one rifled gun apiece these little ships were unable to close to an effective range and simply tried to keep the frigate occupied. While thus engaged, the *Congress* got under way, and with jib and topsails carrying her, she deliberately grounded. Lieutenant Joseph Smith, her young and recently appointed commanding officer, had courageously and wisely sought the protection of shore batteries near Signal Point by beaching his vessel. Unfortunately for him, the current exposed her stern to seaward and left only two guns able to bear on the approaching *Virginia*.

The draft of the Confederate armorclad would not allow her to ram the *Congress* in shallow waters, but she stood to within a hundred yards of the helpless frigate and opened fire. The *Virginia's* cannonade was devastating: within a few minutes more than a hundred of the *Congress's* crew were killed or wounded, and the doomed vessel was on fire. For more than an hour the *Congress* was pounded by the ironclad's heavy guns. Finally, when it was clear that there would be no relief, her colors were hauled down. Among the dead was Lieutenant Smith.

Buchanan ordered the *Raleigh* and *Beaufort to* go alongside the sur-

34. Thomas O. Selfridge, Jr., *Memoirs of Thomas O. Selfridge, Jr.: Rear Admiral, U.S.N.,* 50.

rendered vessel to "take the officers and wounded men prisoners, to permit the others to escape to the shore, and to burn the ship."[35] As the wounded were being lowered into the *Beaufort,* a regiment of Federal troops supported by artillery opened on the Confederate vessel, killing and wounding a number of men. Lieutenant William Parker, commanding the *Beaufort,* blew his steam whistle, recalling the men who had boarded the frigate. He then moved out of range. Buchanan evidently believed that Parker had failed to carry out his orders to burn the ship, and he commanded his flag lieutenant to do so. "I took some eight or ten men in our only remaining boat and pulled toward her," Minor wrote in describing the incident that night.

The *Teazer* [was ordered] to protect me. . . . as I drew near the *Congress* the soldiers on shore opened on me . . . and very soon two of my men and myself were knocked down. I was only down a second or two, and, steering my crippled boat for the *Teazer.* . . . [then I was] taken to the *Virginia,* where it had already been reported that they were firing upon me, and the flag officer, seeing it, deliberately backed our dear old craft up close astern of the *Congress* and poured gun after gun, hot shot and incendiary shells into her.[36]

Standing near a hatchway on the *Virginia,* Lieutenant John R. Eggleston heard Buchanan shout to his executive officer, "Destroy that —— ship! She's firing on our white flag." The flag officer then climbed to the hurricane deck for a better view. Moments later he was shot in the leg and had to be carried below.[37] With flames beginning to consume the dying *Congress,* the command devolved upon Catesby Jones. The *Congress* burned until 12:30 A.M. on the morning of the ninth, when the fire reached her magazine and she blew up.

In the midst of the *Virginia-Cumberland-Congress* engagement, additional ships on both sides attempted to join in the battle. The Confederate James River Squadron consisted of the wooden gunboats *Jamestown, Patrick Henry,* and *Teaser* arrived in time to contribute to the surrender and destruction of the *Congress.* On the Union side, the screw frigates *Minnesota* and *Roanoke* stood for Newport News when firing was heard but grounded two miles from the city. The sailing frigate *St. Lawrence* was anchored outside the capes of Chesapeake Bay and was unaware of the fighting in Hampton

35. William H. Parker, *Recollections of a Navy Officer, 1841–1865,* 257.
36. To Kell, March 8, 1862, quoted in John M. Kell, *Recollections of a Naval Life,* 282–283.
37. Buchanan was wrong. The *Congress* was not firing. Both Buchanan and the regimental commander were criticized for their actions, but both believed that under the circumstances they were doing their duty. See Tindall, "True Story of the *Virginia,*" 34–36.

Roads until informed by the steamship *Cambridge* which towed her into the Roads where she, too, grounded. The *Roanoke* and *St. Lawrence* were able to slip free and retire to Fortress Monroe. The *Minnesota,* however, remained hard aground until 5:00 P.M. when the *Virginia,* accompanied by the *Jamestown* and *Patrick Henry,* left the blazing *Congress,* and turned in her direction. The helpless frigate was saved, though, by the shoal water which prevented the ironclad from closing to less than a mile. After firing ineffectively for some time, Jones decided to break off the engagement. With darkness falling, the Confederate flotilla steamed for Sewell's Point with the *Virginia* exchanging fire with the *St. Lawrence* as the frigate retired toward Fortress Monroe.

The battle lasted approximately five hours, during which two Union vessels were sunk, a third slightly damaged, nearly three hundred Union sailors lost their lives, and another hundred were wounded. The Confederate vessels suffered only minor damage. The *Virginia* lost her ram and two guns, and several plates were loosened although not penetrated. Confederate casualties were fewer than sixty killed and wounded. Captain John A. Dahlgren, commandant of the Washington Navy Yard and a personal friend of Lincoln, described in his memoirs the effect of this news:

Sitting in my office, about 10:30 in the morning, when I should have been in church, the President was announced at the door. I went out. Senator [Orville H.] Browning was with him. He had, he said, "frightful news." The *Merrimac* had come out yesterday, smashed the *Cumberland,* and compelled the *Congress* to surrender. . . . The President did not know whether we might not have a visit here. . . . I could give but little comfort; such a thing might be prevented, but not met. . . .[38]

The "most frightened man on that gloomy day," wrote Welles in his sometimes unreliable but illustrative diary,

was the Secretary of War [Edwin M. Stanton]. He was at times almost frantic. . . . The *Merrimac,* he said, would destroy every vessel in the service, could lay every city on the coast under contribution, could take Fortress Monroe; McClellan's mistaken purpose to advance by the Peninsula must be abandoned. . . . Likely the first movement of the *Merrimac* would be to come up the Potomac and disperse Congress, destroy the Capitol and public buildings; or she might go to New York and Boston and destroy those cities. . . . there was throughout the whole day something inexpressibly ludicrous in the . . . frantic talk, action, and rage of Stanton as he ran from room to room, sat down and jumped up after writing a few words, swung his arms, scolded and raved.[39]

38. Madeleine V. Dahlgren, *Memoir of John A. Dahlgren,* 359–360.
39. Gideon Welles, *Diary of Gideon Welles Secretary of the Navy Under Lincoln and Johnson,* ed. Howard K. Beale, 3 vols., I, 51–52.

In the South, Lieutenant John Taylor Wood carried the news and the flag of the *Congress* to Richmond where he was received by Jefferson Davis. Newspapers and telegraph quickly spread the tidings throughout the Confederacy. Wood returned to Portsmouth that night and the following morning boarded the *Virginia* as she was preparing to get under way.

As Wood neared the armorclad off Sewell's Point, he could hear the signal gun at Fortress Monroe echoing across the quiet waters. In the early morning mist Hampton Roads appeared unusually empty with only two ships visible, the stranded *Minnesota* and another craft that strangely resembled a cheesebox on a shingle or raft. Jones instantly recognized her as the ironclad *Monitor*. In a postwar article he stated that they were not surprised to see her that morning since a pilot had observed the vessel the night before in the light of the burning *Congress*.[40] As most historians know, the *Monitor* was not built solely to challenge the *Virginia*. It was simply a fortunate coincidence for the Union that she was completed in time to reach Hampton Roads before the *Virginia* could finish her destructive work.[41] Upon her arrival, the *Monitor* was ordered to protect the *Minnesota*.

At 6:00 A.M. on March 9, the *Virginia*, followed by the *Patrick Henry, Jamestown,* and *Teaser,* got under way and stood for the grounded frigate. As the ironclad drew within range, she fired a shot through the rigging of the *Minnesota*. The *Monitor* immediately approached the armorclad, determined to keep her away from the helpless frigate. For the next four hours the two ironclads pounded each other mercilessly. Throughout most of the encounter the range was brutally short—less than a hundred yards. The *Monitor's* commanding officer, Lieutenant John L. Worden, hoped to loosen the *Virginia's* armor by firing at point-blank range, while Jones planned to ram or board his opponent. The *Monitor* had a distinct advantage in speed and maneuverability, while the deep-drafted Confederate ironclad was laboring under the additional handicap of having to operate in the shoal waters of the sound. She was able to ram once, but the *Monitor* turned in time and received only a glancing blow that did no damage except to the *Virginia* which developed another leak.

The *Monitor's* evasive action, however, permitted Jones to renew his attack on the *Minnesota,* and he did manage to damage her slightly before the *Monitor* could get between them again. Shortly after this the *Virginia* ran

---

40. Jones, "Services of the *Virginia*," 70–71.

41. Howard P. Nash, Jr., "A Civil War Legend Examined," *The American Neptune,* XXIII (1963), 197–203. For details on the *Monitor's* construction and voyage to Hampton Roads see William C. White, *Tin Can on a Shingle,* and Robert S. McCordock, *The Yankee Cheesebox.*

aground and remained immobile for nearly an hour, while the two Union vessels rained shells on her iron sides. Then, as the *Monitor* moved closer, a Confederate shell exploded against the front of her pilot house, driving powder fragments into the eyes of Worden, who was then looking through the peep holes. This may have saved the *Virginia*. For twenty minutes the *Monitor* now commanded by the inexperienced executive officer Lieutenant Samuel D. Greene, stood clear of her opponent while the temporarily blinded Worden was attended. Greene had decided not to continue the fight but simply to guard the *Minnesota* when he saw that the *Virginia* had worked free.

For a time, Jones wanted to renew the attack on the Union frigate, but his pilots dissuaded him because of the falling tide, and the fact that leaks were forcing the ironclad even lower than usual in the water. Consequently, he returned to the anchorage near Sewell's Point.

Neither ship was seriously damaged, although the *Virginia* had to go into drydock while a number of cracked plates were replaced and other minor repairs made. Tactically the engagement was a victory for the *Monitor*: the *Minnesota* was saved, and this was the Union ironclad's primary objective. Strategic consequences, though, seemed to favor the *Virginia* and the Confederacy: the Confederate ironclad gained undisputed control of Hampton Roads and the James River, enabling her to protect Norfolk and the river approaches to Richmond. At the same time the menacing presence of the *Virginia* seriously affected General George B. McClellan's spring campaign to take Richmond.[42]

It is true that the *Virginia* could not steam beyond the confined waters of Hampton Roads, but the North was unaware of this. On March 10, Welles sent a telegram to his capable assistant, Gustavus Fox, who had hurried to Fortress Monroe: "It is directed by the President that the *Monitor* be not too much exposed, and that in no event shall any attempt be made to proceed with her unattended to Norfolk."[43] The secretary was convinced that the *Monitor* was the only thing that could prevent the *Virginia* from sallying forth and attacking some place along the eastern seaboard. Indeed, the Confederate naval chief endorsed such an idea in a letter to Buchanan written shortly before the latter engaged the Federal fleet. Mallory suggested to the flag officer that he consider attacking New York City. "Once in the bay," he

42. Daly, *How the Merrimac Won, passim;* William N. Still, Jr., "Confederate Naval Strategy: The Ironclad," *Journal of Southern History,* XXVII (1961), 335.
43. *Official Records, Navies,* Ser. I, VII, 83.

declared, "she could shell and burn the city and shipping. Such an event would eclipse all the glories of the combat of the sea . . . and would strike a blow from which the enemy could never recover."[44] In order to understand Mallory's completely unrealistic suggestion, one must remember that he was convinced at this time that the blockade could be broken by the *Virginia* or by the four ironclads then under construction in the West. They were designed as seagoing vessels. Only later would he abandon the notion of building seagoing armorclads within the Confederacy. Certainly Buchanan shared little of this premature enthusiasm. Because of his wound, the flag officer did not reply until March 19:

The *Virginia* is yet an experiment, and by no means invulnerable as has already been proven in her conflict on the 8 and 9. . . . The *Virginia* may probably succeed in passing Old Point Comfort and the Rip Raps [but] . . . she has then to be tested in a seaway. . . . Should she encounter a gale, or a very heavy swell, I think it more than probable she would founder.

Buchanan concluded with what amounted to a warning: "the *Virginia* [is] the most important protection to the safety of Norfolk. . . ."[45]

Norfolk was by then in serious danger, for Major General George B. McClellan had decided to strike at Richmond by way of the peninsula between the James and York Rivers. His reasons were obvious and sound. A direct approach through northern Virginia would be costly, while a move up the two rivers could utilize Union naval superiority—gunboats could protect his flanks and river steamers could carry his troops. By March, troop movement toward his base of operations at Fortress Monroe was under way. Then came the *Virginia's* spectacular attack on the Union vessels off Newport News, followed by the duel with the *Monitor*. On March 12, McClellan telegraphed Fox to inquire whether the *Monitor* could be relied upon to keep the *Virginia* in check. That same day the general's chief engineer informed the assistant secretary of the navy that "The possibility of the *Merrimac* appearing again paralyzes the movements of this army. . . ." In a curiously inconsistent statement, Fox replied that while the *Monitor* was superior to the *Virginia* she might be disabled in a second clash and, therefore, "great dependence upon her" was inadvisable.[46]

McClellan decided to continue as planned with only certain modifications. So long as the *Virginia* was operational, the James River was closed

44. *Ibid.,* 780–781.
45. Buchanan letterbook.
46. *Official Records, Navies,* Ser. I, VII, 100.

to Union movement. Therefore, concentration would be on the York River and its tributaries. Because of the threat of the *Virginia,* he would also be without naval support. As he later said,

the James River was declared by the naval authorities closed to the operations of their vessels by the combined influence of the enemy's batteries on its banks and the Confederate steamers *Merrimac, Yorktown, Jamestown,* and *Teaser.* Flag Officer Goldsborough . . . regarded it (and no doubt justly) as his highest and more imperative duty to watch and neutralize the *Merrimac,* and as he designed using his most powerful vessels in a contest with her, he did not feel able to attack the water batteries at Yorktown and Gloucester. All this . . . materially affected my plans.[47]

In view of this, Union naval forces in Hampton Roads would follow a defensive strategy until the threat of the *Virginia* was removed. Robert E. Lee, whose grasp of sea power equalled his tactical genius, instinctively understood this. On March 18 he wrote to General Magruder, "I do not think she [the *Monitor*] will enter York River and leave the *Virginia* in her rear."[48]

The day after Lee's observation, a new flag officer, Joseph Tattnall, was ordered to the James River command to replace the wounded Buchanan. In spite of Jones's very creditable handling of the *Virginia* against the *Monitor* he was not elevated to command the ironclad. As before, that curious arrangement continued, whereby Tattnall commanded both the squadron and the ironclad.

A legendary figure in naval circles and the "beau ideal of a naval officer," Tattnall had spent nearly forty-eight years in the United States Navy. His appearance was striking: nearly six feet in height with an unusually large head, sunken blue eyes, and a protruding under lip. Because of rather long arms and great strength, he had been feared and respected in his younger days as an expert with the sword and cutlass. A fellow naval officer admiringly wrote years later, "He possessed all the traits which are found in heroic characters, and with suitable opportunities, would have set his name among the great naval worthies who are historic."[49] Like most Southern naval officers he had opposed secession but followed his state, perhaps regretfully—

47. Quoted in Daly, *How the* Merrimac *Won,* 142.
48. Clifford Dowdey and Louis Manarin (eds.), *The Wartime Papers of R. E. Lee,* 132.
49. Bulloch, *Secret Service,* I, 143–144. See also Charles C. Jones, Jr., *The Life and Services of Commodore Josiah Tattnall,* 251–256; Alexander A. Lawrence, *A Present for Mr. Lincoln, the Story of Savannah from Secession to Sherman,* 22–23; Parker, *Recollections of a Naval Officer,* 272.

he later made a remark about his grandfather to one of his young officers: "He was a Tory, sir, stood by his King, sir." [50]

When Tattnall reached Norfolk on March 29 the *Virginia* was still in drydock undergoing numerous repairs and modifications: a new ram was bolted on, wrought-iron port shutters were fitted, the damage to the armor was repaired, the hull was strengthened by an additional two inches of iron plate, and two new guns replaced those that had been damaged. These changes, although strengthening the ironclad, also increased her draft and reduced her speed slightly. Little could be done with the decrepit machinery and Chief Engineer H. Astor Ramsey finally reported that the engines could not be relied upon.

Tattnall was eager to "try" his new command and on April 4 took his flagship out of drydock, Mallory's instructions were characteristically vague and general. He was to "make . . . the *Virginia,* as destructive and formidable to the enemy as possible."[51] A few days later the secretary "hinted" that the Union fleet in the Roads should be attacked as soon as possible, but again no specific orders were issued. This time, however, there were no suggested attacks on New York or any other point beyond the calm waters of Hampton Roads.

On April 2 McClellan arrived at Fortress Monroe to join the bulk of his 60,000-man army. As previously mentioned, the Union general had decided that the York River must be his main channel of invasion. Within the week, Confederate intelligence had discovered the change and informed the War Department. General Lee promptly asked Mallory whether the *Virginia* could be sent to attack the enemy gunboats and transports in the mouth of the York. The secretary forwarded the request to Tattnall, but he also noted that such a venture would dangerously expose Norfolk and the James River.

Poor weather conditions forced Tattnall to wait until April 10, six days after the *Virginia* came out of drydock, before steaming down the river. On that day the James River Squadron moved down and anchored for the night inside of Craney Island at the mouth of Elizabeth River. Craney Island must have been a memorable spot for the old commodore, for it was here in 1813 that as a young midshipman he fought his first battle. On April 11 his squadron entered Hampton Roads to challenge the Union vessels. Tattnall

50. Henry M. Doak, "Memoirs," (Tennessee State Library and Archives, Nashville).

51. *Official Records, Navies,* Ser. I, VII, 751. Tattnall commanded the vessel forty-five days, and all but thirteen of these were spent in drydock or in the hands of yard workers.

had expected the *Monitor* to attack as soon as he threatened the anchored transports, but much to his surprise only three transports were in the area. The Union fleet was beyond Fortress Monroe with the *Monitor* in the channel between the fortress and the Rip Rap battery.

Throughout most of the day the two protagonists steamed back and forth within sight of each other, but neither actually moved within range of the other's guns. Tattnall's vessels captured the transports in a futile attempt to draw in the *Monitor*. Goldsborough clearly refused to dispute control of Hampton Roads explaining to his wife,

Had the *Merrimac* attacked the *Monitor* where she was and still is stationed by me, I would instantly have been down before the former with all my force. . . . The salvation of McClellan's army, among other things, greatly depends upon my holding the *Merrimac* steadily and securely in check and not allowing her to get past Fort Monroe and so before Yorktown. My game therefore is to remain firmly on the defense unless I can fight on my own terms. . . .[52]

To the *Monitor's* paymaster the situation seemed ridiculous: "Each party steamed back and forth before their respective friends till dinner time, each waiting for the other to knock the chip off his shoulder. . . . The same comedy I suppose will be enacted day after day for I don't know how long." Also, he accurately outlined Goldsborough's strategy: "His object is to get the *Merrimac* in deep water where the large steamers fitted up as rams can have a chance at her. . . ."[53]

Union blockading forces off Hampton Roads had been increased to twenty-one vessels by the addition of the new ironclad *Galena,* and the iron-hulled *Naugatuck,* as well as several fast steamers converted into rams.[54]

Tattnall easily perceived Goldsborough's scheme. "The enemy's plan," he wrote to Mallory, "obviously will be to get me in close conflict with the *Monitor,* and, as in that event I must occasionally lose my headway entirely, to seize the opportunity to run into me with the *Vanderbilt* and other vessels. . . ." The flag officer also advised him that he woud act "with proper

52. Louis M. Goldsboro Papers (Duke University Library, Durham, North Carolina).

53. William F. Keeler to his wife Anna, April 11, 1862, in Robert W. Daly (ed.), *Aboard the USS Monitor: 1862: The Letters of Acting Paymaster William Frederick Keeler, U. S. Navy to his Wife, Anna,* 75–76.

54. The *Galena* was a gunboat built on conventional lines but armored. She was a screw steamer, mounting four 9-inch Dahlgren guns and two Parrott rifles, and was launched on February 14 at Mystic, Connecticut. The *Naugatuck* was an iron-hulled vessel designed and outfitted by Edwin A. Stevens at his own expense. She carried one 100-pounder Parrott rifled gun.

prudence," for with the *Virginia* at the mouth of James River the enemy's operations in that direction may be checked."[55]

In short, neither commander had any intention of challenging the other unless there was no chance of failure. Each rightly believed that too much was at stake to risk his ironclad. If the *Monitor* were disabled, the *Virginia* had a good chance of reaching the York River and endangering McClellan, an idea that was definitely being considered. Mallory instructed Tattnall on April 12 to get the *Virginia* ready for "a dash [to the] York River."[56] At the same time, Tattnall had no intention of jeopardizing Norfolk and the control of the James River.

On May 5, Abraham Lincoln and members of his cabinet paid a surprise visit to Fortress Monroe. Three mornings later, while the President was still there, a deserter brought information that Norfolk was being evacuated. Lincoln then ordered Goldsborough to bombard Sewell's Point to ascertain whether the Confederate had abandoned that post and also to draw the *Virginia* out if possible. Six warships, including the *Monitor* and the *Naugatuck,* steamed near the point and opened fire. The *Virginia* was then in the yard, but Tattnall got under way as soon as he heard the bombardment. He had orders to defend the James River at all cost, and it was his impression that a Union attack up river could be materializing. As the Confederate armorclad steamed into the Roads and stood directly for the *Monitor,* the Federal vessels ceased firing and retired below Fortress Monroe. The *Virginia* still refused, however, to be drawn into the channel where the rams were waiting. Instead she steamed in the Roads for more than two hours and then withdrew to her anchorage. The Union flag officer complained to his wife that night, "She kept more in reserve than ever and would not even give me half a chance to run her down. . . ." Nor would he have another chance, because two days later the Confederates themselves destroyed the *Virginia.*

On May 3, General Joseph E. Johnston, in command of Confederate military defenses on the peninsula, had ordered the abandonment of Yorktown and Norfolk. McClellan was already on the peninsula with the bulk of his army, and the Confederate general considered the lines around Yorktown too weak to hold. Norfolk would have to be evacuated, because the withdrawal would open the city to attack from the James. The navy had known for several days (since April 28) that such a movement was imminent and had already begun withdrawing personnel and stores from the naval

55. *Official Records, Navies, Ser. I, VII,* 223–224.
56. *Ibid.,* 225.

yard. On the ninth a conference held to determine the fate of the *Virginia* decided that the ironclad should continue to defend the approaches to Norfolk until all supplies had been removed and then steam up the James River. Tattnall was under the impression that he had several days, but on the tenth, without notifying the flag officer, the military units defending the city evacuated their positions. Upon hearing this the *Virginia's* crew began trying frantically to lighten her sufficiently to ascend the river. The pilots had earlier assured Tattnall that if her draft could be diminished to eighteen feet she would be carried to a point well up the James, but that night they changed their minds, claiming that a shift in the wind direction had reduced the level of the river and that the ship probably could not go beyond Newport News. After questioning the pilots, Tattnall resolved to destroy the ship. Only a few days before he had pleaded vainly for the chance to attack the Union fleet in a do-or-die effort. This time he had no alternative, since lightening the ship had exposed her weakly armored hull. Ironically, Craney Island was chosen as the site to destroy the *Virginia*—the last vessel that the old flag officer would ever command in battle.

She was fired around midnight and blew up after burning for four hours. Her destruction was witnessed by thousands of Union soldiers and sailors. One naval officer reminisced,

It was a beautiful sight to us in more senses than one. She had been a thorn in our side for a long time, and we were glad to have her well out of the way. I remained on deck for the rest of the night watching her burning. Gradually the casement grew hotter and hotter, until finally it became red hot, so that we could distinctly mark its outlines, and remained in this condition for fully half an hour, when, with a tremendous explosion, the *Merrimac* went into the air and was seen no more.[57]

Approximately two weeks after the *Virginia's* destruction, Mallory learned that the *Louisiana* had been blown up below New Orleans. While the *Virginia* had been asserting her dominance over Hampton Roads and the James River, the Confederacy was losing control of the "Father of Waters," the mighty Mississippi, and its tributaries.

57. Franklin, *Memories of a Rear Admiral*, 182–183.

3

Confederate Ironclads and the Defense of the West, 1861–1862

IN THE months after the fall of Fort Sumter the United States formulated its strategy to recover the South. Similar to the plan originally proposed by the aged General in Chief of the Army, Winfield Scott, this strategy called for blockading the Southern coast and capturing the main transportation arteries from Ohio to the Gulf. Control of the Mississippi and its tributaries would provide communication between the interior cities of the North and the Gulf and simultaneously restrict the movement of important supplies from the trans-Mississippi states of Arkansas, Louisiana, and Texas to the heart of the Confederacy.

There can be no doubt that Union leaders fully grasped the importance of the Mississippi Valley: "The Mississippi is the backbone of the Rebellion," said Abraham Lincoln in 1861; "it is the key to the whole situation." Sherman actually considered the opening of the river and the dividing of the Confederacy "far more important [to ultimate victory] than the conquest of Virginia."[1] Although military forces were collected and warships built, no attempt was made to implement this strategy until early in 1862.

Since the rivers were at once natural highways for invasion and barriers against it, they should have been defended jointly by Confederate army and naval forces. For its part, the army did attempt to block the arteries at various points, but naval power was noticeably absent. Moreover, even the war department did not perceive the significance of river operations until it was too late. In February 1862, Union amphibious forces broke the Confederacy's key defensive points in the West by capturing Forts Henry and Donelson on the Tennessee and Cumberland Rivers. This was decisive, for it opened those river routes to invasion. Yet the Confederate government still failed to appreciate the urgency of the situation. Only in the fall of 1861, for instance, did it begin to build gunboats for the defense of the Tennessee

1. John D. Milligan, *Gunboats Down the Mississippi*, xxii. See also Archer Jones, *Confederate Strategy from Shiloh to Vicksburg*.

and Cumberland rivers, and even then the action was carried out by the army rather than the navy. On October 31, 1861, General Leonidas Polk, in command of Confederate forces in western Tennessee, purchased the river steamer *Eastport* for $12,000. The vessel was towed to Cerro Gordo, on the Tennessee River, where she was razed to her main deck. Early in December, Polk asked the naval secretary to assign a naval officer the task of converting the sidewheeler into an ironclad. Mallory complied, and on Christmas Eve Lieutenant Isaac N. Brown was ordered to superintend naval construction on the Tennessee and Cumberland rivers. At that time the *Eastport* was the only "naval construction," but within a month Brown had negotiated the purchase of four additional river steamers for conversion into gunboats. This sudden burst of energy had come too late, however, for the loss of Forts Henry and Donelson had dictated the withdrawal of Confederate forces from central and western Tennessee. The *Eastport* was then captured by Union forces, completed as an ironclad, and attached to the Mississippi Squadron until her destruction during the 1864 Red River expedition.[2]

The loss of Forts Henry and Donelson also necessitated the withdrawal of Confederate forces from Columbus, Kentucky, hence clearing the way for Union forces to move down the Mississippi. In March, General John Pope's army of 18,000 men forced the Confederates to evacuate their positions at New Madrid, and on April 8, the Confederate garrison on Island Number Ten capitulated.

While Union forces were descending the upper Mississippi, preparations had been made for the capture of New Orleans. Early in January 1862, Flag Officer David G. Farragut received command of the West Gulf Blockading Squadron for the express purpose of capturing this important seaport.

As related earlier, Mallory attempted to strengthen naval defenses on the Mississippi in the late summer of 1861 by approving the construction of two ironclads at Memphis and two at New Orleans, but these vessels were still on the stocks when the Union invasion began. Construction difficulties, compounded by vagueness in the Confederate command structure and the lack of co-operation between the services, seriously handicapped the naval

2. Leonidas Polk to Judah P. Benjamin, January 7, 1862, Polk to Mallory, December 11, Benjamin to Polk, October 31, in General Leonidas Polk Papers, War Department Collection of Confederate Records, Record Group 109 (War Records Branch, the National Archives); *Eastport* folder, Vessel File, National Archives Record Group 109; Mallory to Baker, February 7, 1863, construction at Nashville, Tennessee, folder, Confederate Subject and Area Files, National Archives Record Group 45.

program.[3] Neither of the two Memphis vessels was finished in time to aid in the city's defense, and only one of the New Orleans armorclads was able to participate in the battle with Farragut's fleet—and she was not completed.

Memphis and New Orleans were the logical sites for naval shipyards in the West. In fact, a navy yard was built in Memphis in 1844 at the suggestion of Matthew Fontaine Maury. This facility constructed only one warship, however, and in the 1850s the buildings were sold and it ceased to exist.[4]

In 1819, the first shipyard with marine ways was established in New Orleans, and the city became a center of steamboat construction until the outbreak of the war. At least five shipyards with twelve docks were in operation in 1861, and by April 1862 these yards had constructed, converted, or were building more than thirty vessels-of-war. With the exception of the Gosport Navy Yard at Norfolk, New Orleans was the most important shipbuilding center of the Confederacy.[5]

Ironically, the builders of the two ironclads were unable to use the existing yards at New Orleans or across the river at Algiers. Instead they had to erect new facilities at Jefferson City, just north of the city limits. On this location the land was cleared, buildings and ways constructed, and the keels of both vessels laid down by the beginning of October, 1861. Actually there were two separate yards: one was under E. C. Murray who had con-

---

3. In situations where military activities involve both army and naval units, close co-operation between the two services is essential. Although harmonious relations generally prevailed in the Confederate military, there were all the same too many instances of a lack of understanding and co-operation. This was true from the cabinet level down to local commanders. Part of this was because there was no clear policy concerning the command setup. There were senior naval officers in most military districts and, with the exception of Admiral Buchanan at Mobile, these naval officers were below the local army commander in rank. For this reason generals frequently attempted to exercise control over naval units. A unified command would have unquestionably improved this situation, but there was no precedent for a unified command. See Frank E. Vandiver, *Rebel Brass: The Confederate Command System,* 4–5, 72.

4. Walter Chandler, "The Memphis Navy Yard," *West Tennessee Historical Society Papers,* I (1947), 70–71.

5. John H. Neill, Jr., "Shipbuilding in Confederate New Orleans" (M.A. thesis, Tulane University, 1940), 47; *Report of Evidence Taken Before a Joint Special Committee of Both Houses of the Confederate Congress to Investigate the Affairs of the Navy Department* (Richmond, 1863), 75, hereinafter cited as *Report of Evidence.* See also Harrison A. Trexler, "The Confederate Navy Department and the Fall of New Orleans," *Southwest Review,* XIX (1933), 88–102; and William M. Parks, "Building a Warship in the Southern Confederacy," *United States Naval Institute Proceedings,* LXIX (1923), 1299–1307.

tracted to build the ironclad *Louisiana,* while the other was under the general supervision of the Tift brothers, agents of the Navy Department who were to build the *Mississippi,* an armored vessel of their design.[6]

From the beginning there were inevitable and critical delays, chiefly concerning the procurement of necessary materials. Timber was not available locally and had to be brought in by railroad and steamer from the other side of Lake Pontchartrain. Furthermore, an arrangement for obtaining light oak from Florida was rendered totally ineffective by the ever-tightening blockade. To make matters even worse, iron was already in short supply, and the builders lost precious time searching for bolts and other essential items. Wrought-iron plate for armor was particularly difficult to obtain, since there were no foundries capable of rolling the plate. Ultimately, it became necessary to use T-rails as a substitute, and approximately 500 tons of this iron was purchased from the Vicksburg and Shreveport Railroad. The resourceful Tifts were more successful in acquiring plate. Pressured by the government, the Scofield and Markham Iron Works of Atlanta agreed to convert their machinery in order to roll the needed plate, and by December they were producing an average of 150 plates per day.[7]

The greatest difficulty encountered by the Tifts, though, was procuring the *Mississippi's* massive power plant (three engines, sixteen boilers, etc.). While they were en route from Richmond, Mallory telegraphed the senior naval officer in New Orleans ordering him to investigate the cost and time required to manufacture the engines, propellors, and boilers.[8] A circular request for bids was sent to the various machine shops and foundries in the city, and it resulted in two responses. Leeds and Company, New Orleans' largest machine shop, offered to complete the machinery in four months at a cost of $65,000. Patterson Foundry, however, agreed to provide it within ninety days for $45,000 and thereby received the contract. The Tifts promised a substantial bonus if the work were completed by January 31, 1862,

6. The *Louisiana* was 264 feet in length, 62 feet in beam, armed with two seven-inch rifles, three nine-inch shell guns, four eight-inch shell guns, and seven thirty-two pounders when she was destroyed. The *Mississippi* was 260 feet in length, 53 feet, 8 inches in beam, and was designed to carry a battery of twenty guns.

7. One firm agreed to roll plate for the *Louisiana* if Murray would advance $5,000 of his own money, but the agreement was never fulfilled. James M. Merrill, "Confederate Shipbuilding in New Orleans, *"Journal of Southern History,* XXVII (1962), 87–93; *Official Records, Navies,* Ser. II, I, 581.

8. *Ibid.,* 532–533. Because of a miscalculation involving boiler capacity the number of boilers was increased from ten to sixteen. This was a factor in delaying completion of the vessel.

a fruitless gesture, since the last of the machinery was not installed until the following spring.[9]

Two wing shafts and one center shaft were to connect the engines with the propellors. A local foundry provided the wing shafts, although the last one was not completed and installed until April 23. The forty-four-foot center shaft presented a special problem, since it was so large that only the navy yard at Norfolk and Tredegar had the facilities to handle it, and even they could not forge a new one. Tredegar did agree, however, to modify an old shaft, and early in October a satisfactory one was located in a burned vessel on the James River below Richmond. Several weeks were required to remove the cumbersome piece of iron from the hulk and haul it by oxen through the mud to the iron works. Meanwhile, special furnaces and cranes large enough to support the shaft had to be constructed. Work commenced in January and was maintained at a strenuous "around the clock" pace until the machinery was completed. Finally, a special railroad car to carry the finished shaft was built, and it arrived at New Orleans in mid-April.[10]

The *Louisiana's* machinery was less difficult to acquire and install because most of it was transferred from the river steamer *Ingomar*. Nevertheless, her shafts proved troublesome. Like those of the *Mississippi,* they had to be forged, consuming so much time that they were completed and installed only a few days before her destruction.[11] Murray's ironclad was to be propelled by twin centerline wheels and twin screws.

Although the New Orleans builders had a sufficient number of qualified carpenters and mechanics, they were embarrassed by other labor problems. For instance, early in November naval construction in the city was halted by a strike. The workers demanded pay increases of a dollar a day, so that their wages would be equal to those received by carpenters sent from Richmond to work on the *Mississippi.* When it became obvious that the other shipbuilders would not submit to the strikers, the Tifts consented to the demanded pay increase. This ended the strike, but not before it had delayed construction by six days and further antagonized the builders, already resentful of the government's failure to utilize local constructors to build the ironclads.[12]

9. For a detailed description of the *Mississippi's* machinery see the John Roy Diary (Tulane University Library, New Orleans, Louisiana). Roy was an agent of the Navy Department in New Orleans.

10. *Official Records,* Ser. I, VI, 626–627; *Official Records, Navies,* Ser. II, I, 637, 773.

11. *Ibid.,* 761.

12. *Ibid.,* 553–554, 756.

Frequent militia drills were another irritant causing delayed construction. On October 6, Joseph Pierce, a naval constructor sent by the department to assist the Tifts, urged them to ask that those men employed on the *Mississippi* be exempt from military duties. The governor complied with this request until the spring of 1862, when the impending invasion necessitated the full mobilization of the militia, including many of the workers on the ironclads. This was a crucial blow to the constructors who then were trying desperately to complete the vessels. On April 24 the Tifts wrote General Mansfield Lovell, in command of the New Orleans defenses: "The officers of companies are taking from the ship yard our carpenters and laborers, and thus crippling our operations in trying to save the *Mississippi*."[13] Lovell then issued orders exempting the workers in the shipyards.

The labor situation was never stable, although Murray, Pierce, and the Tifts later testified that they had adequate labor. At one time the Tifts were able to lend fifty or sixty men to work on the *Louisiana,* but later when twenty-four hour shifts were required to prepare the *Mississippi* for launching, additional labor could not be located. It was necessary for a steamboat captain to make the rounds of neighboring plantations and borrow several hundred Negroes.[14]

While the builders sought to overcome their difficulties, Mallory had to find some means of strengthening his naval force on the lower Mississippi. The Confederate squadron, under the command of Flag Officer George N. Hollins, consisted of six small wooden vessels carrying a total of nineteen naval guns of assorted sizes. Early in October the small naval force was strengthened when a small party of sailors led by Lieutenant Alexander F. Warley boarded the private ironclad *Manassas* and commandeered her for the navy. This action was not taken without some tense moments. Midshipman James M. Morgan, a member of the boarding party, wrote some years later:

To a polite request that she should be turned over to us came the reply that we "did not have men enough to take her." The *McRae* [Confederate gunboat] was ranged up alongside of her and a boat was lowered. . . . On arriving alongside of the ram we found her crew lined upon the turtleback, swearing that they would kill the first man who attempted to board her. There was a

---

13. *Ibid.,* 553–554.
14. *Official Records,* Ser. I, VI, 626. Governor Moore and members of a New Orleans citizens committee testified that insufficient labor was the major delay in completing the vessels, and that the constructors—particularly the Tifts—refused to hire additional labor when offered. It appears, however, that the offer was made when additional labor was not needed. *Official Records, Navies,* Ser. II, I, 610.

ladder reaching to the water from the top of her armor to the water line. Lieutenant Warley, pistol in hand, ordered me to keep the men in the boat until he gave the order for them to join him. Running up the ladder, his face set in grim determination, he caused a sudden panic among the heroic crew of longshoremen who . . . took to their heels and like so many prairie dogs disappeared down their hole of a hatchway with Mr. Warley after them. . . .[15]

The *Manassas* had originally been converted from a river towboat for privateering purposes. In May 1861, John A. Stevenson, secretary of the New Orleans Pilots Benevolent Association, went to Montgomery for interviews with various governmental officials.[16] To President Davis and others he proposed to "alter and adapt some of our heavy and powerful towboats on the Mississippi as to make them comparatively safe against the heaviest guns afloat, and by preparing their bow in a peculiar manner . . . rended them capable of sinking by collision the heaviest vessels ever built."[17] Stevenson did not contemplate a warship but a privateering vessel, and upon his return to New Orleans he opened subscription books at the Merchant's Exchange. Within a few days, more than $100,000 had been raised, enough to purchase the *Enoch Train,* a river towboat selected because of her heavily constructed bow.[18]

The *Enoch Train* was then taken across the river from New Orleans to a shipyard at Algiers for conversion. On the ways, her masts and superstructure were removed, and a convex iron shield was erected over the main deck. Her bow was extended and strengthened, and a heavy cast-iron prow or ram attached below the water line. After conversion the vessel was fifteen feet longer, five feet wider, and four and one-half feet deeper in draft. She had one stack and, in spite of Stevenson's objections, one bow port, or trapdoor, where an unpointable, untrainable, and practically unloadable thirty-two pound gun was located—a "plaything," as her captain later called it.

15. James M. Morgan, *Recollections of a Rebel Reefer,* 55. For Morgan's account of the *Manassas* see "The Pioneer Ironclad," *United States Naval Institute Proceedings,* LXXIII (1917), 2275–2280. See also Warley to William P. Miles, January 1862, in William P. Miles Papers (Southern Historical Collection, University of North Carolina Library, Chapel Hill). Stevenson and his associates were later paid $100,000 by the Confederate government for the vessel.

16. The best accounts of the *Manassas* are William M. Robinson Jr., *The Confederate Privateers,* 153–164, Charles L. Dufour, *The Night the War was Lost,* 71–86, H. Allen Gosnell, *Guns on the Western Waters: The Story of River Gunboats in the Civil War,* 31–43.

17. Quoted in *Civil War Naval Chronology, 1861–1865,* I, 14.

18. A. W. Sington, Collector, Boston custom house, to O. V. Badge, March 29, Archives Record Group 45.
1883, construction at New Orleans folder, Confederate Subject and Area File, National

The only other openings into the vessel were two hatches, one forward and one abaft the stack. To prevent boarding, pumps were installed to eject steam and scalding water from the boiler over the iron surface. Her inadequate machinery consisted of one high- and one low-pressure engine, both long overdue for the scrap heap.

Christened the *Manassas* after the Confederate victory in Virginia, she was alternately described as looking like a turtle or a long cigar. The New Orleans *True Delta* called her "something very like a whale."

This strange looking craft was launched in the middle of August, and after a trial run in the river opposite New Orleans—viewed by hundreds of curious spectators—she was commissioned, a crew enlisted, and a letter of marque applied for. The *Manassas,* however, was not destined to slip through the blockade and enrich her owners, for she was seized by the navy even before a letter of marque was granted.

Lieutenant Warley, the ironclad's new commander, was not impressed with his vessel, calling her a "bug-bear—no power, no speed, no strength of resistance and no armament. [In addition to the thirty-two pounder] she had a twelve pound old fashion boat gun forward and four double-shot guns. She could steam [not] . . . more than six knots under favorable circumstances."[19]

The *Manassas* was also without a crew, for with the exception of the first mate and, fortunately, the chief engineer, Stevenson's "crew of longshoremen" departed in haste for New Orleans. One is not sure what led to their departure. Perhaps it was the disappointment of losing potential prize money, fear of battle, or fear of Warley, who was a stern disciplinarian ("everybody feared him," wrote Morgan). At any rate, a replacement crew had to be found immediately, and volunteers were requested from the squadron. Consequently, Warley and his crew would have little time to acquaint themselves with their vessels, for Hollins was planning a sortie down the river that night (October 11).

Late in September 1861, a Union blockading flotilla of four vessels had occupied the Head of the Passes, a body of water about fifteen miles from the Mississippi's bars. Since the Mississippi empties into the Gulf through a number of arteries running from the Head of the Passes to various mouths, the Union occupation of this area effectively sealed off New Orleans to blockade-runners.

With the *Manassas* added to his squadron, Hollins decided to attack the blockading vessels. The night of October 11 was ideal, "very dark, the moon

19. Warley to Alfred T. Mahan, March 17, 1883, Area file, Confederate Subject and Area File, National Archives Record Group 45.

had set, and the mist, hanging low over the river, shut in the hulls of the . . . ships . . . their masts and spars only being visible." The *Manassas* led the way, followed by two tugs pulling three fire rafts; astern came the remainder of the small force—*McRae, Ivy, Tuscarora, Calhoun,* and *Jackson.* The plan of battle called for the *Manassas* to steam ahead and ram the most suitable

FIGURE 4

target; a signal would then be given to release the fire rafts among the Federal craft. In the pandemonium that should follow, the rest of the Confederate flotilla would engage the blockaders.

At the Head of the Passes three of the Federal warships, the steam sloop *Richmond,* mounting twenty nine-inch Dahlgren smoothbores, an 80-pound

Dahlgren rifle, and a 100-pound Parrott rifle; the sailing sloop *Preble,* carrying seven 32-pounders, two eight-inch rifles, and one light 12-pounder; and the steamer *Water Witch* with four small guns, were anchored near the eastern bank while the sailing sloop *Vincennes,* armed with fourteen 32-pounders, two nine-inch Dahlgren smoothbores, and four eight-inch rifles, was close to the western bank, all with bows pointed upstream. In command of the squadron was Captain John Pope, whose professional standing would certainly not be enhanced by his actions that night.

Several days earlier a small Confederate gunboat had appeared at the "Head" and fired a few shots, causing Pope to complain that his position was untenable. Nevertheless, there were no precautions against a possible attack by larger forces; no picket boats were out, special lookouts stationed, or preparations of any kind against a night assault. The *Richmond* was taking on coal from a schooner moored along her port side. Dim lanterns were used to facilitate the operation.

At about 4:40 A.M. the *Richmond* was hailed from a nearby vessel, "Ahoy! There is a boat coming down the river on your port bow." Apparently this warning went unheard in the noise of coaling. On the *Preble,* anchored at the head of the line about two hundred yards from the *Richmond,* the captain had just retired when a midshipman burst into his cabin, exclaiming, "Captain, here is a steamer right alongside of us." Commander Henry French—who had gone to bed with his clothes on—immediately rushed on deck. "As I passed out of my cabin . . . I saw through a port an indescribable object not twenty yards distant . . . moving with great velocity toward the bow of the *Richmond.*"[20]

When the *Manassas* reached the Head of the Passes, the dim lights on the *Richmond* were observed, and the ironclad turned toward her. The Confederate vessel was sighted by the *Richmond's* lookouts as she loomed up out of the darkness, but before anything could be done, the ram crashed into the side of the Union vessel. The blow parted the lines holding the coal schooner, and she drifted away. One of the *Richmond's* officers wrote:

I . . . had been soundly sleeping, when I was rudely awakened by a tremendous shock, followed by the sound of the rattle we used as a signal to night quarters. Jumping into my trousers, with my coat in one hand and my sword in the other, I, with the other wardroom officers, rushed on deck. . . . Emerging from the hatchway, I saw on the port side amidships a smokestack just above our hammock nettings from which belched streams of black smoke. . . . the ram . . . cleared herself from us and dropped slowly astern in the darkness.[21]

20. *Official Records, Navies,* Ser. I, XVI, 712–714.
21. Frederick S. Hill, *Twenty Years at Sea,* 149–158.

As the *Manassas* disappeared in the mist, bedlam enveloped the Federal fleet; broadsides were fired into the darkness; a signal rocket from the ram soared into the air; and the warships rapidly slipped their cables as the flagship hoisted the red danger signal. Yet the *Manassas* was in no position to renew the attack. After ramming the *Richmond,* she sheered off and headed for the *Preble.* Unfortunately, the blow had damaged the vessel: her cast-iron ram was broken off, her machinery damaged—one engine completely out of operation, and the smoke stack had collapsed over a ventilator causing choking fumes to spread throughout the vessel. In this crippled condition, she drifted ashore, but later returned upstream.

As the ironclad floated toward the bank, the three fire rafts came on the scene, drifting across the water until they finally lodged on a shoal, having accomplished nothing but lighting the scene in an eerie fashion. For some unexplainable reason the remainder of the Confederate squadron did not enter the Head of the Passes until daylight. By this time all the Federal vessels but the *Water Witch*—which alone remained in the "Head"—had retired down Southwest pass to the bar. At daybreak, the *Water Witch* found herself alone, and she too retreated. When she reached the end of the pass, Pope ordered the vessels to cross the bar. The first one made it safely, but both the *Richmond* and *Vincennes* grounded, the former broadside and the latter stern upstream. While in this helpless position shells began passing overhead—Hollins' flotilla had arrived. After both sides exchanged a number of shells, the Confederate gunboats surprisingly withdrew up the river. Thus Hollins missed an excellent opportunity to capture or destroy the *Vincennes,* which was abandoned by her crew because of a misunderstood signal. Later she was reoccupied, lightened, and passed over the bar.

When Commodore Hollins anchored off Fort Jackson that night, he dispatched a telegram to New Orleans: "Last night I attacked the blockaders with my little fleet, and succeeded, after a very short struggle, to drive them all aground on the Southwest bar, except the sloop-of-war *Preble,* which I sunk. . . . after I got them fast on the sand I peppered them well. . . . A complete success." Although the encounter was certainly not the overwhelming success that Hollins boasted of, it was a tactical victory and something of a morale booster for the Confederacy. Nothing was accomplished by the engagement, however, which quickly became known as "Pope's Run." Even though Federal forces would not reoccupy the Head of the Passes for several months, they still controlled the passes; thus the effectiveness of the blockade continued to increase.

Upon her return to New Orleans the *Manassas* underwent extensive repairs and was ready to come out of the yard when Lieutenant Robert Minor arrived from Richmond to inspect her and the two large armorclads on the stocks above the city. On January 31, 1862, he reported to Mallory that repairs on the *Manassas* were finished and she was ready for service. He also outlined progress on the two ironclads under construction:

The *Louisiana* will be launched on Monday or Wednesday the third or fifth of February—no machinery in—but all ready to be put on board . . . no iron on the roof but the two layers of T rails are ready and will be put on after [she is] launched. Men are working on the launching ways to take advantage of the rise in the river. . . . In three weeks she will be ready for her armament. Has great capacity for fuel, water, and provisions. . . . The vessel is more than two thirds completed now. . . . [The *Mississippi's*] engine keelsons, shaft holes, thrust blocks, and boilers have been in the ship for thirty days and are now waiting for machinery. Timber comes in slowly. Men have been detained three times for want of material to keep them at work. The magazines, shell rooms, and store rooms are all complete forward, but not aft—which cannot be done until machinery is put in. About eighty-five feet of the roof . . . is without iron—commencing from the center and working each way. . . . [The iron] comes in fast enough—being ahead of the woodwork. . . . On the whole the work seems to be very reliable, but all depends upon the principle of construction which remains to be tested. I am informed by Mr. Pierce that from all appearance the gunboat will not be launched before the 25th of March—all depending upon receipt of machinery.[22]

On February 6 a large crowd witnessed the launching of the *Louisiana*. As the box-like craft slid broadside into the river, thousands cheered, and according to the newspaper *True Delta* "everyone present seemed to be impressed."[23] Yet, the vessel was far from being completed; Murray was still frantically trying to locate iron for armor and to install the remainder of the machinery.

The Tifts were pushing ahead rapidly also. By mid-February the woodwork was finished, the boilers had been installed, the iron port frames and doors were nearly ready, and the first shipment of 400 tons of iron plating had arrived, ready to be bolted on. By March the vessel was ready for the center shaft, but since Tredegar was still working on it, the machinery was not even shipped until the 24th.[24]

22. Copy of report in the Minor Diary, in Minor Papers. The "principle of construction" that Minor mentioned concerned the ship's unusual design—there were no frames and no curves. All the surfaces were flat, except the four corners that connected the two ends of the ship with the sides.

23. Quoted in Dufour, *The Night the War was Lost,* 176. Naval agent Roy who was on board the *Louisiana* as she was launched wrote in his diary, "was some what surprised at the easy manner in which she slipped into the water."

24. Correspondence between Mallory and the Tifts concerning the shaft will be found in *Report of Evidence,* 153–204.

To the public, the pace of construction seemed unnecessarily languid. In February leading citizens of New Orleans, who were beginning to doubt the adequacy of defense preparations, organized a Committee of Public Safety. The matter of the uncompleted gunboats naturally caught the attention of this committee. The fact that the constructors were outsiders further stimulated suspicion that work on the vessels was lagging needlessly. As a result, the committee made suggestions to the Tift brothers about initiating night work, using Negro labor, while at the same time complaining unfairly that the Navy Department was failing to meet its local bills. When the Tifts' explanations proved unsatisfactory, the committee turned to the local naval and military authorities, and finally to President Davis himself.[25]

Later the committee became involved in another controversy with the Tifts, this time over launching the *Mississippi*. At the end of February and again a month later constructor Pierce recommended that the vessel be launched immediately because of the rising river. The Tifts vetoed this idea, saying that it would delay completion by at least a month.[26] The Committee of Public Safety heard of the matter and it, too, demanded immediate launching. A member of the committee later testified that the Tifts "positively refused," and that Mallory had supported them. The discord between the committee and the naval agents was still not healed when New Orleans fell, and would become a major point in the later congressional investigation of the Navy Department.

Completion of both vessels was still held up by the continuing lack of iron. On March 19 the *Picayune* appealed to the people for iron to use on the *Louisiana* and counseled them to "charge as much as your patriotism will admit." Two days later Nelson Tift reported to Mallory that the *Mississippi* was being delayed because of the "nonreceipt of the balance of iron . . . from Atlanta." The delay was caused by inadequate transportation facilities. Vir-

---

25. *Official Records,* Ser. I, VI, 575–576, 831–832; *Official Records, Navies,* Ser. II, I, 714–715. The failure of Tifts's paymaster to pay the bills was not his fault nor the Navy Department's. On February 22, 1862, Mallory wrote to Secretary of the Treasury, C. G. Memminger, "The operations of the Department and the credit of the Government is damaged by the delays incurred in placing funds in New Orleans to meet expenditures. . . ." Records of the Confederate Treasury Department, Legal and Fiscal Branch, Record Group 365 (The National Archives). See also Mallory to Memminger, January 11, 1862, Records of the Confederate Treasury Department, National Archives Record Group 365, and Benjamin to General Mansfield Lovell, February 27, 1862, in *Correspondence Between the War Department and General Lovell Relating to the Defenses of New Orleans Submitted in Response to a Resolution of the House of Representatives Passed Third February, 1863,* 58.

26. *Official Records, Navies,* Ser. II, I, 595.

tually all rolling stock had been commandeered by the army and it took direct presidential intervention to secure the release of several flatcars. Once flatcars became available the movement of iron was resumed, and the last shipment arrived on April 23.[27]

In the United States Navy before the war, station commanders had supervisory control over naval construction within their district. Actual building was left to constructors, contractors, or agents of the department; but the local commanding officer had the authority to make inspections and recommendations and to see that the work in general was satisfacory. This was not true, however, of Confederate station commanders at New Orleans. Flag Officer Hollins, John K. Mitchell, and William C. Whittle, all of whom commanded the New Orleans Station at various times during construction of the ironclads, had no authority over naval building.[28] In the spring of 1862, Mallory initiated a change in this policy, prompted by the constant delays in construction, the growing criticism of the department and its agents in New Orleans, and the urgent need to complete the vessels as soon as possible. On March 15 he telegraphed Mitchell to assume complete control of the *Louisiana* if, in his opinion, the contractor were not doing everything possible to expedite her completion. Mitchell notified Murray of this order but left the vessel in the hands of the builder. In the latter part of March, Commander Arthur Sinclair was ordered to assume command of the *Mississippi* when she was commissioned, and until that time to aid the Tifts in completing the vessel. Sinclair, a Virginian and former commander in the United States Navy, according to his later testimony, did more than just give aid: "I was daily aboard superintending her construction—often three or four times a day."[29] Nevertheless, the Tifts remained in charge of construction.

Anxiety for the two ironclads was increasing daily—and for good reason. On February 20, Flag Officer Farragut arrived at Ship Island, off the coast of Mississippi, to assume command of the United States Navy's Western Gulf Blockading Squadron, and it quickly became apparent that his major objective was the capture of New Orleans. By April 1, all but two of his squadron were over the bar and in the Mississippi River. Four days later, Mallory ordered Whittle to work day and night completing the armorclads

27. *Ibid.*, 592, 593; *Official Records,* Ser. I, VI, 626; voucher, construction at New Orleans folder, Confederate Subject and Area File, National Archives Record Group 45.

28. *Official Records, Navies,* Ser. II, I, 474, 494–495, 440.

29. *Official Records,* Ser. I, VI, 608; for Mitchell's order see *Official Records, Navies,* Ser. I, XVIII, 834. From April, 1862, until the end of the war all naval construction was placed under the supervision of station commanders.

and advised the Tifts, "Spare neither men nor money. . . . Can not you hire night gangs for triple wages?"[30] The Tifts responded by offering a bonus to the Patterson Foundry if the *Mississippi's* machinery were ready by April 25. But this was a futile gesture, since machinery parts and the remainder of the plating had not arrived. In view of this, only a skeleton force was needed to work on the *Mississippi,* and many of Titt's employees were actually aiding Murray on the *Louisiana.*

On April 19, Union mortar boats opened a heavy bombardment upon Forts Jackson and Saint Philip, located some seventy miles below New Orleans. The following day, Commander Mitchell was ordered to assume command of naval forces in that vicinity and to take the *Louisiana* down with him. The armorclad, however, was not completed: part of her machinery was not installed (only the wheels were in working order), the forcastle and forward hatch combings were still without plate, the guns were not mounted, and a full complement was not on board. Nevertheless, on Easter Sunday, April 20, the lines holding the vessel to the levee were cast off, and her two large center wheels set in motion. Much to the concern of the crew and assembled workers, she could not stem the current and began to drift downstream. The ironclad was taken in tow by two tugs and moored to the bank above Fort Saint Philip the following day.

Mitchell's command, aside from the *Louisiana,* consisted of the wooden steamers *McRae, Jackson, Governor Moore, General Quitman,* the *Manassas,* and several launches and tugs. Only the *McRae* with seven guns had a respectable battery; the remainder were armed with fewer than three guns apiece. Mitchell had few illusions about stopping Farragut with this hodgepodge force. As he later told Mallory, "our chief hopes rested upon the completion of the *Louisiana.*"[31] During the interval from April 21 to 24, while the mortars continued their destructive fire on the forts, workmen brought down on the tugs labored day and night trying to complete the vessel. Her crew also toiled to mount as many guns as possible, but when the battle began, only six were ready. The commander of Fort Jackson strongly urged Mitchell to place the ironclad below the fort and attempt to dislodge the mortar boats. Mitchell refused, insisting then, and later in his defense, that placing the vessel under fire at that time would have further delayed finishing her. He held stubbornly to this view in spite of appeals from the army commander and his subordinates, as well as a suggestion from Flag Officer Whittle. On April 23, however, he informed the flag officer that the *"Louisiana*

---

30. *Ibid.,* 836–837, 290, Ser. II, I, 607.
31. *Ibid.,* Ser. I, XVIII, 292.

[has] . . . so far progressed as to encourage the hope and belief that the next day she might be moved to the position proposed by [the fort commander] General Duncan." The "next day" was too late.

At 2:00 on the morning of April 24, two red lanterns were hoisted to the mizzen peak of the *Hartford,* Farragut's flagship. This was the signal for his fleet to get under way in an attempt to pass the forts guarding the river entrance to New Orleans. Farragut was virtually unknown outside of naval circles when he received the command early in 1862. A southerner by birth, he had spent a brief period as a youth in the city that he was ordered to capture. His orders called for him to reduce the forts, using Porter's mortars as long as necessary, and then to place the city under guns until troops could arrive to take over. Ships were assembled and taken over the bar into the passes, and on April 18 Porter opened a deliberate bombardment of the forts which continued at intervals until the attack began.

Farragut divided his fleet into three groups. The first under the command of Captain Theodorus Bailey consisted of six gunboats and two sloops-of-war. They were to engage Fort Saint Philip. The second group was led by the *Hartford,* followed by the sloops *Brooklyn* and *Richmond.* Six gunboats brought up the rear. The ships proceeded in a column in order to pass through the narrow opening in a boom of hulks that had been chained together by the defenders to block the river just below the forts. The battle opened immediately after the second vessel, the *Pensacola,* passed through the barrier. As both forts opened fire and the Union ships replied with broadsides of grape and canister, Confederate vessels joined in the fight.

Ready for the Federal attack, Mitchell ordered his gunboats to sortie within minutes of the first exchange of shots. Six converted riverboats of the "River Defense Fleet,"[32] were supposed to co-operate with the naval vessels, but not one of them fired a shot or attempted to ram a single enemy vessel. All but one surrendered.

The *Manassas* was moored to the bank above Fort Saint Philip with her bow pointed upstream.[33] Lieutenant Warley, her captain, expected an attack and had lashed his vessel to a tug inshore of her in order to swing the ram

32. The "River Defense Fleet" was composed of converted river steamers manned by personnel under the direct orders of General Lovell. They were rams with only two small guns as armament.

33. For Warley's account of the *Manassas'* participation in the battle see Warley to Mahan, March 17, 1883, Area file, Confederate Subject and Area File, National Archives Record Group 45; to editor of the Charleston *Daily Courier,* August 18, 1862; *Official Records, Navies,* Ser. I, XVIII, 302–04, 336–337; Warley, "The Ram *Manassas* at the Passage of the New Orleans Forts," *Battles and Leaders,* II, 89–90.

around. When the battle began, Warley quickly cut his lines to the bank and, aided by the tug, steamed toward the gun flashes on the river. The silhouette of an enemy warship was soon observed, but as the *Manassas* stood for her, she collided with one of the fleeing "River Defense" vessels. The ram was undamaged, but by the time she could swing clear, the enemy ship had disappeared in the darkness. Warley then made for the next vessel in line, but misjudging her speed he only grazed her side. Moments later the Confederate officer spotted a side-wheeler angling across the river and recognized her as the old *Mississippi* (Union vessel) on which he had made an around-the-world voyage some years before.

Lieutenant George Dewey, the *Mississippi's* executive officer, had the deck, while the commanding officer directed the ship's battery below. Years later Dewey recalled in his *Autobiography* that a newspaper artist observing the battle from the foretop had pointed out the ironclad's approach:

Looking in the direction which he indicated I saw what appeared like the back of an enormous turtle painted lead color, which I identified as the ram *Manassas.* . . . There was no time in which to ask the advice of the captain. . . . I called to starboard the helm and turned the *Mississippi's* bow toward the *Manassas* . . . but . . . Warley . . . wheeling in . . . managed to strike us a glancing blow abaft the port paddle-wheel.

The effect of the shock was that of running aground. The *Mississippi* trembled and listed and then righted herself. . . . The impact of the ram, which would have sunk any other ship in the fleet, had taken out a section of solid timber seven feet long, four feet broad, and four inches deep.[34]

The collision swung the two vessels side to side, but after the Union gunners frantically fired a broadside, which passed over the *Manassas,* the slightly damaged *Mississippi* churned on up the river.

By this time the *Manassas* was nearly to the barrier with most of Farragut's fleet above. Warley considered attacking the mortar boats below, but heavy fire from the excited gunners in the forts, who were firing at everything that floated in the river below, persuaded him to pursue those enemy vessels steaming toward New Orleans.

After moving several hundred yards upstream, Warley observed a ship lying athwart the stream under the guns of Fort Jackson. This was the *Brooklyn* which had crossed to the other side after becoming entangled with part of the barrier and received a severe pounding from the guns of Saint Philip. It was here that Warley found her: "I ordered resin thrown in the furnaces to make steam rapidly, drew the valves all open, and ran into her,

---

34. George Dewey, *Autobiography of George Dewey, Admiral of the Navy* (New York, 1916), 63–65.

firing my gun loaded with a 5-second shell when within a few feet. I struck her fairly abreast of the mainmast with a tremendous crash, and a force that threw everyone from their feet."[35] The *Brooklyn* was jarred fore and aft but her chain armor (anchor chains secured to the vessel's sides) saved her. Damage was slight, her starboard gangway was crushed, and as the ironclad fell astern, a leadsman in the chains on the *Brooklyn* threw his lead at a couple of men standing in a scuttle forward of the ram's smokestack and knocked one of them overboard.[36]

Warley then attempted to break up a one-sided fight between the gallant *McRae* and several Union gunboats, and when they disengaged, he pursued them up the river. By this time it was daylight, and as the battle-weary ironclad rounded Quarantine Point, she came in sight of the remainder of Farragut's fleet.

Observing the ram's appearance, Farragut shouted: "Signal the *Mississippi* to sink that damn thing."[37] The *Mississippi* along with the *Kineo,* which evidently anticipated the order, stood toward the *Manassas.* The ram was barely making headway, and as the *Mississippi* bore down on her, Warley avoided the blow and ran his vessel ashore. "I considered that I had done all that I possibly could do to resist the enemy's passage of the forts," he later explained, "and that it then became my duty to try and save the people under my command."[38]

Shortly after noon on April 25, Farragut's fleet rounded the last bend in a drizzling rain and appeared within sight of New Orleans. The flag officer was appalled by the scene that met his eyes; "The levee of New Orleans was one scene of desolation; ships, steamers, cotton, coal, etc., were all in one common blaze and our ingenuity much taxed to avoid the floating conflagration. . . . the [Confederate ironclad] *Mississippi,* which was to be the terror of the seas . . . soon came floating by us all in flames. . . ."[39]

The *Mississippi* had been launched on the day the *Louisiana* was ordered to the forts. But when Farragut started up the river, she was still far from completion: her main propeller was in place, but the other two were

35. *Official Records, Navies,* Ser. I, XVIII, 336–337.
36. *Ibid.,* 198.
37. B. S. Osbon, *A Sailor of Fortune: Personal Memories of Captain B. S. Osbon,* 198. Osbon was Farragut's signal officer.
38. *Official Records, Navies,* Ser. I, XVIII, 303. The *Kineo's* captain apparently planned to board the ram but was ordered to search for a vessel ashore farther down the river. Hollingsworth to Ransom, March 20, 1869, Colburn to Ransom, September 17, 1869, Smith to Commodore [Ransom], January 23, 1868, all in Area Seven file, National Archives Record Group 45.
39. *Official Records, Navies,* Ser. I, XVIII, 158–159.

still on the wharf; the hull was sheathed, but the shield was still unarmored; her rudder was not installed; and her guns were not mounted. At 5:40 A.M. Commander Whittle learned that Farragut had passed the forts. He immediately summoned Sinclair, and ordered him to take command of the *Mississippi* and either get her up the river or destroy her. Sinclair later recounted his efforts before a Congressional investigating committee:

One the morning of the 24th, I employed, through the Messrs. Tifts, the only two steamers then available—the *St. Charles* and the *Peytona*— to come immediately to the ship and endeavor to get her up the river. They did not come, however, until a late hour. . . . The steamers came about 8 oclock at night, and made as an excuse for their failure to come earlier the want of engineers and hands. . . . I furnished the steamers with hands and an engineer, and after some difficulty we started. But we found it impossible to do anything with the vessel on account of the strong current. . . . We tugged at her the whole of that night unsuccessfully, for, instead of making any headway, we lost ground considerably. . . . [In the morning] I went to the city and endeavored to get additional steam power. I found on getting there that the crews of the vessels had left them. . . . While there I saw the enemy coming up, and then I regarded the case as hopeless.[40]

Sinclair had left orders with his executive officer, Lieutenant James I. Waddell, that if enemy vessels were sighted, the ironclad should be put to the torch. As Waddell prepared to burn the ship, five men, one carrying a rope, came on board and asked for Nelson Tift. Informed that he was not present, "with an oath they cried out, 'He is a traitor and we brought this rope to hang him.'" Waddell then told them that "a train [had been laid] to the magazine, and the vessel would be fired in a few minutes. They retired quietly, and in a few minutes I fired her. . . ."[41] As her lines burned she began drifting down the river toward the city she was supposed to defend and the enemy she was built to defeat.

By now Farragut had possession of the city, but the forts remained in Confederate hands. Under these bastions lay the *Louisiana* which had emerged from the engagement of April 24 undamaged. She remained in position above Fort Saint Philip until April 28 while the engineers assembled the last of the machinery. Mitchell's intention is not clear. The report which he wrote later in prison said only that "during the night of Sunday the 27th we had so far succeeded in operating the propellers that we expected early the next day to make a fair trial of them in connection with the paddle

40. *Ibid.*, 351–352.
41. James I. Waddell, *C.S.S. Shenandoah: The Memoirs of Lieutenant Commanding James I. Waddell,* ed. James D. Horan, 15. See also *Report of Evidence,* 194–195.

wheels." It is clear that he did not seriously consider an attack on the Union vessels above, for he added that "little confidence was felt [in the machinery] . . . being of sufficient power . . . to enable the *Louisiana* to stem the current."[42] Years after the war, one officer speculated that Mitchell was planning to make a dash for Mobile, but this seems doubtful because of the limited supply of provisions and coal and the questionable status of the vessel's machinery.[43] At any rate, by daylight all thoughts of operations were irrelevant since an offer to surrender the forts had already been dispatched to Union naval forces. Mitchell decided to destroy the armorclad after a fruitless meeting with the army commander and a council with his own officers. She was set on fire, and when the securing hawsers burned away, the ironclad drifted out into the stream and blew up—only a few hundred yards from the Union gunboats awaiting the forts' surrender.[44]

The fall of the largest city and most important port in the Confederacy was a tremendous blow to Southern morale. It aroused such a furor that a congressional investigation occurred, and both the army and navy held courts of inquiry. Although the reports of these investigative bodies blamed no particular individual or group for the disaster, the public never completely exonerated the navy. This was in large part because of the erroneous belief that the *Mississippi* and *Louisiana* could have saved the city had their completion not been prevented by negligence on the part of the navy and its agents. One indication of this is the fact that the Tifts were threatened at New Orleans and later at Vicksburg.[45]

No one person was responsible for the failure to complete the two ves-

42. *Official Records, Navies,* Ser. I, XVIII, 298.

43. James M. Baker, "Reminiscences" (MS. in J. Thomas Scharf Papers, Maryland Historical Society, Baltimore).

44. John Wilkinson, *The Narrative of a Blockade-Runner,* 52–57. Porter said that Mitchell deliberately tried to blow up the Union vessels, and after the Confederate officer surrendered, he was subjected to somewhat harsh treatment (close confinement, etc.) until a letter from Mitchell to Welles stopped it.

45. The New Orleans situation is a good example of the problems and friction arising out of the vague command set up in the Confederacy (see footnote three of this chapter). A number of writers have suggested that the lack of a unified command was a significant factor in the city's capture. There was considerable friction between army and naval commanders, but it is extremely doubtful that a unified command would have saved the city. It would not have hastened completion of the ironclads, nor would it have prevented Farragut's successful attack. For support of the significance of a unified command see Dufour, *The Night the War Was Lost,* 340–341, and his article, "The Night the War was Lost: The Fall of New Orleans; Causes, Consequences, Culpabilities," *Louisiana Historical Quarterly,* XXXIV (1961), 157–176. See also Scharf, *Confederate States Navy,* 301; J. R. Soley, "The Union and Confederate Navies," *Battles and Leaders,* I, 628.

sels on time, although errors were made by everyone concerned, particularly Mallory. He alone was responsible for sending the Tifts to New Orleans, instead of utilizing local shipbuilders. Perhaps a more serious error was his failure to designate someone on the scene, such as the station commander, as co-ordinator for the department, the constructors, and the city. Nonetheless, the cause of the failure lies less with individuals than with the fatal delays brought on by inadequate facilities, poor transportation, and insufficient materials. The construction of these two ironclads clearly illustrates the difficulties that the Confederacy would encounter in its attempts to create an ironclad navy.

Even if the *Louisiana* and *Mississippi* had been completed in time, it is doubtful that they could have materially affected the outcome of the battle. It is quite likely that these ships were basically faulty. The *Mississippi* was designed by an individual with absolutely no experience in naval construction, and she was remarkably unorthodox from her box-like structure to her power plant. Lieutenant Minor cautioned Mallory about one particular problem, that her heavily armored ends might be too heavy. (He had earlier said that her "ends were drooping" which is not surprising considering her size and weight). The CSS *Columbia* later broke her back because of a similar problem. All Confederate ironclads were notoriously slow, and in spite of her three engines and triple screws, there is nothing to indicate that the *Mississippi* would have had adequate speed. In fact, with her immense size and shape, it was likely that she could not have stemmed the current and would have been most difficult to handle.

The *Louisiana* was obviously a failure. Chief Engineer Wilson Young-blood wrote to Mitchell while a prisoner that "I do not think [the machinery] . . . would have been able to handle the vessel, the wheels being put in the middle of the vessel, one right abaft the other, so that the after wheel could do no good whatever. . . . when the wheels were working, they would force the water out under the stern so that it would form an eddy around the rudder so that she would not steer, and if we tried [to] steer her with the propellers, she could not stem the current. Consequently she was unmanageable in the Mississippi River."[46]

When the news reached Richmond of this disaster in the West, Mallory gloomily recorded in his diary: "The destruction of the Navy at New Orleans was a sad, sad blow, and has affected me bitterly, bitterly."

---

46. *Official Records, Navies,* Ser. I, XVIII, 318. Two recent books on the naval side of the war point out that completion of the two ironclads could have resulted in Farragut's defeat. See Dufour, *The Night the War Was Lost,* 336; Virgil C. Jones, *The Civil War at Sea,* II, 75.

4

The *Arkansas*

IN MEMPHIS the news of New Orleans' fall panicked the senior naval officer into ordering the destruction of one ironclad on the stocks and the removal of a second, the *Arkansas,* to "Some swamp until she can be completed."[1] On April 26, 1862, the *Arkansas* was towed from Memphis by the steamer *Capitol* for refuge on some lower tributary of the Mississippi. More than a month passed, however, before a Union force threatened the city, and the attack came from up rather than down the river.

The *Arkansas* might have been completed in time to participate in the city's defense had she not been moved. Her woodwork was finished except for the captain's cabin, and the hull was armored from the main deck to approximately a foot below the water line; the casemate was without iron, however, and the machinery, including the two engines and boilers, was on board but inoperative.

The two armorclads had been laid down in October 1861 at Fort Pickering, a landing below Memphis. The contract called for them to be completed and turned over to the Navy Department on or before December 24, 1861. The usual difficulties in locating and transporting materials and hiring workmen so delayed construction, however, that the builder, John Shirley, decided to complete one vessel at a time. Even so, progress was slow. As late as March, the *Arkansas*'s executive officer wrote, "Our work goes on very slowly, and it seems impossible to get it done faster." Neither was he impressed with the vessel; "she is such a humbug, and badly constructed," he wrote to his wife.[2]

1. Quoted in Cynthia E. Moseley, "The Naval Career of Henry Kennedy Stevens as Revealed in His Letters, 1839–1863" (M.A. thesis, University of North Carolina, 1951), 305–306. When Island No. Ten fell, the naval commander in Memphis was ordered to have the *Arkansas* towed to New Orleans, but Farragut's success made this impossible. The two ironclads were sister ships. They were 165 feet in length, 35 feet in beam, with a draft of 11 to 12 feet. Their machinery was to include two horizontal direct-acting noncondensing engines with four boilers, driving twin screws.
2. Moseley, "The Naval Career of Henry Kennedy Stevens," 303–304.

General Beauregard, who had taken command of the "Army of the Mississippi" and the military district that included Memphis, wanted her completed as quickly as possible, badly constructed or not. On March 18 he ordered Lieutenant John J. Guthrie, a naval officer apparently attached to his staff, to inspect the two vessels under construction at Memphis and to "remain and overlook their construction in the interest of the service. . . ."[3] A few days later the naval officer reported that "one has the keel laid, the ribs and frame work in place, and with present prospect, will not be ready to launch in less than six weeks. The other is much further advanced, will soon float. . . ."[4]

Beauregard, concerned by the continued advance of Union forces down the Mississippi, was not pleased with the vessel's progress. He even offered to detail an unlimited number of carpenters from his command if the constructor would furnish him a list of names and their units.[5] To the general's intense irritation, Shirley, whose appeals had largely been ignored in the past by army officers reluctant to part with their men, made no effort to provide a list. He may have felt that additional labor was not needed. On April 24 he wrote to Beauregard that "one of the boats will surely be ready in fifteen days, and the other in thirty days. . . ."[6] Unfortunately, not even fifteen days were available, for on the following day the news of the loss of New Orleans arrived and the day after that, one ironclad was destroyed and the other, the *Arkansas*, was under tow down the Mississippi.[7]

Lieutenant Charles H. McBlair assumed command of the *Arkansas* before she left Memphis and took the vessel up the Yazoo River to Greenwood, Mississippi. For nearly a month she lay moored to a pier in the rain-swollen stream with machinery, guns, and stores cluttering her deck. McBlair evidently was unequal to the task of finishing her. One of the ship's officers recalled that the "leading citizens" of Greenwood telegraphed Richmond for a more "energetic officer" to take charge. Beauregard, too, demanded action. On May 19 he asked the commanding officer at Vicksburg whether work

3. *Official Records, Navies,* Ser. II, I, 763, 780; voucher on construction at Memphis, Tennessee, folder, Confederate Subject and Area File, National Archives Record Group 45.

4. *Official Records, Navies,* Ser. I, XXII, 838.

5. John Shirley folder, Citizens File, National Archives Record Group 109.

6. To Thomas Jordan, March 22, 1862, construction at Memphis folder, Confederate Subject and Area File, National Archives Record Group 45; see also John Adams folder, letter of March 22, 1862, Citizens File, National Archives Record Group 109.

7. The *Arkansas* was commissioned on April 25.

was being done on the *Arkansas*. When a negative reply was received, he urged the Navy Department to replace McBlair. Mallory complied.[8]

On May 29 Lieutenant Henry K. Stevens, the *Arkansas*'s executive officer, wrote his wife: "Today I was astonished to see Lieutenant I. N. Brown come on board and show an order from the Secretary to take command of the *Arkansas*."[9] Brown immediately took command, and McBlair left for Richmond to report to Mallory that he had been "insulted" by his successor. Brown was also wrathful: "I came near shooting him," he wrote of McBlair, "and must have done so had he not consented and got out of my way."[10]

Brown, a Kentuckian by birth and the son of a Presbyterian minister, had spent nearly twenty-eight years in the United States Navy before the war. The story of the *Arkansas* is to a great extent the story of the sheer determination of Brown, a man of prodigious energy and drive. One officer wrote admiringly, "Brown is a pushing man." To another he was "the right man in the right place. He is not afraid of responsibility and there is nothing of the Red Tape about him. . . ."[11]

Brown decided to move the vessel back to Yazoo City; the annual drop in the river after the spring floods, the inacessibility of Greenwood, and the lack of facilities had made the move imperative. By June 4 the *Arkansas* was back at Yazoo City, tied up to the east bank of the river adjacent to the town's southern limits.

Before the war, Yazoo City had been a bustling cotton-shipping port of more than a thousand inhabitants, but the war had disrupted its river trade. Cotton was no longer brought by wagons to the docks to be loaded on steamers; the boats themselves were either confiscated by the Confederate government or were taken far up the river to avoid the approaching Union Navy. In addition, the town's population had declined as more and more of its male citizens drifted off to war. As a river port, however, Yazoo City still had

8. Mallory to McBlair, May 24, 1862, McBlair folder, ZB File. See also Beauregard to General Daniel Ruggles, May 19, 1862, Daniel Ruggles Papers (Department of Archives and History, Jackson, Mississippi); Moseley, "The Naval Career of Henry Kennedy Stevens," 307–308; Charles W. Read, "Reminiscences of the Confederate States Navy," *Southern Historical Society Papers,* I (1876), 349; Alfred Roman, *The Military Operations of General Beauregard in the War Between the States, 1861 to 1865,* I, 370.

9. Moseley, "The Naval Career of Henry Kennedy Stevens," 307–308.

10. *Official Records, Navies,* Ser. I, XVIII, 647. See also Diary of Acting Master's Mate John A. Wilson, National Archives Record Group 45.

11. John Grimball to his father, July 2, 1862, John Grimball Collection (Duke University Library, Durham, North Carolina).

facilities and equipment used to repair steamboats plus the largest sawmill on the river.

Brown's actions clearly demonstrated that his reputation for efficiency was well deserved. Establishing his headquarters at a local plantation, he immediately arrested and imprisoned several workers for insubordination. Orders were issued to press into service all blacksmiths and mechanics that could be found. Brown met with local planters and appealed to them for slave labor and overseers. Two hundred men were obtained from the nearest army detachment. Work was to go on twenty-four hours a day, seven days a week, and all workmen were required to live on board a steamer anchored alongside the *Arkansas*.

Officers and men were sent far and wide searching for badly needed equipment and materials. Plantations were stripped of their forges; ordnance stores were acquired from the army at Vicksburg and from the naval laboratory in Atlanta; more than a hundred solid shot were cast in Jackson, and some powder was manufactured at Yazoo City.[12] Brown later attempted to claim provisions, clothing, small boats, sidearms, chains, and an anchor from the *General Polk* and *Livingston* (refugee gunboats anchored below the town at Liverpool Landing), but before these items could be taken, the vessels were destroyed by the Confederates to prevent their falling into enemy hands.

Six of the ironclad's battery of ten heavy guns were brought from Memphis and the remainder were obtained from the two stranded gunboats. Four gun carriages mounted on railroad iron chassis were brought from Memphis, and the other six were built at Jackson. One officer wrote later that the Jackson carriage builders were inexperienced. Under Stevens's supervision, however, they did the work, and in less than two weeks he appeared at the shipyard "with four ox teams and the carriages."

Work on the *Arkansas* progressed rapidly, accelerated by the knowledge that a powerful enemy fleet was within only a few days' or possibly a a few hours' steaming distance. The steamer *Capitol* was brought alongside, and her hoisting engine was rigged up to drive a number of drills for fitting the railway T-rail iron that was to cover the shield. At night lanterns and pine flares lighted up the ship. During the day the workmen toiled under a hot summer sun, and when men fell from the heat or malaria, others took their place. The work never stopped. Stevens wrote to his wife, "I have not much

12. Diary of Meta Grimball (Southern Historical Collection, University of North Carolina Library, Chapel Hill); Harriet Castlen, *Hope Bids Me Onward*, 63. This book is actually an edited compilation of the letters and writings of Lieutenant George W. Gift, CSN. The originals are now in the Ellen Schackleford Gift Papers (Southern Historical Collection, University of North Carolina Library, Chapel Hill).

time for writing now, as my whole day from five in the morning until seven in the evening is taken up, and I am then pretty tired."[13]

General Earl Van Dorn, who had assumed immediate command at Vicksburg, was concerned over the two powerful fleets converging on that city—the sea-going steamers of Flag Officer Farragut moving up from New Orleans and the river gunboats of Flag Officer Charles H. Davis descending the river from Memphis. On June 23 Van Dorn sent a telegram to President Davis requesting that the *Arkansas,* when completed, be placed under his orders. Davis agreed, saying that the commander of the ironclad was ordered to report to him. Van Dorn was determined to use the vessel against the approaching Union naval forces. "It is better to die game and do some execution than to lie and be burned up in the Yazoo," he wrote the military commander at Yazoo City.[14]

The capture of New Orleans had opened the Mississippi as far as Vicksburg, and early in May, Farragut sent seven vessels up the river "to keep up the panic as far as possible." On May 7 Farragut himself followed, arriving below Vicksburg on May 24 with the *Hartford,* two large steamers, and eight small gunboats. Fourteen hundred troops under General Thomas Williams accompanied the small fleet, but both commanders agreed that the force was not adequate to take the city. Farragut returned down the river but in a few weeks was back again. He was determined to run past the Vicksburg batteries and link up with the Union gunboats assembled above the city. This was accomplished, and on the last day of June, Flag Officer Davis joined him with most of his flotilla.

On June 20, after five weeks at Yazoo City, the *Arkansas* got under way for Liverpool Landing, some twenty-five miles downstream, where a raft of logs and earthwork had been constructed to obstruct the river against Union warships. The vessel was not finished, but the rapid falling of the river made it necessary to move into deeper water as soon as possible. Workmen labored feverishly to complete her, and by the end of the month she was nearly ready. Because of the difficulties in filling her complement of two hundred and thirty-two officers and men, the ironclad did not start down the river until July 14.

Brown's orders were to descend the Yazoo and attack the "upper fleet of the enemy to the cover of the Vicksburg batteries." Brown explained in a letter written to Alfred T. Mahan after the war that his objective was "the

13. Moseley, "The Naval Career of Henry Kennedy Stevens," 309–310.
14. *Official Records, Navies,* Ser. I, XVIII, 650. Charles H. Davis replaced Flag Officer Andrew H. Foote as commanding officer of the U. S. Navy's gunboats on the Mississippi and its tributaries. Foote had asked to be relieved because of a foot wound.

fleet at Vicksburg—a daylight combat and passage . . . [through the city] was the original plan."[15] Vicksburg, however, was to be only a stopping point for taking on coal; the ironclad was to "sweep the river below and run to Mobile as soon as out."[16] The latter part of the plan was never attempted because of the considerable damage the *Arkansas* suffered in the actions of July 15 and because Farragut took his fleet below the city that night.

The *Arkansas* left the obstructions at Liverpool Landing early on the morning of July 14. For the next twenty-four hours she steamed slowly down the narrow, twisting Yazoo River, her voyage interrupted occasionally to correct minor problems. By daybreak the following day she had entered "Old River," an old channel of the Mississippi the Yazoo followed before it broke through a neck of land into the present channel. It was in the old channel, as the morning mist disappeared before the rising sun, that the outlines of three vessels steaming up the river were observed. Within minutes they were identified as an ironclad and two wooden gunboats—obviously enemy.

The three vessels were the ironclad *Carondelet,* the wooden gunboat *Tyler,* and the army ram *Queen of the West.* They were on a reconnaissance up the Yazoo to locate the *Arkansas* and ascertain the force necessary to destroy her. For some time the Union commanders opposite Vicksburg had had knowledge of the approaching completion of a ram, but they were unaware that she had been finished. In fact, Farragut wrote to Union Naval Secretary Welles on July 10, "I do not think she will ever come forth."

As soon as the approaching *Arkansas* was identified (she showed no colors), the *Tyler* opened fire from her lead position and began backing down the river toward the other Federal vessels. Meanwhile both the *Carondelet* and the *Queen of the West* came about and headed downstream at full steam. Commander Henry Walke, the *Carondelet's* commanding officer, was later criticized for exposing to the *Arkansas* his vessel's poorly armored and armed stern rather than her heavily armored bow. Walke defended his action:

Being a stern-wheel boat, the *Carondelet* required room and time to turn around. To avoid being sunk immediately, she turned and retreated. I was not such a simpleton as to 'take the bull by the horn,' to be fatally rammed. . . . If I had continued fighting, bows on, in that narrow river, a collision, which the enemy

15. Brown wrote this to Mahan when the latter was getting material for his first book, *The Gulf and Inland Waters.* See letter of May 9, 1883, in Area 5 File, National Archives Record Group 45.

16. *Official Records, Navies,* Ser. I, XIX, 136–137; Grimball to mother, July 31, 1862, Grimball Collection; Charles I. Graves to Maggie, July 14, 1862, Charles I. Graves Papers (Southern Historical Collection, University of North Carolina Library, Chapel Hill); Castlen, *Hope Bids me Onward,* 49–50.

desired, would have been inevitable, and would have sunk the *Carondelet* in a few minutes.[17]

Brown meanwhile ordered the pilot to "stand for" the *Carondelet*. Brown and Walke had been messmates and friends before the war; until the engagement was over, neither was aware of the presence of the other. Brown concentrated his fire on the Union ironclad, ignoring the *Tyler* and the army ram. He planned to ram her, and for nearly an hour the *Arkansas* closed slowly on her intended victim. She was within two lengths of the *Carondelet,* too close for her bow guns to fire; the Confederate commander noted, "I found myself going over the tops of the young willows and drawing as the vessel did 13 feet I feared getting inextricably aground and so ordered the helm aport almost touching the side of the *Carondelet* as the *Arkansas* sheered off."[18] As the Confederate ram passed, she fired a full broadside with depressed guns into the hull of the Union vessel. Evidently one of the shots from the stern gun swept away the wheel ropes, for the *Carondelet* ran ashore, "hanging to the willows," as Brown reported to Mallory.

With the Union ironclad out of the fight, the *Arkansas* gave her attention to the *Tyler,* several hundred yards above the *Queen of the West*. The *Tyler's* captain, Lieutenant Commander William Gwin, knew he was in serious trouble. His vessel, a river steamboat cut down and altered with one thirty-two pounder in the stern, was no match for her heavily armored opponent. Nevertheless, he managed to keep from two to three hundred yards ahead of the *Arkansas*—not a comfortable distance, but it did prevent the Confederate ironclad from closing and possibly ramming. At the same time, a very effective fire was poured on her from the *Tyler*. One shot struck the shield and knocked Brown temporarily unconscious. A second shot crashed through the pilot house, broke off the forward rim of the wheel, and mortally wounded the Yazoo River pilot. The *Arkansas* suffered further structural damage when a number of shots and shells penetrated the smokestack and severed the breechings (connections between the stack and furnaces). The damage was serious, for she lost her effectiveness as a ram. Steam pressure dropped from one hundred and twenty to twenty pounds—barely sufficient to keep the engines going—just as she neared the Mississsippi, and by the time she reached the Union fleets, she was moving at less than three miles

17. Henry Walke, *Naval Scenes and Reminiscences of the Civil War in the United States, on the Southern and Western Waters During the years 1861, 1862, and 1863. With the History of the Period Compared and Corrected from Authentic Sources* (New York, 1877), 307.

18. Brown to Mahan, November 25, 1883, Area 5 File, National Archives Record Group 45.

per hour. Damage to the breechings resulted in temperatures soaring to a suffocating one hundred and twenty degrees on the gundeck and to over one hundred and thirty degrees below in the fire room. As the battered Confederate ram steamed slowly into the sluggish Mississippi, the *Tyler* and her consort were rushing as rapidly as their paddle wheels would carry them toward the anchored Union fleets.

Twelve miles above Vicksburg, the Yazoo flows into the Mississippi. Approximately halfway between Vicksburg and the mouth of the Yazoo, the various vessels that made up the squadrons of Flag Officers Farragut and Davis lay at anchor—more than thirty in all. The transports were generally lined up on the Louisiana side of the river; the warships occupied the Vicksburg side. Nearest to the Yazoo and to the approaching Confederate vessel were the wooden-hulled rams manned by army personnel and under the command of Lieutenant Colonel Alfred Ellet. There were four of them, all unarmed side- and stern-wheelers. The rams were followed in line by the eight deep-draft vessels of Farragut's squadron, veterans of the New Orleans campaign that had run the Vicksburg batteries on the night of June 28. Downstream from Farragut's ships lay the river ironclads under Flag Officer Davis. Anchored in line were three center-wheeled vessels armed with thirteen-gun batteries known as "Pook Turtles"; the *Sumter,* a Confederate gunboat captured at Memphis; and the *Essex,* a converted river ferryboat. Below Davis' ironclads—and closer to Vicksburg—were a number of small mortar boats.

There was no indication that the *Arkansas* or any other enemy vessel was expected. Not one vessel had fires lighted and enough steam to get under way quickly. At approximately 6:00 A. M., firing was heard up the river, but as Davis wrote later, "most of us came to the conclusion that the firing was upon guerrilla parties."[19] As the firing grew louder, some suspicions were aroused. The captain of the ironclad *Benton* asked Davis' permission to raise steam immediately, and on the *Hartford* some men began casting loose the gun tackles, apparently without orders. At 7:15 A. M. the *Tyler* and the *Queen of the West* were observed rounding a bend, followed by the *Arkansas.*

Brown was worried about his lack of speed and directed the pilot to steer close to the anchored men-of-war to decrease the possibility of being rammed. The *Arkansas* slipped past the rams, but as she came abreast of Farragut's vessels, they opened fire. The *Kineo* fired first, followed by the *Hartford.* Aroused by the cannonade, Farragut appeared on the flagship's

19. Charles H. Davis Jr., *Life of Charles Henry Davis Rear Admiral 1807–1877,* 262–263.

deck in his nightgown and "seemed much surprised."[20] As the *Arkansas* continued down the line, the Union warships in turn sent broadsides crashing at her armored side. Most of the shots glanced off, but not all. One from the *Hartford* penetrated the railroad iron, a bale of cotton, and twenty inches of wood backing before exploding. Fragments from this shell killed four men on the thirty-two-pound broadside gun. The gunnery officer wrote: "The Captain of the gun standing at my right was knocked down by the concussion and so great was the shock that he lost his mind and never recovered."[21] A second shot exploded near a gun port killing a sponger; a third smashed through the starboard side killing two men and a powder boy and wounding three others. Another shell removed the colors, but Midshipman Dabney Scales scrambled up the ladder under fire and replaced them—a futile gesture for they were again carried away.

Damage was by no means confined to the Confederate ship. The ram *Lancaster* was anchored at the head of the Union fleets, evidently as a picket. She was the first vessel able to raise enough steam to get underway. She tried to ram the Confederate armorclad, but a fortunate shot from the *Arkansas* hit a steam drum. The escaping steam poured through the ship, scalding many men. A witness described the horror he felt as "the scalded men jumped overboard, and some of them never came to the surface again."[22]

It took the *Arkansas* thirty minutes to reach the end of the Union line. The *Benton,* Davis's flagship, was the last warship in line, other than the mortar boats. Although she had had time to build up steam, the Confederate vessel had passed, with an exchange of broadsides, before the *Benton* could maneuver into the current. The *Benton* and a sister ship followed the ram until she rounded the bend directly above Vicksburg and came under cover of the Confederate land batteries.

When the firing was heard coming from up the river, soldiers and civilians at Vicksburg began lining the banks. One spectator estimated that more than 20,000 people assembled on the heights above the river near the bend in the river. Generals John C. Breckenridge and Van Dorn viewed the entire fight from the dome of the courthouse. The fleets were in plain view, and when the *Arkansas* appeared, the spectators began yelling and cheering

20. Bartholomew Diggins, "Recollections of the war cruise of the *USS Hartford,* January to December, 1862–1864," (MS in New York Public Library, New York City).

21. Dabney Scales to Mahan, April 30, 1883, Area 5 File, National Archives Record Group 45; see also Reminiscences of Arthur D. Wharton in Arthur D. Wharton folder, ZB File; Hinds County *Gazette* (Raymond, Mississippi), December 9, 1874.

22. *Official Records, Navies,* Ser. I, XIX, 747.

as if it were a "horse race."[23] As the battle progressed "clouds of dense white smoke" began to cover the river, and as a newspaper reporter wrote, "only the continuous roar announced that [she] . . . still lived."[24]

At 8:50 A.M. the *Arkansas* reversed her engines, preparing to moor at a wharf opposite the courthouse. General Van Dorn, instead of waiting for the vessel to dock, was rowed out in a small boat. A member of his staff said later: "The smoke was still rolling around . . . the survivors of the crew, stripped to the waist and blackened with gunpowder, were just beginning to clean decks, and altogether it was the most frightful scene of war that was ever presented to my eyes."[25] Another officer who was in charge of a company of cannoneers acting as stretcher-bearers described the frightful carnage that he found in the gunroom; "the embrazures, or portholes, were splintered, and some were nearly twice the original size; her broadside walls were shivered, and great slabs and splinters were strewn over the deck of her entire gunroom; her stairways were so bloody and slippery that we had to sift cinders from the ash pans to keep from slipping. . . ."[26] When she made fast to the wharf, a number of curious soldiers and civilians crowded on board, but recoiled when they saw "blood and brains bespattered every [where], whilst arms, legs, and several headless trunks were strewn about."

Shortly after the vessel was moored, all dead, wounded, and sick were removed. A detachment of army volunteers also departed, since their orders required them to go only as far as Vicksburg. This so depleted the ship's crew that there were not enough men left to handle the guns. Brown's efforts to obtain additional recruits were entirely unsuccessful. He became so desperate that he agreed to take volunteers from the army to serve on board for terms of one week. One officer wrote, rather bitterly, "It is a shame for the Department to keep us here, half manned with green soldiers . . . [when] there is a good crew of sailor men, the *Virginia*'s, in a shore battery near Richmond. . . ."[27]

23. L. S. Flatau, "A Great Naval Battle," *Confederate Veteran*, XXV (1917), 459. See also Roland Chamber Diaries (Department of Archives, Louisiana State University, Baton Rouge); John S. Kendall, "Recollections of a Confederate Officer," *Louisiana Historical Quarterly*, XXIX (1946), 1239; Peter F. Walker, *Vicksburg: A People at War, 1860–1865*, 114.

24. Article in the Chicago *Tribune* quoted in Walke, *Naval Scenes and Reminiscences*, 313–314.

25. Clement L. Sulivane, "The *Arkansas* at Vicksburg in 1862," *Confederate Veteran* XXV (1917), 496.

26. Flatau, "A Great Naval Battle," 459.

27. Dabney Scales to father, July 29, 1862, copy of letter on file in Naval His-

The *Arkansas* had been heavily damaged. The iron rails on her port side were loosened considerably in some places and completely blown off in others; the smokestack was riddled until it resembled a nutmeg grater; all the boats were shot away; a shot had broken the cast iron ram; and the hawse-pipe had been destroyed. Nevertheless, Van Dorn telegraphed President Davis that the vessel would be repaired quickly, "and then ho! for New Orleans."

"As the boys says, 'I told you so,' " Farragut wrote to Davis a few hours after the *Arkansas* had passed. "We were all caught unprepared for him, but we must go down and destroy him. I will get the squadron underway as soon as the steam is up. . . ." Davis was as cautious as Farragut was impetuous and persuaded him to hold off the attack until late in the afternoon. Davis agreed to engage the upper batteries with his ironclads while the seagoing warships descended the river in two columns. In a tone reminiscent of Nelson, Farragut said in his orders for the attack: "No one will do wrong who lays his vessel alongside of the enemy or tackles the ram. The ram must be destroyed."

Farragut's vessels did not get under way until 7:00 that evening, two hours later than planned, and darkness had descended before they were in sight of Vicksburg. While a vigorous fight was going on between the Union ironclads and the Vicksburg batteries, the two columns steamed down the river, guided on the west side by large fires lighted by Federal soldiers. As the fleet neared the city, the port column swung to within thirty yards of the eastern bank, preparing to attack the *Arkansas*. But the ram could not be seen; all that they could do was fire at her estimated position and gun flashes. Frustrated, Farragut said later, "[I] would have given [my] . . . commission to have [had] a crack at her."[28]

On the *Arkansas* there had been no indication that another battle was pending until a messenger arrived with a note stating that the enemy fleet was preparing to get under way. This was shortly after Davis's vessels had opened fire on the upper batteries. For the third time that day the remaining crewmen, exhausted, dragged themselves to their guns and fired at the Union ships passing by. Only one shell hit the *Arkansas*, but it pierced the port side a few inches below the water line, killing two men and wounding three in the engine room.[29] The encounter lasted about an hour.

---

torical Division, U.S. Navy Department. Casualties were ten killed, fifteen seriously wounded, and more than sixty slightly wounded.

28. Quoted in Charles L. Lewis, *David Glasgow Farragut,* II, 287.

29. One officer later recalled that one of those killed was a pilot who had a

Thus ended what was probably the most humiliating day in Farragut's career. Meekly, he wrote to Welles, "It is with deep mortification that I announce to the Department that notwithstanding my prediction to the contrary, the ironclad ram *Arkansas* has at length made her appearance and took us all by surprise." Flag Officer Davis, however, not only refused to be perturbed by the incident, but actually wrote admiringly of it. "It was certainly a very exciting and pleasing sight so far as the gallantry of the thing was concerned," he told his wife.[30] The Union naval secretary was somewhat less impressed, writing in his diary that it was the most disreputable affair of the war. He also wrote to both of the commanders instructing them to destroy the ironclad "at all hazards."

Farragut needed no urging; in fact, it seemed to Davis that he needed to be calmed down. Davis wrote,

What annoys me is that Farragut invites me to join him in placing both squadrons under the guns of the batteries, thus risking the great trust we hold. . . . I fear that I shall be dragged into a violation of my clearest sense of duty by his impetuosity. Conceive the fatal consequences of the loss of this six hundred miles of river . . . and yet my friend the admiral says we are to act "regardless of consequences." This is the language of a Hotspur. . . .[31]

Davis urged caution and attempted to destroy the ram with mortar fire. It took five days of planning and more than twenty communications to devise a satisfactory plan for the mortar attack. When it proved unsuccessful, Farragut's patience was sorely tried.

On July 20 Colonel Ellet wrote Davis offering to take command of one of his rams personally and attack the *Arkansas* if Farragut and Davis would engage the batteries. A conference followed in which details of the operation were, supposedly, worked out. The *Queen of the West* commanded by Ellet and the ironclad *Essex,* recently arrived from St. Louis under the command of Commander William "Wild Bill" Porter, brother of David D. Porter, would attack the *Arkansas* from above, while the *Sumter* attacked from below. According to Ellet, the plan of attack called for Porter to "grapple the *Arkansas* and drag her into the stream and fight her broadside to broadside lashed together." At the same time Ellet was to dash in and ram her exposed

premonition of his fate. "When the fleet was passing down . . . he did not go into the pilot house but stayed below looking over at the engines. The single shot that struck us . . . struck him fairly in the middle of the body and literally tore him into a thousand pieces." Wharton, Reminiscences, BZ File.

30. Davis, *Charles Henry Davis,* 262–263.
31. *Ibid.,* 264–266.

beam. Incredibly, Porter later wrote to Ellet that he was not even aware that Ellet and his ram were to participate in the attack.[32]

Shortly before daybreak on the morning of July 22, three of Davis's vessels, the *Benton, Louisville,* and *Cincinnati* moved down and opened fire on the upper batteries. At 4:14 A.M. the *Essex* started downstream. A few minutes later the *Queen of the West* followed. A most unfortunate misunderstanding occurred as Ellet's vessel passed the *Benton.* Davis, on board the latter, shouted, "good luck," but Ellet thought he yelled, "Go back!" and immediately swung the ram about. Precious time was lost before the confusion could be straightened out, and by this time the *Essex* was out of sight.

The situation on the *Arkansas* was critical. She was moored to the bank with her bow pointed upstream and was practically helpless. There was no steam to get under way, and there were only enough men on board to man three guns. Porter attempted to ram cross current, but as the *Essex* bore in, the Confederate crew threw off the bow lines and swung her prow out toward the oncoming ironclad. The *Arkansas* fired her guns as they were brought to bear, but with little effect. The *Essex'* fire, on the other hand, was most damaging. One shot struck the *Arkansas* near the forward porthole of the port side, breaking off the ends of the rails and throwing metal among the gun crews. Several men were wounded. A second shot penetrated the shield, crossed diagonally to the starboard side, and hit a broadside gun. This shot killed several men and wounded others. These shots were fired at so close a range that, as one officer wrote, "our men were burnt by the powder from the enemy's guns."[33] By this time Brown's crew was so decimated that only two guns could be used, even with his officers "pointing and firing them in person."

When the *Arkansas*'s bow swung toward the *Essex,* the Federal vessel grazed her side and slipped up on the bank. For ten minutes she remained aground—the target of every Confederate gun within range. She finally backed clear and steamed downstream, under continuous fire until out of range. Although Porter's battered ironclad was hit at least forty-two times, damage was slight, and only one man was killed and three wounded. In the meantime Ellet's *Queen of the West* was running the gauntlet of fire from

32. Alfred Ellet to Charles Ellet, July 24, 1862, David Porter to Alfred Ellet, November 27, 1862, in Charles Ellet Papers (University of Michigan Library, Ann Arbor); W. D. Crandall, and I. D. Newell, *History of the Ram Fleet and the Mississippi River Brigade,* 110; Milligan, *Gunboats Down the Mississippi,* 87–90.

33. Dabney Scales to his father, July 29, 1862, copy of letter in Naval Historical Division, Navy Department. See also George W. Gift, "The Story of the *Arkansas,*" *Southern Historical Society Papers,* XII (1884), 168–169.

the batteries on the bluffs at Vicksburg. Because Ellett misjudged his speed, he passed the Confederate vessel and was forced to ram against the current. The Confederate armorclad rolled heavily but suffered little damage. In return the *Arkansas*'s two guns raked the Union steamer from stem to stern. Ellet immediately headed back upstream and once again the *Queen of the West* came under the curtain of fire from the cannon overlooking the river. Although heavily damaged, she suffered no casualties.

This failure was the last straw. Farragut, who had been reluctant to ascend the river in the first place, decided to return back down the river. Two days after the abortive attack on the *Arkansas,* the troops were embarked on transports, and by mid-afternoon the entire fleet was standing down the river. Farragut went all the way to New Orleans but left two of his gunboats, as well as the *Essex* and the *Sumter,* at Baton Rouge to watch for the Confederate ironclad in case she ventured down. Less than two weeks later the *Arkansas* followed.

On August 2, Lieutenant Stevens, the executive officer, sent a hastily written note to his sister: "We are ordered off tomorrow and expect a pretty tough time of it. . . . Our destination is Baton Rouge. It is not just to send us in our condition, but I am ready to do what I can." The "condition" that Stevens referred to was not encouraging. Damages sustained during the attack of July 22 were still being repaired, and the engines were so defective that the chief engineer warned that they might break down at any time. Her crew had finally been filled, but with untrained volunteers from various artillery regiments in Vicksburg. Finally, the *Arkansas* would have to go into action without her commanding officer, for Brown was in Granada, Mississippi, on sick leave.[34]

At 2:00 A.M. on August 3, the *Arkansas*'s lines were cast off, and while Vicksburg citizens slumbered, she slowly got under way, with Stevens in command. A veteran of twenty-two years of naval service, Stevens was greatly admired by the crew. He was deeply religious. He wrote to his mother after the battles and ordeals of July 15 asking her to pray for him. "I myself," he wrote, "feel most grateful for all [God's] mercy. It is to his protecting arm alone that we are here this day." While informing his wife of his safety, he noted, "We have been shown that we need not trust to iron sides nor cotton

34. Moseley, "The Naval Career of Henry Kennedy Stevens," 312; Isaac N. Brown, "The Confederate Gunboat *Arkansas,*" *Battles and Leaders,* III, 579. When Brown received word of the *Arkansas's* impending movement, he left immediately for Vicksburg but arrived too late. Still suffering from illness, but grimly determined to rejoin his ship, he took the train for Tangipahoa, Louisiana. He arrived in time to collect the ship's crew and bring it back to Mississippi.

protection, but the uplifted arm of God." When his promising career was cut short by a Minié ball a few months later, a fellow officer wrote a fitting epitaph: "No deck E'er drunk better blood than his. He was a brave, skillful and talented officer, and a pious gentleman."[35]

As the *Arkansas* steamed down the Mississippi, a small Confederate army of 3,000 men moved into position to assault Baton Rouge. The men were under General John C. Breckinridge, the former Vice-President of the United States and presidential candidate in the election of 1860. Defending Baton Rouge was a Union force of approximately the same number of men under General Thomas Williams. The Union general had entrenched his men around the city with the flanks resting on the river. Protecting the flanks were the gunboats *Essex, Gayuga, Kineo,* and *Katahdin.* Breckinridge believed that a successful attack depended on the *Arkansas*'s ability to drive off the Union vessels and bombard Union positions in the town, but the Confederate ironclad was unable to carry out her part of the plan.

Twenty-four hours after the ironclad got underway for Baton Rouge, her engines developed so much trouble that Stevens anchored for repairs. As the engineers worked on the machinery under the feeble light of kerosene lamps, Breckinridge launched his attack. By the time the repairs were completed (8:00 A.M.), the Federal lines were breaking, and Williams's troops were beginning to fall back toward the river.

In 1862 Baton Rouge was located on a long, straight section of the Mississippi that extended four miles above the city. Shortly after the *Arkansas* reached this part of the stream, within sight of Baton Rouge, her starboard engine suddenly stopped. The port engine continued racing at full speed, forcing the vessel to ground on some cypress stumps. The chief engineer recommended calling off the attack. He reported to Stevens,

From my examination of all the defects in the . . . engines, it will be impossible for me to put them in fit condition to render efficient aid to propel the ship into action. . . . The steam drum has now the entire weight of the gun deck. If it should be possible to use the ram, in my judgment the weak condition of the ship would carry it (the drum) away. . . .

Stevens then asked him whether the engines could be stopped and the vessel backed, and if so how long it would take. The engineer replied that it would take fifteen or twenty minutes.[36]

35. George Gift to Ellen, March 6, 1863, Ellen Shackleford Gift Papers.
36. Charleston *Daily Courier,* March 24, 1863. Stevens evidently sent home copies of various documents including the engineer's reports and they were quoted by one of the lieutenant's relatives in a biographical article after his death in February 1863.

While the engineers worked wearily on the machinery, the remainder of the crew strove to clear the ironclad from the stumps. By sundown she was free with her engines working again. Coal had been located on a landing several miles upstream, and Stevens decided to move up to the landing, fuel his ship during the night, and attack the Union vessels early the following morning. On the way up the river, a crank pin in the starboard engine broke, and again the vessel was forced to anchor for repairs.

Throughout the day the battle for Baton Rouge raged. The Federals were slowly giving ground. Breckinridge anxiously awaited the arrival of the *Arkansas,* but all that he heard from the river were the guns of the Union gunboats as they poured a direct fire into his ranks. Late in the afternoon he withdrew his exhausted troops to the suburbs; they had been in the lines without water and food for sixteen hours and under heavy fire most of the time.

During the night, news of the *Arkansas's* approach reached Porter on the *Essex.* At 8:00 A.M. on August 6, the *Essex* led the small Union flotilla up the river in search of the ram. On the *Arkansas,* the crank pin was replaced at about the time Porter's vessel was raising anchor, and as the Confederate armorclad was building up steam, the Union vessels came within sight. Stevens immediately determined to steam a few hundred yards upstream, turn and attack the *Essex* first, then the other gunboats. As the *Arkansas* moved out into the stream, Porter believed that she was trying to escape, and he opened fire—although he was out of range. The Confederate vessel had steamed only a few yards when both engines broke down within a minute of each other, and she drifted helplessly back to shore.[37]

Stevens then prepared to abandon ship. The engines were broken up with axes, the magazines were opened and cartridges scattered; and shells were placed on the gun deck between the guns. The guns were then loaded, primed, and readied to fire, and finally the wardroom bedding and cotton lining in the shield were set on fire. The vessel meanwhile began to drift out

37. Masters Mate Wilson says in his diary that when they got under way upstream they were going back to Vicksburg; the idea of attacking was given up after Stevens held a conference with his officers. Stevens mentions the conference, but does not say what was decided. Moseley, "The Naval Career of Henry Kennedy Stevens," 318–319. For a slightly different account see W. P. Park to Marcus J. Wright, October 23, 1893, Records of the 1st Regiment Tennessee Heavy Artillery, National Archives Record Group 109. The Arkansas's engines were new, manufactured in Memphis, but they were poorly constructed and never worked properly. Stevens later expressed suspicion of the builder of the engines because he fled to the North. More than likely, the failure of the engines was just another example of the Confederacy's inability to manufacture power plants adequate for warships.

into the river, and Stevens, the last to leave, had to jump over the stern and swim ashore.

The *Essex* and the other Union vessels had remained at a "respectful" distance from the *Arkansas,* sending shells in her direction, but without effect. They made no attempt to close even after the ironclad began drifting down the river.[38]

After being fired, the *Arkansas* drifted slowly downstream for more than an hour. As the fire reached the guns, they were discharged. " 'It was beautiful,' said Lieutenant Stevens, while the tears stood in his eyes, 'to see her, when abandoned by commander and crew, and dedicated to sacrifice, fighting the battle on her own hook.' "[39] About noon the *Arkansas* finally blew up.

When Breckinridge was informed of the ironclad's destruction, he decided not to renew the attack and withdrew his troops from the city.

Thus ended the service of the last of the five armorclads originally laid down by the Confederate government. Mallory had believed that these vessels would not only destroy the Union blockade, but ultimately carry the war to enemy waters and attack New York, Washington, and other cities along the eastern seaboard. Only the *Virginia,* however, gained a position from which such an operation was possible, and she was unseaworthy. The naval secretary was despondent over their destruction, but he was also impressed by the achievements of the *Virginia* and *Arkansas.* The fact that neither was destroyed by enemy fire, but by their own crews, convinced him even more of their importance. He determined that every effort should be made to build up a powerful ironclad navy in the Confederacy.

---

38. Porter claimed that shells from the *Essex* destroyed the Confederate ram, and Farragut at first supported his claim. After hearing from the other gunboat commanders, however, he changed his opinion, and wrote to Welles that the vessel was blown up by her own crew. Benjamin Butler claimed that Porter was in his office when a Confederate staff officer on an errand of business under a flag of truce informed them that she was set on fire by her crew. Porter refused to believe it. Benjamin F. Butler, *Butler's Book,* 483–484; *Private and Official Correspondence of General Benjamin F. Butler during the Period of the Civil War,* II, 140–141, 164, 176, 178–180; Fairfax to Wise, August 22, 1862, Henry A. Wise Letterbook (New York Historical Society, New York City); *Official Records, Navies,* Ser. I, XIX, 120; G. M. Williams, "The first Vicksburg expedition, and the Battle of Baton Rouge," in *Papers read before the Wisconsin Commandery of the Loyal Legion of the United States,* II, 52–69.

39. *Official Records, Navies,* Ser. I, XIX, 138. See also George W. Burgess, "The ram *Arkansas* and the battle of Baton Rouge," *East and West Baton Rouge Historical Society Proceedings,* II, 34–37; Sarah Dawson, *A Confederate Girl's Diary,* 150.

5

1862, the Year of Transition

THE YEAR 1862 was particularly significant for the Confederate ironclad program. Mallory and a few progressive naval officers and congressmen had long believed that armored vessels would offset Union naval superiority, but the final decision to concentrate on ironclad construction came only in the summer of 1862 after the successes of the *Virginia* and the *Arkansas*. This emphasis on armored ships henceforth would be the major objective of Confederate naval policy.

Although the Confederate navy had five ironclads under construction at the beginning of 1862, most of its efforts were still spent in converting and building wooden gunboats. A great many naval officers doubted both the feasibility of ironclads and the South's ability to construct these vessels. As naval constructor Porter wrote: "I received but little encouragement from anyone while the *Virginia* was progressing."[1] Moreover, the Union amphibious operations of late 1861 which resulted in the capture of Forts Clark and Hatteras on the North Carolina coast and Port Royal in South Carolina actually accelerated the building of wooden gunboats.[2] In both state legislatures and the Confederate Congress there were new demands that gunboats be constructed as rapidly as possible for river and harbor defense. Even more important, though, was the October 22 proposal of Matthew Fontaine Maury, one of the most revered officers in Confederate naval service. Recognizing the lack of facilities necessary to build large warships, he averred that the South could construct a large number of small steam gunboats with "neither cabin, nor steerage, nor any accommodation on board."[3] Shortly before Christmas 1861, Congress authorized the construction of one hundred of these small vessels and appropriated two million dollars for the work.

1. Quoted from a letter in the Charleston *Daily Courier,* March 19, 1862.
2. For a succinct statement on the effects of these operations see James M. Merrill, *The Rebel Shore: The Story of Union Sea Power in the Civil War,* v–vi.
3. *Official Records, Navies,* Ser. II, II, 98–104. For a detailed account of Maury's gunboats see Francis L. Williams, *Matthew Fontaine Maury: Scientist of the Sea,* 382–390.

Meanwhile, state legislatures were also showing concern with warship construction. The Mississippi Legislature appropriated $50,000 for the building of light-draft gunboats; the Tennessee Legislature petitioned Congress to authorize the construction of river gunboats for defense of the Cumberland and Tennessee rivers; the Louisiana Legislature debated a resolution to allocate funds for gunboat construction; the Alabama General Assembly on November 8 passed an act appropriating $150,000 for the "construction of an iron clad gunboat and ram for the defense of the bay and harbor of Mobile;" and in December the South Carolina General Assembly set up a special committee to investigate the possibility of building war vessels. From all the gunboats built at state initiative, only those constructed under the authority of the Alabama and South Carolina General Assemblies were ironclads, and they were turned over to the Confederate government.

In December, a special commission appointed by the Alabama Legislature purchased the *Baltic,* a lighter used to transport cotton from Mobile to ships in the lower bay, and within a month the work of converting her into an ironclad was proceeding rapidly. There was little difficulty in obtaining labor and material since Mobile was a small-boat and shipbuilding center before the war, and except for the iron plate, essential materials could be found locally. On May 27 conversion was completed, and the vessel was turned over to the Confederate government. Flag Officer Victor Randolph, commanding the Mobile Naval Station, accepted the vessel but rebuked the commission for being "greatly imposed upon by the mechanics and . . . [taking] a most unreasonable time . . . occupied in [her] completion."[4]

The *Baltic* was 186 feet in length, 38 feet in beam, with a draft of approximately 6 feet. She was armed with four guns, fitted with a ram, and powered with two high-pressure engines connected to side wheels. A nondescript vessel in many ways, she was unmanageable, slow, and unliveable for her crew. One of her officers described her as "rotten as punk, and . . . as fit to go into action as a mud scow."[5] But she remained the only Confederate

4. to Governor Shorter, May 1862, Area file, Confederate Subject and Area File, National Archives Record Group 45. See also *Baltic* Construction Papers, Military Records Division, Navy Records, File 34 (Department of Archives and History, Montgomery, Alabama), and Mallory to Baker, March 5, 1863, construction at Mobile folder, Confederate Subject and Area File, National Archives Record Group 45.

5. *Official Records, Navies,* Ser. I, XXI, 886. See also Buchanan to Mallory, September 26, 1862 in Buchanan letterbook, and a memorandum dated February 24, 1863, in the Gustavus V. Fox Papers (New York Historical Society, New York City). Lieutenant John Grimball while serving on the ram which he referred to as his "Castle [and] . . . a rather warm one," wrote that "our sleeping quarters are cool and

ironclad operating in Mobile Bay until the *Tennessee* was completed in 1864.

Early in 1862, South Carolina also started an ironclad construction program at the recommendation of a committee appointed by the General Assembly the previous December. Three hundred thousand dollars were appropriated for the project, and in February the chief of the state military department consulted with Mallory about building warships. The naval secretary strongly disapproved of the idea, noting that the navy was already utilizing all available facilities and labor to build gunboats. Duly impressed with Mallory's argument, the General Assembly dismissed its committee. In March, however, Captain Duncan N. Ingraham, CSN, in command of naval construction at Charleston since November 1861, was appointed to the command of naval forces in South Carolina waters. Within a few days Ingraham was able to persuade both Mallory and the General Assembly to reconsider their respective positions. The result was the appointment of a new "gunboat commission," which recommended the immediate construction of an ironclad similar to the *Palmetto State,* recently laid down in Charleston under the direction of the Navy Department. The assembly agreed and appropriated the necessary money for what was to become the *Chicora.*[6]

These two vessels would be under construction throughout the spring and summer months. The usual problems confronted the builders. Ship timber was not available and had to be cut. Following Ingraham's futile appeal to local planters for white oak, the assembly authorized the builders to cut timber, "wherever most accessible, provided . . . [they] will not cut shade and ornamental trees, without consent of the owners."[7] The vessels were ready for their armor in June, but an unfortunate delay occurred when the army refused to release sufficient railroad cars to transport the heavy metal to Charleston. No sooner was this problem overcome than a second frustrating delay materialized because the Treasury Department failed to pay its bills promptly. Consequently, July and most of August had passed before all of the armor plate had reached the yards.

---

airy, being nothing more than on deck between the wheel house under a awning." To his mother, September 12, 1862, Grimball Collection.

6. Report of the Chairman of the Military Committee, August 30, 1863, *Journal of the Convention of the People of South Carolina held in 1860, 61, and 1862 together* with the Ordinances, Reports, Resolutions, etc., 612–613; Charles C. Cauthen, *South Carolina Goes to War, 1860–1865,* 150; *Charleston, South Carolina: The Centennial of Incorporation, 1883,* 232. See also Francis T. Chew Journal (Southern Historical Collection, University of North Carolina Library, Chapel Hill), and the Memoirs of James H. Tomb in the William V. and James H. Tomb Papers (Southern Historical Collection, University of North Carolina Library).

7. Charleston *Daily Courier,* April 3, 1862.

On August 23 the *Chicora* was launched and turned over to the Navy Department in accordance with instructions from the assembly to sell the vessel to the Confederate government and use the money to construct a second one. Within a month her commanding officer took charge, officers and men reported on board, and her battery was received and mounted.

For some unexplained reason, however, progress on her sister ship the *Palmetto State* was not as advanced. Her captain, Lieutenant Alexander F. Warley, received his orders as early as August 25. After commanding the *Manassas* in the "Head of the Passes affair," he served on the ill-fated *Louisiana,* and was on board when she surrendered at Fort Jackson. Exchanged early in August, he subsequently reported to Charleston, where he assumed responsibility for completing the vessel and preparing her for service. Understandably, he wrote a few weeks later, "God knows when we will be ready."[8] The launching of the *Palmetto State* on October 11 was an unusually elaborate affair, primarily because a substantial amount of the cost of the vessel was paid by donations from the women of South Carolina.[9] A local correspondent for the Richmond *Whig* described the occasion:

All places affording a view of the boat and of the site of the ceremonial were thronged at an early hour, and a large proportion of the spectators were of the fair sex. At an early stage of the proceedings General Beauregard and staff . . . arrived and took position on the upper deck, which, being elevated some distance above the surrounding wharves, formed the rostrum for the occasion. . . . At the appointed hour, the exercises were opened with prayer. . . . Colonel Richard Yeadon . . . then delivered an oration. . . . [after the speech] the orator handed a check for thirty thousand dollars to Captain Ingraham, and then proceeded to perform the baptism. . . . Just as the ceremony had been concluded, the other gunboat, the *Chicora,* came steaming up from the wharves, and with colors flying fore and aft saluted her consort. . . . The pleasing ceremonial being over, the ladies were invited into the workshop of the Messer's Marsh, where they partook of a bountiful collaration [sic]. . . .

Early in November both vessels were operating with the Charleston Squadron.

South Carolina later built another ironclad, the *Charleston,* and turned her over to the Confederate government. One hundred and eighty feet in length and thirty-four feet in beam, she carried four Brooke rifles in broadside

8. to Robert Minor, September 27, 1862, in Minor Papers. Launching was delayed several days because the water off the ways was not deep enough. More than 2,000 tons of mud had to be drained from the floor of the river. Voucher, August 23, 1862, construction at Charleston folder, Confederate Subject and Area File, National Archives Record Group 45.

9. See below, pp. 85–87 for the Charleston Ladies Gunboat Association.

and two nine-inch smoothbores as pivots. She was ready for service early in 1864 and became the flagship of the Charleston Squadron.

Little change occurred in the navy's shipbuilding program during the early months of 1862. Riverboats were still being converted into vessels-of-war, Maury's gunboat project was beginning, and the five initial ironclads were still under construction. Work on the *Virginia,* however, rapidly progressed, and Mallory's enthusiasm grew as the vessel neared completion. On February 27 he reported to the President that the five ironclads under construction and others of this type would "keep our waters free from the enemy. . . ." Five days later he replied to a resolution of the House of Representatives, "as to what additional means in money, men, arms, and the munitions of war are . . . necessary . . . for the public service," that fifty light-draft ironclads for local defense and four armored cruisers could be used immediately.[10]

No action had been taken on this recommendation when the *Virginia* fought her celebrated combat in Hampton Roads. It was this engagement that dramatically justified Mallory's faith in ironclad vessels-of-war. A few days after the battle, a Confederate naval officer wrote that "as to the wooden gunboats we are building, they are not worth a cent." Congress evidently shared this sentiment, for on March 17 the House of Representatives passed a resolution declaring that it was "of the utmost importance that this Government should construct with the least possible delay as many small ironclad rams as practicable," and authorized the President to suspend the act approving the construction of Maury's wooden gunboats.

At first Mallory evidently favored converting the wooden gunboats (of which fifteen were already under construction) into ironclads. After a series of conferences on the matter, however, he recommended to the President that the wooden gunboats already on the stocks be completed as planned while the remainder of the two million dollars appropriated for Maury's vessels be reallocated to the building of additional armored ships. On May 1 Congress gave Mallory the authorization he desired.[11]

The secretary had not waited for congressional approval to expand his ironclad program. Already, in the latter part of February, Ingraham was empowered to negotiate a contract for the construction of a 150-foot harbor-defense ironclad which became the *Palmetto State.* On March 7 a shipbuilder in New Orleans received a contract to build a large ironclad ram, and a few days later Commander John K. Mitchell, also in New Orleans, was ordered

10. *Official Records, Navies,* Ser. II, I, 796; II, 152.
11. *Ibid.,* I, 751.

to engage builders for an unspecified number of 150-foot-class vessel. At the navy yard in Norfolk, still another of this class was laid down. By May 1, Mallory had sanctioned at least twelve new ironclads to be built either by contract or in navy yards.[12]

For a brief period during the spring and early summer months of 1862, the navy enjoyed a refreshing amount of popular support. Ironically, this stemmed from the erroneous belief that the new ironclad fleet would save the Confederacy, as one newspaper expressed it, by driving "from our waters the whole blockading fleet." This optimistic faith germinated with the publicity gained by the *Virginia*'s exploits, and even the loss of New Orleans strengthened these ideas, for it was commonly believed that Farragut was able to capture the city only because the *Mississippi* and *Louisiana* were not completed. The ability of the *Arkansas* to run the gauntlet of Federal ships anchored off Vicksburg without being sunk further intensified faith in the ironclads' invincibility.

The overwhelming majority of the people (and apparently newspapers were no better informed) never realized that the ironclads laid down in 1862 and later were not designed to break the blockade, but to protect the harbors, rivers, and inlets of the South.[13] At some time in 1862, Mallory recognized that the blockade could be raised only by an attack from outside the Confederacy by the ironclads and other vessels that were being converted or constructed in Europe. Various advisers (particularly Brooke) had earlier convinced the secretary that seagoing armored ships could be built in the Southern states in spite of deficiencies in skilled labor and facilities. The validity of this idea was shaken when it was demonstrated that the *Virginia* was not seaworthy, followed by doubts (never to be proven or disproven) concerning the Mississippi vessels. Naval Constructor Porter had long insisted that the Confederacy's limited facilities should be utilized to construct small, shallow-draft, ironclads that were simple to build. After inspecting Porter's plans for such vessels (modified from the original 1846 model), Mallory agreed to the construction of one small armored vessel at Charleston and another at Norfolk. Others were to be laid down as soon as Congress allocated the necessary funds.

Late in March 1862, disagreement between Porter and Brooke grew into open controversy when the constructor wrote a letter to Richmond newspapers claiming credit for the *Virginia*. Brooke made no attempt at that time to refute Porter's claim; however, Mallory later testified before a congressional committee that Brooke's design was the one adopted. Nevertheless,

12. For the contracts see the appendix to *Report of Evidence,* 457–472.
13. Still, "Confederate Naval Strategy: The Ironclad," 330–343.

after 1862, Brooke's advice and influence concerning the ironclad program was not as strong with the naval secretary. Mallory pointedly ignored his continuing insistence that seagoing casemated vessels should be built in the South; the naval lieutenant also became disgruntled when the feature which he considered his own—the submerged ends—was discarded by Mallory in later models. By the middle of July, Brooke was writing,

I can not get up any feeling of interest in my work, it is all a task, Mallory asked me about getting up some iron clad vessels, I told him I had not thought of it lately. That in fact my interest in them was not what it was before. . . . That Mr. Porter's conduct, and results generally, had killed the interest I took in such matters.[14]

Porter's influence had increased significantly by the fall of 1862, not only regarding construction, but the ironclad program in general. Indeed, his influence may have been decisive since Mallory's ironclad policy did change toward building only harbor defense vessels. The naval secretary later wrote, "Certainly they [the ironclads] are unseaworthy, as vessels usually are that are built as these were, for harbor defense chiefly. . . ."[15]

Unfortunately for Mallory, the public did not share his appraisal of ironclad capability. Had the situation been otherwise, criticism later directed at the navy might have been less extreme.

In the spring, however, enthusiasm for the navy, particularly ironclads, was conspicuous in a number of ways: newspaper editorials as well as letters to the editors were fervent about the possibilities of the new weapon; public visits to the yards where the vessels were under construction became extremely popular; and the idea of raising funds to build gunboats became almost a rage in the South. Men's clubs, military units, banks and other private businesses, town councils, and women's organizations either donated money, or their services to collect money.

Probably the most zealous disciples of this mania for building ironclads were the women. Patriotic ladies' societies with names such as "Ladies' Gunboat Funds," "ladies' gunboat associations," and "ladies' defense associations," were organized for the purpose of raising funds to build ironclads. Apparently the first of these societies appeared in New Orleans late in 1861, and from there the idea spread to Mobile, Charleston, and elsewhere. By the spring and summer of 1862 they were scattered throughout the South. The Charleston *Daily Courier* printed in its March 1 issue a letter from a Summerville, South Carolina, lady suggesting that the paper "open a list for contributions" and enclosing a dollar to inaugurate the proposal. The *Courier*

14. July 11, 1862, quoted in Brooke, "John Mercer Brooke," II, 849.
15. *Official Records, Navies,* Ser. I, XV, 699–701.

endorsed the suggestion, and within a week more than a thousand dollars was donated. On March 14, the Columbus (Georgia) *Enquirer* reported, "We see in the Charleston papers a young lady has started a subscription to build a gunboat at Charleston. We propose that her example should be followed in Georgia." Before a week had passed, ladies in twelve Georgia cities and towns had formed organizations and were forwarding to Savannah the funds collected.

On March 17, the Richmond *Dispatch* appealed for funds to build an ironclad warship in Virginia and mentioned the women of South Carolina and Georgia who were endeavoring to raise money for a similar purpose. Evidently this appeal was at first responded to by men rather than by women, but on the twenty-eighth a letter to the editor was printed in the *Dispatch* which mentioned the fact that the ladies of Williamsburg had formed a society for the purpose of aiding in the construction of an ironclad gunboat. On April 4 the Ladies' Defense Association of Richmond was formed.

Newspapers throughout the Confederacy began carrying in their editions lists of contributors and the amounts various organizations had collected. On April 8 the Montgomery *Advertiser* reported that $200 had been collected by the city's "gunboat fund." Rivalries developed among various communities. "The ladies of Savannah . . . have already raised over $3,600.00 . . ." declared the Sandersville *Central Georgian,* "What will the ladies of Washington County do. . . ?"

The ladies engaged in a variety of activities to raise money. They solicited objects to be sold at bazaars or raffled off—jewelry, china sets, silverware, watches, vases, musical boxes, and books. "Gunboat Fairs" were held to obtain funds. In Charleston, Mrs. Mary B. Chesnut noted in her famous diary that she "gave the girls . . . a string of pearls to be raffled for at the Gunboat Fair." On April 14, 1862, she wrote, "Our Fair is in full blast. We keep a restaurant. . . ." and on the fifteenth, "Two thousand dollars were made at the Fair."[16] In Alabama "gunboat quilts" were made and auctioned off, while in Americus, Georgia, a tableau and charade exhibition was prepared and the proceeds donated to the gunboat fund. Concerts were held, collections were taken at prayer meetings and Sunday Schools, although a Savannah donor warned that no work should be done to a vessel on the Sabbath, for "we do not want it to be sunk at the first engagement."

There is no way to determine the exact amount raised by these organizations, but evidently they collected a considerable sum. The "gunboat fund" at Charleston raised $30,000, and the Ladies' Defense Association of

16. Mary B. Chesnut, *A Diary from Dixie,* 212.

Richmond amassed at least that amount. Three ironclads, the *Charleston, Fredericksburg,* and *Georgia* were called "Ladies Gunboats," or as one critic derisively said, "petticoat gunboats." The *Palmetto State* was also constructed partly with funds contributed by ladies in Charleston and other communities in South Carolina.[17]

Several associations desired actually to build gunboats. A North Carolinian asked for specifications of an ironclad, and the President of the Mississippi Gunboat Association wrote to President Davis and Flag Officer Buchanan for information about building a gunboat in Columbus.

One ironclad, the *Georgia,* was built entirely from funds collected in the state of Georgia. It was a co-operative venture: women's organizations, businessmen, the state and city of Savannah governments with advisors from the army and navy, set up a committee to solicit funds and govern the building of the vessel. They at first wanted to construct a "gunboat ram" but later agreed on a "floating battery." Plans submitted by a local builder were accepted, and by the beginning of April she was on the ways. The vessel was launched on May 20, but her casemate, armor, machinery, and battery were not ready until the fall of 1862. Commissioned the *Georgia,* she was 250 feet in length, 60 feet in beam, armed with a battery of ten guns. She was supposed to be self-propelled, but her engines were too weak and tugs or tow boats had to be used to move her. Although a Northern newspaper correspondent called the ironclad a "monstrous creature," many Georgians were disappointed in her. One local gentleman sardonically called the vessel a "mud tub," and a prominent member of the local gunboat association referred to her as a "splendid failure." In September he wrote, "She has been taken down between the forts and they are obliged to keep her engines at work the whole time to prevent her sinking. She leaks so badly. The officers held a consultation a day or two after she went down [river], to decide on the propriety of throwing over her coal to keep her afloat. . . ."[18] One of her officers despairingly wrote, "being shut up here in these swamps, in an iron-

17. Mrs. Chesnut reported in her diary on April 23, 1862, "We are fighting a battle over the new gunboat's name. Dr. Gibbes, Mrs. Picken's [the governor's wife] knight errant, wants to call it *Lucy Holcombe* for her. We wanted to call it *Caroline* for old darling Mrs. Preston; but if we are to have a female name I say let it be: *'She Devil'* for it is the Devil's own work it is built to do. The ironclad was named the *Palmetto State.*

18. Susan M. Kollock (ed.), "Kollock Letters," *Georgia Historical Quarterly,* XXXIV (1950), 241–243; Lawrence, *A Present for Mr. Lincoln,* 77, 134; George A. Mercer Diary (MS and typescript copy in Southern Historical Collection, University of North Carolina Library, Chapel Hill), March 15, May 20, 1862; Charles Nordoff, "Two Weeks at Port Royal," *Harper's New Monthly Magazine,* XXVII (1863), 116.

box (for she is not a vessel) is horrible. . . . She is not a fit command for a sargeant of marines."[19]

Although the women's gunboat societies would linger on well into 1863, their popularity was at its peak in the spring of 1862. When the navy came under increasing public disapproval in the summer and fall, interest began to decline, and by 1863 only an occasional donation was received.[20]

Public censure of the navy was an inevitable consequence of the disasters suffered in the early spring of 1862: the loss of New Orleans, Memphis, and Norfolk, and loss of all but five of the ironclads laid down in 1861. Another factor contributing to the growth of public dissatisfaction was the increasing effectiveness of the blockade. This was reflected by the fact that the very editors who lavished praise upon the sea service after Hampton Roads now began to vituperate against Mallory and his department. "A little less blowing, do, has become a popular song in the navy," suggested the editor of the Richmond *Whig*. Poor Mallory was even subjected to the wrath of those enthusiastic ladies who somehow held him accountable for the destruction of the ironclads. DeLeon, in his travels, heard the story of one group of women who visited an ironclad with the naval secretary serving as guide, an act frequently performed. At the tour's end, he commented that they had seen everything worth seeing. One lady is supposed to have replied sarcastically, "Everything but one . . . the place where you blow them up."[21]

19. Charles F. M. Spotswood to John K. Mitchell, April 14, 1863, John K. Mitchell Papers (Virginia Historical Society, Richmond, Virginia). See also *Official Records, Navies,* Ser. I, XV, 696; Montfort to his wife, March 26, 1862, in Miscellaneous Letters from Georgia Soldiers (MS. in Georgia State Archives, Atlanta), II, 91.

20. Thomas C. DeLeon, *Belles, Beaux and Brains of the 60's,* 415–416. Information, lists of contributions, etc., about the gunboat associations can be found in Confederate newspapers, particularly for the period beginning in February 1862, and ending in the summer months. See especially the Charleston *Daily Courier,* Charleston *Daily Mercury,* Savannah *Morning News,* Savannah *Republican,* Macon (Georgia) *Daily Telegraph,* Mobile *Advertiser and Register,* Montgomery *Advertiser,* Richmond *Daily Dispatch,* Columbus (Georgia) *Daily Enquirer.* See also Jefferson Davis to Mrs. J. W. Harris and others, August 21, 1862, in Dunbar Rowland (ed.), *Jefferson Davis, Constitutionalist: His Letters, Papers and Speeches,* V, 328; Franklin Buchanan to Mrs. J. W. Harris, October 25, 1862, in Buchanan Letterbook; Mallory to C. G. Memminger, April 16, 1864, Records of the Confederate Treasury Department, National Archives Record Group 365; M. Quad, *Field, Fort and Stream,* 85; Matthew P. Andrews, *The Women of the South in War Time,* 296–297; Scharf, *Confederate States Navy,* 671–672; Catherine C. Hopley, *Life in the South,* II, 257; Mary A. Snowden Papers (The South Caroliniana Library, University of South Carolina, Columbia).

21. DeLeon, *Belles, Beaux and Brains,* 415–416.

As Secretary of the Navy, Mallory was the natural victim of most of the public, newspaper, and congressional criticism directed against the navy. Moreover, because he was a member of Davis's cabinet, criticism of him would necessarily affect the administration. Early in August, attacks upon the naval secretary from the floors of Congress became steadily more abusive and reached a peak when the chairman of the Senate Naval Affairs Committee, Charles M. Conrad of Louisiana, introduced a resolution calling for the abolition of the Office of Secretary of the Navy, and placing its direction of the navy under the War Department. Mallory was distressed at these assaults and confided in his diary, "I am as sick as I am disgusted with the carpings and complaints of ignorance and persumption, that I have not built a navy! I feel confident of having done my whole duty, of having done all that any man could have done with the means at hand." To his wife he poured out his mortification:

I have much to be proud of and nothing whatever to regret in my administration. . . . Knowing that the enemy could build one hundred ships to our one, my policy has been to make such ships, so strong and so invulnerable, as would compensate for the inequality of numbers. Thus the *Merrimac,* the *Arkansas,* the *Mississippi, Louisiana,* etc. . . . and the destruction of these vessels—by no fault of mine—just as everybody saw their gigantic power and the consequences thereof, brings upon my head the rage of the ignorant, the rabble and the prejudiced. . . .[22]

Under obvious mental pressure and after consulting with several friends, Mallory demanded an investigation of his department. In a letter to the President explaining his decision, he predicted that "the triumphant vindication of its course must result." The investigation was subsequently held, and after several hundred pages of testimony was taken, the department was fully exonerated.

While Mallory was struggling with his political headache, a crisis developed that threatened to destroy his fledgling naval program. When the Confederate Navy was organized in 1861, naval establishments were concentrated in the large shipping ports such as Norfolk and New Orleans where shipbuilding and subsidiary facilities were available. But the disastrous loss of these localities and others in the spring of 1862 forced the decision to place naval facilities in the interior whenever possible.[23] Although this provided more security from attack, it had the serious disadvantage of de-

22. August 31, 1862, Stephen R. Mallory Papers (University of Florida Library, Gainesville).

23. Still, "Facilities for the Construction of War Vessels in the Confederacy," 291.

centralization. There was no one point where everything needed to construct and fit out a ship-of-war was located. Shipyards were in various localities, ordnance stores and laboratories in other places, and foundries, machine shops, iron works, and rope walks, were in still other locations.[24] Transportation was obviously essential, but transportation within the Confederacy, particularly railroads, was never adequate; and as the war progressed it became increasingly inefficient. A majority of the railroads were small lines with different gauges; there was a chronic shortage of operating equipment and rails which continued to deteriorate because of no replacement; skilled labor was scarce; and the competition between the Confederate government and the various state governments for use of the rails all contributed to mounting chaos. Although the Confederate government gradually monopolized railroads, the navy found its use curtailed because of army control. Mallory, naval officers, builders, and contractors constantly complained, with some justification, that their requirements were ignored by the army. For example, Captain William F. Lynch, CSN, reported to the Secretary of the Navy that "Fourteen car loads of plate iron arrived last evening, and for a week past we have had two car loads waiting transportation to Kinston and Halifax [North Carolina]. The whole rolling capacity of the road, except passenger trains, has been monopolized by the army, and I fear the completion of the gun boats at those places will be delayed." The note was passed on to the Secretary of War, who replied, "at present the food and forage necessary for our armies in the field demand our entire transportation."[25] This illustrates the failure of logistical co-operation which troubled the navy throughout the war and contributed to the destruction of many ironclads and other vessels while they were still on the ways.[26]

The new interior sites (some of which were not served by railroad lines) included Richmond; Edward's Ferry and Whitehall, North Carolina; Columbus, Georgia; Yazoo City, Mississippi; Selma, Montgomery, and Oven Bluff, Alabama; and Shreveport, Louisiana. At Richmond a navy yard was located in a suburb known as Rocketts. Here the *Richmond,* towed from the Gosport yard shortly before Norfolk fell, was being finished; the "ladies gunboat"

24. *Ibid.,* 292–294. "Rocketts," the navy yard at Richmond, was referred to by one young officer in his diary as nothing more than a "shed." Francis W. Dawson Papers (Duke University Library, Durham).

25. Seddon to Mallory, March 18, 1864, in Secretary of War Letterbooks, National Archives Record Group 109.

26. There are a number of letters in the Shelby Iron Company Papers (University of Alabama Library, Tuscaloosa) and in the official papers and letterbooks of Governor Zebulon B. Vance of North Carolina (North Carolina Department of Archives and History) about the navy and the transportation problem.

Fredericksburg was on the ways, and a third ironclad (*Virginia II*) was laid down. In North Carolina, Gilbert Elliott and William P. Martin received contracts to build two ironclads and a wooden gunboat, but only the *Albemarle,* built at Edward's Ferry, was completed. A sister ship, the *Neuse,* was laid down at Whitehall, while two 150-foot-class ironclads were negotiated for at Wilmington. On the Chattachoochee River in Georgia, a small yard was established in Columbus and a *Fredericksburg* class vessel, the *Jackson* —175 feet in length, 35 feet in beam—was built. Yazoo City, Mississippi, became the site of a yard, not by design, but because the unfinished *Arkansas* was towed there from Memphis. Afterwards three other warships including two ironclads were laid down at Yazoo City, but they were never launched. At Oven Bluff, Alabama, some sixty miles up the Tombigbee River from Mobile, the wooden hulls of three ironclads were built, but the incompetence of the contractors plus the location of the yard near a malaria-ridden swamp prevented the completion of the vessels. They were later towed to Mobile but were still without armor and machinery when the city surrendered in the spring of 1865. The keels of four ironclads were laid at Selma, but only three (*Tuscaloosa, Huntsville,* and *Tennessee*), were completed, while a side-wheel armored ship, the *Nashville,* was built at Montgomery. All were taken to Mobile to receive armor, machinery, and battery. Shreveport, Louisiana, on the Red River, was probably the most unsuitable site selected to build warships. Two ironclads were contracted for, but only the *Missouri* reached operational status.[27]

Most of these yards were primitive—a small clear area on a beach, or the bank of a river, creek, or inlet. The water at the end of the shipways had to be deep enough for launching, and the timber and other necessary materials accessible. Fixed equipment was usually limited to a small mill, blacksmith shop, and a few forges. These yards were probably unsuitable for building large seagoing steamers, but Mallory believed that they would be adequate for constructing small armored vessels.

Eighteen ironclads were laid down in these yards in the fall of 1862. The most formidable problems to overcome, other than labor and materials, was how to get the vessels from their building sites to their operational areas. The yards were generally located miles up muddy, shallow, and winding rivers, accessible to riverboats with slight drafts, but not to deep-drafted vessels. Even though the new ironclads were flat-bottomed, they were still handicapped by eight- to twelve-foot drafts—too deep when the rivers were

27. Still, "Facilities for the Construction of War Vessels in the Confederacy," 292–293.

low. At Mobile the problem was solved by using camels. These were watertight structures attached to the bottom of a vessel's hull, after which the water was pumped out and their buoyancy lifted the vessel. The *Tennessee* was successfully carried over the bar into Mobile Bay in this manner. However, the usual course was to take advantage of high water, particularly in the spring when heavy rains created flood stage on the rivers. For the *Missouri* and *Neuse* nothing worked, and they were destroyed near their yards.

Not only shipyards but other naval facilities were moved inland: ordnance stores and laboratories were established at Richmond; Charlotte, North Carolina; and Atlanta, Georgia; a marine machinery works was started in Columbus, Georgia; naval foundries for casting guns were erected at Richmond and at Selma, Alabama. By the beginning of 1863 most of these establishments were in operation.

Without apologies, Mallory could boast to his wife, "I am working with unsinking perseverance in getting up iron clad ships, and am certain of success. The obstacles in the way would deter most men. . . ."[28]

The year 1862 was indeed one of transition for the Confederate navy. The successes of the first ironclads resulted in Mallory's decision to deemphasize building wooden gunboats in favor of ironclads. At the same time the naval secretary was convinced that the department should concentrate on building small harbor-defense vessels in the Confederacy and attempt to obtain seagoing armorclads in Europe. By 1863 the smaller ironclads were joining the various Confederate naval squadrons.

28. August 21, 1862, Mallory Papers.

6

Characteristics of the Ironclads

THE NEW armorclads that Mallory was "getting up" were described by contemporaries as "gunboxes," "iron gophers," and "iron elephants." These descriptions certainly were apt, for the lines of beauty that characterized the sailing ships-of-line were not present in the ironclads. No one, however, denied that the appearance of the "monsters" was formidable.

It is nearly impossible to generalize about these vessels, for even those that in theory were of the same class usually differed noticeably because of modifications.[1] One characteristic structural feature, however, made them somewhat similar in appearance: the ironplate casemate or shield with sloping sides, on a hull with an extremely low freeboard. With the exception of two conversions—the *Manassas* and the *Baltic*—every Confederate ironclad placed in commission had an armored shield to protect its guns and machinery. There was nothing original in the casemated vessel. The Stevens battery, as well as the first French floating batteries (the *Lave* class), were of this type.

The *Virginia* was the prototype Confederate ironclad. Although she had several obvious weaknesses, as an experimental ship she proved to be successful. The Hampton Roads engagements fully vindicated the casemated type of vessel in the judgment of the Confederate Navy Department. Mallory remained convinced throughout the war that this type of armorclad was the most suitable for the Confederacy to construct. Less than two months before General Lee surrendered at Appomattox Court House, the secretary was writing,

For river, harbor, and coast defense, the sloping shield and general plan of armored vessels adopted by us . . . are the best that could be adopted in our

1. For the classification of all Confederate naval vessels, including ironclads, into major classes and types, see *Dictionary of American Fighting Ships*, II, 490–492.

situation. . . . In ventilation, light, fighting space, and quarters it is believed that the sloping shield presents greater advantages than the Monitor turret. . . .[2]

No attempt was made to standardize the first ironclads constructed from the keel up within the Confederacy. The two Memphis vessels were to be sister ships, but the *Louisiana* and *Mississippi* built in New Orleans were quite different. However, all of these early armored vessels (including the *Virginia*) were apparently designed to operate in coastal waters, as well as in rivers and harbors.[3] This is one reason they were unusually large (all were more than 200 feet in length) in contrast to the later ironclads.

Other characteristics included a long casemate and a relatively high freeboard (compared with the later ironclads). The New Orleans vessels also included rather unorthodox propulsion units: the *Louisiana* was propelled by two wheels and two screws, and the *Mississippi,* by three screws.

The most popular hull design used by the Confederate Navy in ironclad construction was inaugurated early in 1862 when the *Richmond* was laid down at the navy yard at Norfolk. The design was adapted from a model of an armored vessel developed by Constructor Porter in 1846. This model was for a seagoing ironclad 150 feet in length, 40 feet in the beam, with a 19-foot draft.[4] Porter submitted it when Mallory first considered building an ironclad, and later a modified version was approved as a harbor-defense vessel.[5] The *Richmond* was the first ship built to this design.

This hull design was characterized by a flat bottom with some dead-rise, built-on knuckle,[6] with a tapered stern and stem. The original dimensions were 150 feet in length, 34 feet in beam, and 11 feet in draft, but larger vessels were later built by this plan. Because the data regarding Confederate ships are inadequate, it is difficult to determine exactly the number of ironclads built with similar hulls. Evidence, however, indicates that at least twenty of those placed under construction incorporated this design.[7]

2. Mallory to Albert G. Brown, February 18, 1865, folder on design of Confederate ships, Confederate Subject and Area File, National Archives Record Group 45.
3. One of the *Arkansas*'s officers described her as combining the qualities of the "flat bottomed boats of the West, and the Keel-built steamers for navigating in deep water." Castlen, *Hope Bids Me Onward,* 64–65.
4. Porter, *Norfolk,* 330, 342.
5. The length remained the same, but the beam was reduced to thirty-four feet and the draft to eleven feet.
6. The knuckle was where the side of the shield joined with the side of the hull and formed an angle. See Figure 5.
7. See Figure 5. Specifications regarding Confederate ironclads are at the most approximate. Those ironclads built to this design include the *Richmond, Chicora, Raleigh, Palmetto State, North Carolina,* and *Savannah* (150-foot class); the *Virginia*

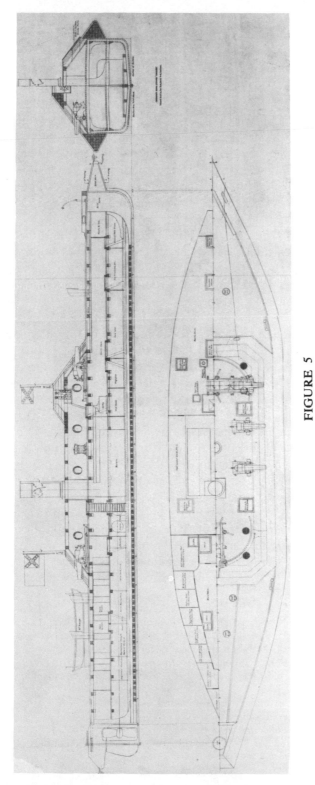

FIGURE 5

Detailed drawing of CSS *Tennessee*: inboard profile, gun deck, berth deck, sections.

A second hull type was used by Confederate shipbuilders on the "home water" ironclads; the only noticeable difference between this hull and that of the *Richmond* were the flared side in place of the built-on knuckle, giving it the shape of a diamond from the ends, and a completely flat bottom. This design was used on iron-plated vessels that were built adjacent to very shallow water. For example, the *Albemarle* and *Neuse* were constructed to operate in only a fathom of water.[8]

The shield designed by Porter for the *Virginia* was flush with the ends of the hull and was elliptical in shape. The curved ends (found only on the *Virginia*) gave way to flat ends inclined to the same degree as the sides. The length of casemates decreased gradually until those on the vessels under construction in the latter part of the war were from 70 to 80 feet.[9] This development was the result of a number of factors: the need for space to handle anchors and mooring gear, the increasing scarcity of iron, the necessity for increasing the size of the guns and thickness of the armor, and the need for a shallower draft. The weight of the shield also contributed to the unseaworthiness of the vessels; they were topheavy and subject to capsizing, even in calm waters. Lieutenant William H. Parker wrote that the *Palmetto State* was more buoyant than the *Virginia* "yet I have seen the time when we were glad to get under a lee [shelter] even in Charleston Harbor."[10] As a consequence of the reduced size of the shield, the bow and stern pivot gun mount became standard on Confederate armorclads.[11]

The use of inclined armor to deflect projectiles and thus increase resistance was not new; in fact, it was almost as old as the use of armor on warships. Inclined armor had been proposed in Spain in 1727, in England in 1805, and in America during the War of 1812 and periodically afterwards. In the decade before the outbreak of the American Civil War, experiments concerning the relative merits of vertical and inclined armor were conducted in England and France. Mallory was aware of these tests, but accurate data

---

11 and *Charleston* (180-foot class); *Milledgeville* (175 feet); *Columbia, Texas,* and *Tennessee* (216 feet); *Nashville* (270 feet); and the two 160-foot vessels under construction at Oven Bluff, Alabama, that were never completed.

8. See Figure 6. In addition to the *Albermarle* and *Neuse,* the *Huntsville, Tuscaloosa,* and *Mobile* (150 feet), and the *Fredericksburg* and *Jackson* (175 feet) were built to this hull design.

9. The *Columbia* and *Texas* had casemates seventy-seven feet in length and the *Milledgeville's* was seventy-three feet.

10. Parker, *Recollections of a Naval Officer,* 193–194.

11. This allowed for fewer guns in a ship's battery without seriously affecting her firepower.

were not available. In the fall of 1861, the Confederacy conducted its own tests on Jamestown Island. The tests indicated that for fighting at short range —for which the ironclads were primarily designed—the inclined side was favored over the vertical. On the other hand, several naval officers, including John Brooke, believed that armored vessels with vertical sides were more seaworthy.[12]

Experiments were also conducted to determine the most suitable degree of inclination and thickness of iron plating for armor. Brooke, in charge of the tests, later reported that a target formed of wood approximately twenty-four inches thick, faced with three layers of one-inch plate, inclined at an angle of about sixty degrees from the perpendicular, was tested at three hundred yards range with an eight-inch shot, and the projectile "penetrated the iron and entered 5 inches into the wood."[13] The amount of inclination was later increased, determined primarily by the vessel's breadth.

Armor plating was also tested and analyzed on the island. Brooke was aware that investigation in England had proven the superiority of solid plate over laminated armor of similar thickness, but laminated plate was adopted from necessity. The South was not equipped with proper machinery to produce iron plates of the thickness of those fabricated abroad. Experiments were conducted first with one-inch armor. Later, however, when it was discovered that two-inch could be rolled and drilled, that thickness became standard on Confederate ironclads. A majority of the vessels were plated with a double layer of two-inch armor, the inner belt horizontal and the outer perpendicular. The last armorclads placed under construction had three layers of two-inch plate. Mallory wanted the mills to roll three-inch plate if possible, but there is no evidence to indicate that iron of this thickness was rolled.[14]

When plate was not available, railroad T-rail iron was substituted. A stationary floating battery armored in this fashion was employed successfully in Charleston harbor during the Fort Sumter bombardment. The Jamestown Island tests also proved the utility of T-rails, although it was generally ad-

12. *Official Records, Navies,* Ser. II, II, 86, 174; Brooke, "John Mercer Brooke," II, 769; Brooke to Warley, January 4, 1864, folder on design of Confederate vessels, Confederate Subject and Area File, National Archives Record Group 45. The only ironclads built within the Confederacy with vertical sides were the *Arkansas* and *Tennessee,* built at Memphis.

13. *Official Records, Navies,* Ser. II, I, 785–786.

14. Mallory to Buchanan, July 1, 1863, Area file, Confederate Subject and Area File, National Archives Record Group 45. The *Milledgeville, Tennessee, Virginia II,* and *Columbia* were all designed to carry six inches of armor.

mitted that iron plate was superior.[15] Railroad iron was used to armor the *Arkansas, Louisiana,* and *Missouri.* But whether rails or plates were used, there was never enough of either to go around. Consequently, a large number of ironclads under construction were never completed because of the lack of iron for armor.[16]

The hurricane or shield (top) deck of the casemate was not armored but was covered with iron grating (or wooden in some cases, such as that of the *Fredericksburg*), and served as the main source of ventilation. This deck was not strong enough to carry a battery, and its obvious weakness to plunging fire was a constant worry to officers. The pilothouse, usually located forward of the stack, was armored.

The barrage of criticism leveled at the navy throughout most of the war inevitably included the ironclads. "As a means even of harbor defense our [ironclads have] . . . not been able to command success," the editor of the weekly Wilmington *Journal* wrote on August 11, 1864. One week later he suggested certain improvements: "There must be protection for their steering apparatus, and some mode of giving draft to the furnaces and affording an escape for smoke, and at the same time dispensing with smoke stacks projecting above the deck." In that same edition appeared a letter, evidently from a naval officer defending his branch of the service: "is it not unreasonable to expect our hastily and unskillfully constructed vessels to compete with those of the enemy? . . . Your remark that the Navy has proved a failure . . . can only mean that the Navy has failed to achieve an impossibility."

The most outspoken critic was General P. G. T. Beauregard. In November 1863, he wrote to Congressman William P. Miles of South Carolina outlining what was wrong with the ironclads:

Our gunboats are defective in six respects. First they have no speed. . . . Second they are of too great draught to navigate our inland waters. Third they are unseaworthy by their shape and construction. . . . Fourth they are incapable of resisting the enemy's 15 inch shots at close quarters. . . . Fifth they cannot fight at long range, their guns not admitting an elevation greater than from 5 degrees to seven degrees. . . . Sixth they are very costly, warm, uncomfortable, and badly ventilated, consequently sickly. . . .[17]

15. Brooke, "John Mercer Brooke," II, 797–798; *Official Records, Navies,* Ser. II, I, 578.

16. It is difficult to decide which ironclads were not completed *solely* because of the lack of iron for armor. Nevertheless, it seems that three at Mobile, two at Savannah, two at Charleston, and one at Wilmington were definitely destroyed before completion, and the fatal delay was because iron was not available.

17. *Official Records,* Ser. I, XXVIII, pt. 2, 503–504.

Mallory attempted to answer Beauregard's and others' criticism, but he was not very convincing.[18]

In January 1864, Congress passed a resolution (suggested by Beauregard) instructing the House Committee on Naval Affairs to "inquire whether the vessels constructed for harbor defense are adapted to the purpose."[19] No records or minutes of the committee have been located, but various officers including those commanding squadrons and naval districts were asked to submit their opinions and recommendations on the ironclads. The replies were generally favorable.[20] Probably as a result of a recommendation from this committee, Mallory, in February, appointed a board of naval officers to "report upon the best form of construction, shield, battery, etc., for ironclads. . . ."[21] Brooke, Porter, Williamson, and two line officers were nominated to the board, which continued to function until the end of the war.

Although the casemated ironclad remained the standard "home-water" vessel constructed within the Confederacy, the board did recommend the adoption of a new design—a double-ended ironclad with two octagonal casemates. They were similar in appearance to the Union "double-turreted" monitors, but since the casemeates were not moveable turrets, pivot guns had to be utilized. At Richmond and Wilmington, vessels of this type were laid down. A third was approved for Charleston, but construction was never started. In February 1865, the naval secretary sanctioned the building of a small Monitor-type vessel at Columbus, Georgia, but apparently materials were not even collected for the proposed armorclad.[22] In that same month, however, Mallory wrote to the chairman of the Senate Naval Affairs Committee, "it is believed that the sloping shield presents greater advantages than the Monitor turret. Our engineers, builders and mechanics have greatly improved in the art of construction and equipment since we built the first *Virginia*. . . . Every vessel built should be, and is, an improvement upon the preceeding [*sic*] [one] . . . and we are profiting as well by their successes as

---

18. *Official Records, Navies,* Ser. I, XV, 699–701. See also Mallory to Seddon, October 23, 1863, War Department Papers, National Archives Record Group 109.

19. "Proceedings of the Confederate Congress," *Southern Historical Society Papers,* LII, 233.

20. See for example letters of Buchanan and Tattnall in *Official Records, Navies,* Ser. I, XV, 708–709; XXI, 873.

21. *Ibid.,* IX, 801.

22. Brooke, Williamson and Graves to Mallory, November 7, 1864, Letterbook of the Office of Hydrography and Ordnance, National Archives Record Group 109; Warner to Mallory, February 3, 1865, construction at Columbus, Georgia, folder, Confederate Subject and Area File, National Archives Record Group 45.

by their failures."[23] These improvements did not affect their over-all appearance, outside nor in.

The interior structure of the vessel was simple. The gun deck was that part of the main deck located inside the casemate. By swinging hammocks between the guns and in other unoccupied spaces, the interior of the shield became the crew's berthing quarters. The second deck, below the main deck, was also a berth deck, containing the captain's cabin and wardroom aft, and crew's quarters and messing spaces forward. The third deck included forward and after storerooms, shell rooms, and magazines; in the hold, amidships, were located the boilers and other machinery.

Living and working conditions on board these vessels were almost intolerable, particularly during the summers and whenever the enemy was being engaged. Ventilation was primitive or nearly nonexistent, and there is no evidence that blowers were ever fitted. The only fresh air came from the gratings on top of the shield and from the ports along the sides. The excessive heat, dampness, and lack of light resulted in a high rate of illness, low morale, desertion, and inefficiency among the crews. Lieutenant James Baker was disgruntled about the habitability of the *Huntsville*: "she is . . . terribly disagreeable for men to live on," while a fellow officer at Mobile in describing the lack of comfort on the *Baltic* wrote, "I begin to think that in our Navy it does not exist and that one has no right to expect it."[24] No Confederate ironclad was subject to such condemnation for her discomforts as was the *Atlanta*:

I would defy anyone in the world to tell when it is day or night if he is confined below without any way of marking time. . . . I would venture to say that if a person were blind folded and carried below and then turned loose he would imagine himself in a swamp, for the water is trickling in all the time and everything is so damp.[25]

Various remedial measures were tried. Raphael Semmes, when in command of the James River Squadron, ordered his captains to send their men ashore to exercise a few at a time. Later, a board of naval surgeons visited the squadron and recommended that a whisky ration be issued to

23. To Brown, February 18, 1865, folder on design of Confederate ships, Confederate Subject and Area File, National Archives Record Group 45.

24. Grimball to mother, September 12, 1862, Grimball Papers; James Baker to cousin, n. d., Wirt family Papers (Southern Historical Collection, University of North Carolina Library, Chapel Hill); George Gift to Ellen Shackleford, June 10, 1863, Gift Papers; Ruffin Thomson to "dear Pa," June 2, 1864, Ruffin Thomson Papers (Southern Historical Collection, University of North Carolina Library, Chapel Hill).

25. *Official Records, Navies,* Ser. I, XIII, 819–820.

the crew every morning with their coffee. The general practice, however, was to seek quarters outside of the ships. The crews of the *Tuscaloosa* and *Huntsville* slept in cotton warehouses during the "sickly season." The *Tennessee*'s crew was quartered on a covered barge anchored near the vessel. The *Albemarle*'s men slung their hammocks under a shed, leaving only a watch on board at night, and tenders were used by the Wilmington squadron, the *Missouri,* and the *Arkansas.* This alleviated the problem while in port, but inadequate ventilation continued to plague the ships when they were operating.[26]

There was nothing unusual about the engineering installations on board Confederate ironclads. The engines were generally high pressure, reciprocating, single expansion. There were various types, determined by the position of the cylinders.[27] The boilers were also quite common—the horizontal-fire-tube boiler with a double (return) flue. A few of the vessels (for example, the *Missouri* and *Tennessee*) had fans to assist the draft through the fires for the purpose of generating steam more rapidly, but natural draft was usually relied upon. The number of boilers per vessel varied considerably; the *Mississippi* had sixteen, but the *Albemarle* had only two.

The marine engines and boilers used on the ironclads built within the Confederacy were notoriously inadequate and constantly in need of repair. The absence of qualified machinists and insufficient tools and materials were the principal reasons.

The method of propulsion consisted of either wheel or screw or a combination of both, as in the *Louisiana* (two wheels and two screws). A majority of them were screw steamers with either one or two propellers. Mallory apparently favored building a number of sidewheel ironclads similar

26. Richard Harwell (ed.), *A Confederate Marine,* 22; Robert Davis, *History of the Rebel Ram Atlanta with an Interesting Account of the Engagement which Resulted in Her Capture,* 9; Dabney M. Scales Diary (Southern Historical Collection, University of North Carolina Library, Chapel Hill).

27. The only drawing of a Confederate ironclad showing its machinery which the writer could locate is of the *Savannah.* The original is located in the Museum of Arts and Sciences at Columbus, Georgia. The *Tuscaloosa,* carried from 135 to 150 pounds of steam. Buchanan to Mallory, April 6, 1863, Buchanan Letterbook. Commander I. N. Brown wrote that the *Arkansas* had at least 120 pounds on July 15, 1862. The *Savannah's* power was provided by a low-pressure engine. *Official Records, Navies,* Ser. I, XV, 708–709. The *Atlanta* had vertical engines; the *Albemarle, Neuse, Columbia,* and *Texas* had horizontal engines; and the *Nashville, Baltic,* and *Missouri* had inclined engines. For the *Atlanta,* see *ibid.,* XIV, 275; for the *Columbia,* see *ibid.,* Ser. II, I, 251; for the *Texas,* see report of Commander William Radford, April 25, 1865, construction at Richmond folder, Confederate Subject and Area File, National Archives Record Group 45. For the *Albemarle* see *Official Records, Navies,* Ser. II, I, 251.

to the *Nashville,* because steamboat machinery could be easily adapted; but only two others were laid down, and they were never completed. The center-wheeler *Missouri* and the converted sidewheeler *Baltic* were the only other nonscrew ironclads constructed within the Confederacy.

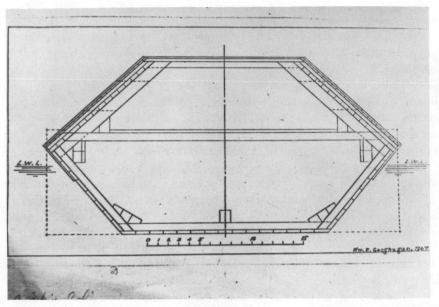

FIGURE 6
Midship section of *Albemarle* and *Neuse* class (Smithsonian Institution).

The universal slowness of these ironclads was partly a result of the inadequate power and propulsion plants. Curiously, some officers defended the lack of speed. Constructor Porter stated that his "model was not calculated to have much speed, but was intended for harbor defense only. . . ."[28] These vessels were also rams however, and were considerably less effective in this function because of their slowness. Their weight and inadequate machinery also made them difficult to steer and maneuver, even in calm waters.

Of all aspects of the Confederate shipbuilding program, the marine engineering industry was by far the most backward, as it was in the United States as a whole.[29] There was little scientific study of engineering before

28. Richmond *Examiner,* April 11, 1862.
29. John G. B. Hutchins, *The American Maritime Industries and Public Policy, 1789–1914* (Cambridge, 1941), 330–331.

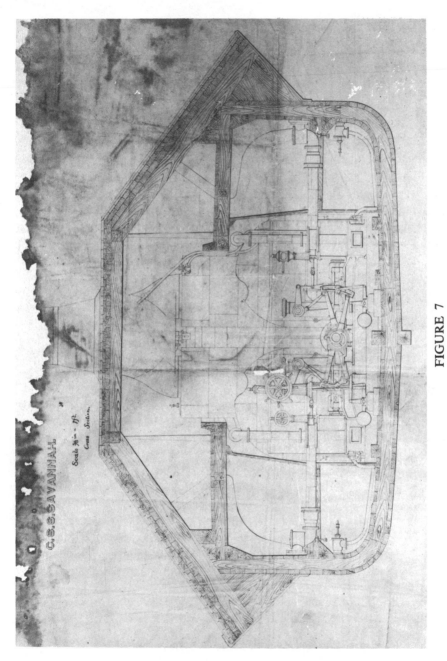

FIGURE 7

Contemporary drawing of CSS *Savannah* by Chief Engineer James Warner, CSN. Original in Columbus (Georgia) Museum of Arts and Crafts, Inc.

the war; construction of marine engines was frequently by rule of thumb. This was true throughout the war, in the North as well as in the South. All parts were generally made by hand, and although the concept of interchangeable parts for engines was quite common in the arms industry, it had not reached the marine engineering industry. In a field where all knowledge was empirical, it was inevitable that the Confederacy's first engines and other machinery would be inefficient. Nevertheless, Confederate marine engines, like the vessels themselves, improved with time, and by the end of the war a few satisfacory engines were being produced. This was particularly true of those built at the Columbus Naval Iron Works, at Columbus, Georgia.

The navy was more fortunate in arming its ironclads than in providing motive power for them. Under the capable leadership of men such as John Brooke and Catesby ap R. Jones, the production of naval ordnance increased steadily throughout the war. There was really never a shortage of guns for the navy, although for the first year or so of the war most ship batteries were a rather heterogeneous lot. With the introduction of the Brooke guns, however, some standardization gradually appeared.

The Brooke guns originated in the summer of 1861 when Mallory ordered Brooke to design a 7-inch "rifle cannon" for the *Virginia*.[30] The design was approved and a contract made with Tredegar to cast six of them. Brooke then designed a 6.4-inch rifle, of which twelve were ordered. Eight-inch rifles and 11-inch and 12-inch smoothbores were later cast, but for ironclad batteries the 7-inch and 6.4-inch guns were the principal types used. The guns were made of cast iron with a wrought-iron ring shrunk onto the piece at the breech, in the manner perfected by the Northern foundryman, R. P. Parrott for his rifled field artillery. By strengthening the powder chamber, these rings increased the safety of the guns and enabled them to carry the heavy charge necessary in firing rifled projectiles. Where Parrott used only one band, Brooke double-banded and even triple-banded his breech rings. Brooke's guns were also considerably heavier than Parrott's of the same bore diameter. For example, the 8-inch Parrott weighed 16,500 pounds while the 8-inch Brooke weighed 22,000 pounds.[31]

Smoothbores were carried at one time or another by nearly all of the armorclads, but in contrast to the Union navy, which advocated them during and after the war, the Confederate navy concentrated on rifled guns.

30. Brooke, "John Mercer Brooke," II, 799; Dew, *Ironmaker to the Confederacy,* 119.

31. Eugene B. Canfield, *Notes on Naval Ordnance of the American Civil War, 1861–1865,* 7; Walter W. Stephen, "The Brooke Guns from Selma," *Alabama Historical Quarterly,* XX (1958), 462–475.

In 1863 the navy began equipping its ironclads with spar torpedoes. This weapon consisted of an egg-shaped copper vessel containing from fifty to seventy pounds of powder, fitted to a long pole attached to the bow of the vessel. Upon approaching an enemy ship, the torpedo would be lowered beneath the water and exploded on contact with the hull. The *Atlanta* was probably the first Confederate ironclad to be armed with the spar torpedo. Captain Francis D. Lee, CSA, developed a spar torpedo while working on his torpedo ram at Charleston. By the spring of 1863 torpedoes of his design were fixed on wooden launches and the Charleston ironclads. For that reason, Lee has generally received credit for the weapon. Early in October, 1862, however, General George A. Mercer at Savannah wrote in his diary, "I have proposed to the General to endeavor to initiate an experiment. . . . it is to attach a concussion shell to an arm running out from the ram of a gun boat, and then destroy the enemy's vessels by striking them below the iron plates. . . . I never heard anyone suggest the above idea, but I have mentioned it to several, and all agree with me that it is perfectly practicable." The idea is logical and rather simple, and each may have developed it at the same time without knowledge of the other. Or Mercer may have suggested it to Beauregard who passed it on to his scientifically-minded engineer. Both Mercer and Lee were in Beauregard's command. Mercer later wrote that his idea was to be experimented with.[32] In 1864 the commanding officer of the *Charleston* rigged up a type of "barrel" contact mine to be rolled off the stern of the vessel. Neither weapon was ever used in action by ironclads against enemy vessels, although at least one of the squadrons—the James River Squadron—carried out training exercises at torpedo attacks.[33] Ironically, Beauregard apparently understood the potential of the torpedo as a naval weapon better than did most naval officers.

32. Mercer Diary, October 1, 13, 1862; Milton F. Perry, *Infernal Machines: The Story of Confederate Submarine and Mine Warfare* (Baton Rouge, 1965), 75–77.
33. Scharf, *Confederate States Navy*, 753–754; *Official Records, Navies,* Ser. I, XXX, 665; XVI, 418.

Charleston Squadron. CSS *Charleston* on right; vessel on left is probably *Palmetto State* or *Chicora*. *Civil War Naval Chronology*, Part VI (Washington, D.C.: Government Printing Office, n.d.).

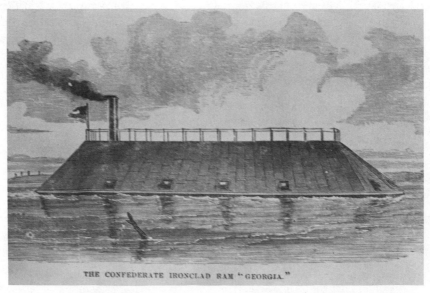

THE CONFEDERATE IRONCLAD RAM "GEORGIA."

The Confederate Ironclad ram *Georgia*. From *Harper's Weekly*, 1863.

Confederate ram *Atlanta* on James River after capture by *Weehawken*. Courtesy National Archives,

CSS *Virginia. Official Records, Navies.*

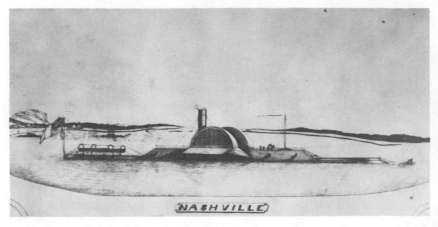

The *Nashville*. Drawing in National Archives.

CSS *Manassas*. Official Records, Navies.

CSS *Richmond. Official Records, Navies.*

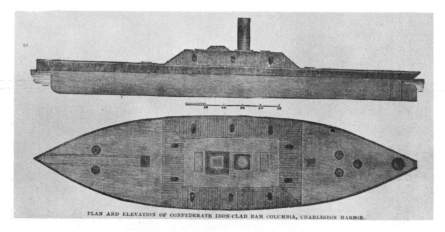

Plan and Elevation of the Confederate ironclad ram *Columbia,* Charleston Harbor. From *Charleston, South Carolina: The Centennial of Incorporation, 1883* (1884).

CSS *Arkansas*. Negative of a contemporary drawing by Acting Master Samuel Milliken, CSN. Original in the National Archives.

The *Chicora*. From Francis T. Miller, *Photographic History of the Civil War* (1912).

The Confederate ram *Baltic* defending Mobile Harbor.

7

Beauregard and the Charleston Squadron

GENERAL PIERRE GUSTAVE TOUTANT BEAUREGARD announced on September 24, 1862, that at the direction of the War Department he was assuming command of the Department of South Carolina and Georgia. Although disappointed in this command and in some disgrace with the Administration for supposedly "abandoning" his army after Shiloh, the swarthy Creole was determined to use the position to regain the field command he so ardently desired.[1]

Beauregard, like Robert E. Lee, instinctively understood the importance of sea power—in coastal defense, at least. He also believed in a unified command, provided that naval forces operating within his department were under his direct command. In fact, the general attempted with a degree of success to exercise de facto control over Confederate naval forces in South Carolina and Georgia, particularly in regard to operations. In shipbuilding, however, his efforts at control were unsuccessful; Mallory, who intensely disliked and mistrusted Beauregard, kept a tight rein on all matters concerning naval building.

On the day the change of command took place at Charleston, Beauregard wrote a note to Commander John R. Tucker, whom he mistakenly believed to be in command of the navy there, inquiring when the ironclads would be ready for service. Tucker, of course, informed the general that Commodore Duncan M. Ingraham was in command. Beauregard then "requested" that Ingraham attend a meeting with his staff concerning "harbor defense."

Ingraham had been in Charleston nearly a year commanding a small flotilla of wooden gunboats and supervising the construction of other vessels, including the two ironclads. Although the slightly-built flag officer was intelligent and cultured and no one questioned his personal courage, he was

1. Beauregard's health declined after Shiloh, and after the retreat from Corinth in June 1862 he took leave without informing the government. He was replaced in command of the Army of Mississippi by Braxton Bragg. T. Harry Williams, *Beauregard: Napoleon in Grey,* 199–200.

considered by many of his younger officers to be too deliberate and "overly cautious; a perfect old woman."[2] Nevertheless, he was one of the most respected officers to give up the flag when his home state of South Carolina seceded. He was a veteran of more than fifty years of active service, which he had begun as a midshipman during the War of 1812. In 1853, while commanding the sloop of war *St. Louis* on station in the Mediterranean, he threatened to fire on an Austrian warship if Martin Koszta, a Hungarian follower of Louis Kossuth in the uprising of 1848–49, were not released. Koszta had fled to the United States after the uprising failed but later returned to Europe where he was imprisoned by Austrian authorities. He was released by diplomatic action, and Ingraham returned home to receive a hero's welcome.[3]

Beauregard's conference was prompted by the pending naval attack against Charleston, which everyone knew was coming. The blockade established early in the war had become increasingly effective, particularly after Port Royal was taken and had begun to serve as an advance supply depot. Nevertheless, it was far from airtight; rakish blockade runners still slipped brazenly in and out of the harbor at will. For several weeks northern newspapers—a constant source of valuable information to the South—had been printing articles about the ironclad fleet that was soon to be on its way to destroy Charleston, that symbol of rebellion. The news was correct, and Confederate authorities knew it—what they did not know was how to stop it. Beauregard, a professional army engineer, demonstrated his mastery as he built fortifications and placed cannon to cover every approach to the harbor. He needed, however, more guns and a boom of linked logs and rails which would be placed across the harbor. A naval force was also needed, and Ingraham promised at the meeting that the two ironclads would be ready in two weeks, "as an important auxiliary to the works defending all parts of the harbor. . . ."[4]

The flag officer was not far from wrong; both the *Chicora* and the *Palmetto State* were at anchor in the harbor by the middle of October, Lieutenant Robert Minor, working in the Office of Ordnance and Hydrography

2. Arthur Grimball to his mother, February 11, 1863, Grimball Papers. See also James H. Tomb Memoirs; Parker, *Recollections of a Naval Officer,* 293; and George H. Bier to "George," January 29, 1863, Area file, Confederate Subject and Area File, National Archives Record Group 45.
3. For a detailed account of the incident see Ander Klay, *Daring Diplomacy: The Case of the First American Ultimatum.* See also Allen Johnson and Dumas Malone (eds.), *The Dictionary of American Biography,* IX, 476–477.
4. *Official Records, Navies,* Ser. I, XIII, 808–810.

in Richmond, was informed in a letter from a Charlestonian dated October 6 that "the ironclads here are in a state of completion. The officers on . . . the *Chicora* are all there, the other, the *Palmetto State,* has only two or three officers here at present."

A month later all the officers had reported on board the *Palmetto State,* but neither vessel had her full crew. This development was most exasperating, for when a recruiting office was opened months before (in February) no trouble was anticipated. Charleston was a port and, in spite of blockade-running, many merchant vessels with their crews were stranded. A number of experienced sailors shipped, but not nearly enough. The naval commander then followed what was becoming common practice throughout the Confederacy by appealing to the local military authorities for "volunteers who had some sea-experience." The army officers were generally co-operative at that time, and a number of seamen were allowed to transfer to the navy. Beauregard was particularly helpful, ordering unit commanders to make out a list of "all seamen in their respective commands immediately." In November the flag officer was still requesting men, but shortly before Thanksgiving a draft arrived from the Yazoo River completing his complement for both ironclads.[5]

Ingraham was fortunate in his enlisted personnel; there were probably more trained seamen in the Charleston Squadron than in any other "home-water" group. A large number of them were foreigners, and unlike the Confederate Army, which had never before enrolled Negroes, there were three free Negroes "regularly enlisted" on board the *Chicora.* He also had a nucleus of battle-trained veterans—many of the transfers from the Yazoo River had served on the *Arkansas.* In contrast to most vessels and squadrons in the Confederate service (except cruisers fitted out in foreign ports), the Charleston Squadron was well trained and well disciplined; the crews generally had the respect of their officers.[6]

If the adage "a clean ship is a good ship" has any merit, then the two

5. Pemberton to Cooper, September 23, 1862, Department of South Carolina, Georgia, and Florida Letterbooks, National Archives Record Group 109; Ingraham to Beauregard, November 1, 17, 1862, *Palmetto State,* Vessel File, National Archives Record Group 109. Parker wrote, "Occasionally we got a man from the army—and we kept a bathing arrangement on the wharf, where all recruits were bathed and their clothes were boiled, before being allowed to come on board, for obvious reasons." Parker, *Recollections of a Naval Officer,* 292.

6. Ben Labree (ed.), *Camp Fires of the Confederacy,* 266–267; F. B. C. Bradlee, *A Forgotten Chapter in Our Naval History: A Sketch of the Career of Duncan N. Ingraham,* 19; James H. Rochelle, *Life of Rear Admiral John Randolph Tucker,* 51; Memoirs of Charles T. Sevier (Tennessee State Library and Archives, Nashville).

Charleston ironclads must have been "good ships." A number of visitors were impressed by the cleanliness of the vessels. Lieutenant William H. Parker, executive officer of the *Palmetto State,* later proudly wrote, "when these two vessels had been in commission a short time, they were fine specimens of men-of-war and would have done credit to any navy. . . . They were the cleanest iron-clads, I believe, that ever floated, and the men took great pride in keeping them so."

Parker, however, was not so complimentary of the vessels themselves, and rightly so, for there were serious weaknesses. Because their engines had been taken from small steamers, both were extremely slow and under-powered; designed to steam seven or eight miles per hour, they were for-tunate to make five miles per hour in calm water. One account relates that the *Chicora,* while acting as picket between Forts Sumter and Moultrie, was compelled to cast anchor because she was unable to stem the ebb tide, a force of slightly more than two miles per hour. Although her engines were kept at full power to relieve the strain on her cables, she continued to drag.[7] As with other vessels of that class, they were also topheavy and difficult to steer.

Since Beauregard was not pleased with the performance of the two ironclads, he was most interested when Captain Francis D. Lee, one of his young officers, showed him the plans of a torpedo ram. Captain Lee, a native of Charleston and an architect by profession, had joined the army shortly after his state left the Union. He was appointed an officer in the engineers and assisted in the construction of Fort Wagner on Morris Island. His interest lay, however, with the more technological aspects of engineering, particularly explosives. He began to experiment with mines or torpedoes as they were then known and, determined to find a method of taking these "infernal machines" to the enemy, he designed a "torpedo ram." His proposed vessel would be similar in shape to a cigar, submersible (with only the smokestack, pilot's cockpit, and the top of the armored hull above water), and armed with a spar torpedo.[8]

Before Beauregard's arrival in Charleston, Lee had had absolutely no success in gaining support for his project. Beauregard, however, was im-

7. Francis Lee to Beauregard, February 8, 1864, Department of South Carolina, Georgia, and Florida Letterbook, National Archives Record Group 109. For criticism of the machinery see the Memoirs of James H. Tomb, and Maffitt to Davis, June 7, 1880, *Jefferson Davis,* VIII, 474.

8. Francis Lee to Beauregard, February 8, 1864, Department of South Carolina, Georgia, and Florida Letterbook, National Archives Record Group 109; Perry, *Infernal Machines,* 64.

mediately receptive to the plan. On October 8 he wrote enthusiastically to the governor of South Carolina that the proposed ram "would be worth several gunboats" and recommended that funds from the state gunboat appropriation be allotted to build the vessel. He added in a later note, "I believe an ordinary gunboat will effect but little against the enemy's new gigantic monitors. . . . we must attack them under water, where they are the most vulnerable if we wish to destroy them and the torpedo ram is the only probable way of accomplishing that desirable end."[9] The governor and the General Assembly were impressed enough to provide substantial funds.

In the meantime, Beauregard, characteristically, had not awaited the results of his petition to the state before seeking the necessary approval from Confederate authorities. He had sent Lee off to Richmond to present the plan to the secretary of war and had appealed to Congressman William P. Miles to "push" Lee's idea. Although Miles did what he could, the captain was generally given the "run-around" by Richmond officials. He went from the adjutant general to the secretary of war, who in turn sent him to the secretary of the navy; all expressed interest but promised little or nothing.[10] He did not return empty handed, however. Permission was given by the War Department to build the vessel.

With this approval and the funds obtained from the state, Lee started to work. An unfinished gunboat hull was obtained; machinery from the old tug *Barton* was purchased when the engine and boiler turned over by the navy were found to be worthless. Lee requested timber, armor plate, and other material from Flag Officer Ingraham, but his requests were turned down.

Inevitably, the Navy Department was somewhat cool toward the project. Although Beauregard wrote Mallory that he "never desired to remove the construction of . . . [the] torpedo ram from the competent naval officer in command of the station," the project was all army, and Ingraham resented it.[11] Mallory also believed in his ironclads then and later and did not want to turn over machinery and iron plate for this vessel when there was not enough for the various ironclads under construction. Unfortunately, Beauregard took the navy's supposed refusal to co-operate as a personal affront, and it furthered his growing antagonism toward the sea service. Nevertheless, Beauregard was anxious to attack the blockading squadron, and the two ironclads would have to do.

9. *Official Records*, Ser. I, XIV, 631; Roman, *Beauregard*, II, 37–38.
10. Lee later said that Mallory promised him "a boiler and two engines suited to the vessel."
11. *Official Records, Navies*, Ser. I, XIII, 814.

Ingraham, however, was extremely reluctant to take his harbor defense ironclads beyond the bar. A naval officer in the Charleston Squadron wrote,

Beauregard told me that some time since the English and French commanders had told him that if he would send the vessels down and raise the Blockade for *twenty hours* they would sail out and proclaim the Blockade raised—that he had suggested it to Ingraham and that he was afraid that the motive power of the vessels was not great enough. How in the Devil is he going to find that out unless he tries? I suppose he will wait until the Yankees have accumulated three or four of their heavy Ironclads and then send us to certain destruction. . . .[12]

Throughout most of January, the commodore was able to procrastinate because of unpleasant weather; the sea was rough off the bar, and even steaming in the harbor was risky for the wallowing rams.[13]

Time was running out. Monitors were on their way, and when they joined the blockading fleet Confederate chances for a successful attack would all but disappear. On January 6, five ironclads were ordered to the South Atlantic Blockading Squadron. Twelve days later, the armor-belted warship *New Ironsides* was observed steaming into Port Royal, followed by the monitor *Montauk*. Three days later the *Passaic* arrived bringing with her the news that the *Monitor* had foundered in a storm off Hatteras.

Rear Admiral Samuel Francis Du Pont, the tall, dignified, and wealthy naval officer in command of the South Atlantic Blockading Squadron, decided to send the *Montauk* and *Passaic* to Savannah and to station the *New Ironsides* off Charleston when she was ready (her smokestack was being cut down and other modifications made). Information obtained from deserters led him to believe that the Confederates were planning an immediate attack with a recently completed ironclad—the *Atlanta*—on his blockading forces off Savannah. The *Montauk,* under tow, arrived off Ossabaw Bar on January 24 and three days later joined in an attack against Fort McAllister. The *Passaic* and *New Ironsides* remained at Port Royal; inclement weather prevented the monitor from leaving for Savannah, and the ironclad frigate was not ready. On January 28 the weather began to moderate enough for the steamer *James Adger* to get underway for Wassaw Sound with the *Passaic* in tow. With the *New Ironsides* still in Port Royal, there were no Union ironclads off Charleston when the seas began to subside.

At 10:00 o'clock Friday evening, January 30, Flag Officer Ingraham hurried on board his flagship, the *Palmetto State,* and ordered preparations to get under way immediately. This action was not totally unexpected; for

12. George H. Bier to "George," January 26, 1863, Area file, Confederate Subject and Area File, National Archives Record Group 45.
13. Parker, *Recollections of a Naval Officer,* 193–194.

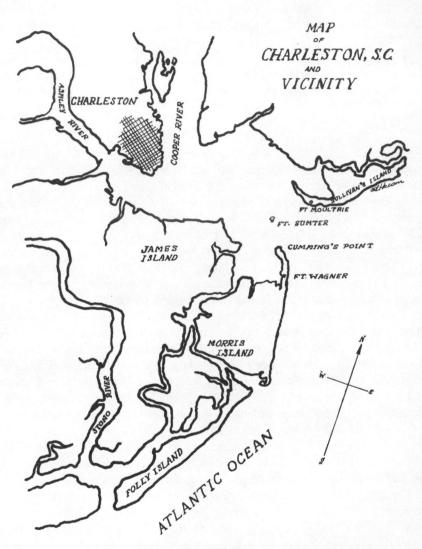

FIGURE 8

several days rumors had foretold an attack on the blockading fleet, and earlier that evening the crews of both ironclads were observed covering the pale blue paint of the shields with a greasy slush. At 11:15 P.M., under a beautiful moonlit cloudless night, lines were cast off the flagship, and she stood slowly for the bar eleven miles away. Fifteen minutes later the *Chicora* followed.

While under way down the main channel to the bar, the Confederate commanders ordered all but the watch on duty to rest before the coming engagement. On the *Palmetto State* hammocks were piped down, but the men, tense with excitement, got up an "impromptu Ethiopian entertainment," presumably a minstrel show. Parker wrote,

After midnight, the men began to drop off by twos and threes, and in a short time the silence of death prevailed. . . . Visiting the lower deck, forward, I found it covered with men sleeping in their pea-jackets. . . . on the gun-deck a few of the more thoughtful seamen were pacing quietly to and fro. . . . in the pilot-house stood the Commodore and Captain, with the two pilots; the midshipmen were quiet in their quarters (for a wonder), and aft I found the lieutenants smoking their pipes, but not conversing. In the ward-room the surgeon was preparing his instruments on the large mess-table; and the paymaster was, as he told me 'lending a hand.'[14]

Early in the morning both vessels reached the bar and hove to to await high tide.

At 4:30 A.M., just before dawn, the two ironclads crossed the bar. There were some anxious moments as they slipped over with little more than a foot of water to spare. The moon had set, and a thick haze enveloped the blockading vessels. Ingraham, however, could make out the *Mercedita*—a converted merchantman armed with nine guns, including a 100-pound Parrott rifle—off the bar, and he ordered the *Palmetto State's* captain, John Rutledge, to ram her. On the Confederate vessel

the port shutters were closed, not a light could be seen from the outside, and the few battle-lanterns lit cast a pale weird light on the gun-deck. . . . As we [Parker wrote] stood at our stations, not even whispering, the silence became more and more intense. Just at my side I noticed the little powder boy of the broadside guns sitting on a match-tub, with his powder-pouch slung over his shoulder, fast asleep, and he was in this condition when we rammed the *Mercedita*.

Although blockade duty was dreary and boring most of the time, it could be arduous, especially at night when the runners would try to slip through the line. On the *Mercidita,* her exhausted captain, Henry S. Stellwagen, had retired at 4:00 A.M. after chasing a vessel which proved to be only a troop steamer. He was in a state of drowsiness when he heard his executive officer, Lieutenant Trevett Abbot, who was still topside, exclaim: "She has black smoke. Watch, man the guns, spring the rattle, call all hands

14. *Ibid.,* 295–296.

to quarters!" Stellwagen put on his coat and bounded up the poop ladder from which he saw "smoke and a low boat" which he at first believed was a tug. Recognizing the possibility of collision, he angrily shouted: "Steamer, ahoy! Stand clear of us and heave to! What Steamer is that?" He hesitated to order the guns fired although they were manned and ready. He hailed again. This time there was a reply, but except for the word "Halloo," it was indistinct. A second later he heard another shout, "This is the Confederate States steam ram ————!" Stellwagen yelled "Fire! Fire!" but it was too late. The *Palmetto State*'s prow crashed into the starboard quarter of the *Mercedita;* at the same time a shell from her bow 7-inch gun entered a few feet above the waterline, passing through both boilers before exploding on the port side. The vessel was instantly filled with steam; water poured into the holes made by the ram and shell; men were killed and scalded.

The *Mercedita* was helpless, dead in the water, apparently sinking, her guns unable to fire. Stellwagen had no choice but to surrender. A boat was lowered after several minutes of hesitation and delay, and Abbot rowed over to the Confederate ironclad, which had by this time drifted clear. Once on her deck (he later told Du Pont that he had trouble gaining a foothold because of the grease), he was taken to the flag officer to whom he reported the name of his vessel, the number of her crew, and her condition.

Ingraham evidently had trouble deciding what to do with *Mercedita's* crew. There was no room on board the ram; the blackader's small boats were inadequate (and apparently worthless because their plugs had been removed); he needed his crew; and the unarmed vessels that were supposed to take possession of prizes had for some unexplained reason remained above the bar. His procrastination bothered the impatient officers looking on. Abbott later reported to Du Pont that one officer said, "Commodore, you must think quick for we must get along!" Daylight was rapidly approaching. He finally asked the Union officer to give his word of honor for "his commander, officers and crew," that they would not serve against the Confederacy until regularly exchanged. Abbott agreed and returned to what he thought was a sinking ship. In parting he was assured that the vessel "will not go lower than the upper deck" because of the shallow water.[15]

At about the time the *Palmetto State* was ramming the *Mercedita,* the

15. Quoted in a letter from DuPont to his wife, February 2, 1863, Journal Letters of Samuel F. DuPont to his wife, September, 1862 to July, 1863 (typed copies in the possession of Rear Admiral John D. Hayes, Annapolis, Maryland). For accounts of the engagement between the *Palmetto State* and *Mercedita* see *Official Records,* Ser. I, XIII *Navies,* 579–581, 617–618; Parker, *Recollections of a Naval Officer,* 295–296.

Chicora was passing to the starboard of her consort, standing for another blockader. The *Chicora* was commanded by a Virginian, John Randolph Tucker. Tucker had planned to ram, but according to one of the engineers, the chief pilot dissuaded him with the argument that the vessel's power might not be great enough to pull her clear after ramming.[16]

In his report, Tucker mentioned first engaging a "schooner rigged propeller," which was probably the *Mercedita*. Tucker wrote that after firing a few shots, "We then engaged a large side-wheel steamer twice our length from us on our port bow, firing three shots into her with telling effect." This was the *Keystone State,* a converted merchantman with a battery of three 8-inch Dahlgren smoothbores and seven lighter guns. Her commanding officer was William E. LeRoy, called "Lord Chesterfield" by a fellow officer because of his dogmatism on "good breeding and gentlemanly bearing." He was characterized as "a great stickler for etiquette and red tape, nervous and easily excited. . . . He had the Episcopal prayer service read every afternoon (generally by himself) on the berth deck and prompt attendance to these services by any officer was a sure passport to his good will."[17]

Moments after the 5:00 A.M. bell sounded on the *Keystone State,* a shot from a nearby gun was heard. This was the usual announcement of a sighted blockade runner, and LeRoy immediately had the crew beat to quarters and the cables slipped. A steamer was then observed approaching out of the mist; a challenge rang out, and when no intelligible reply was heard, the *Keystone State* opened fire, swinging to the east to bring her broadside guns to bear. The *Chicora* returned the fire; one shell entered the blockader's berth deck, "tearing the hammock racks . . . to pieces, setting fire to some of the wood work, rudely disturbing the watch asleep in their hammocks and wounding and killing several men." The *Keystone State* was then turned into the wind toward the open sea in an attempt to extinguish the flames. LeRoy worked his vessel up to twelve knots, and though the ironclad continued firing, she rapidly fell astern.

After about ten minutes of steaming into the wind, the fire was brought under control, but almost immediately a second one broke out near a shell room. By the time that fire was out, it was full light, and objects were visible at a distance. After a brief discussion between LeRoy and his executive officer, the *Keystone State* was brought about toward the sound of firing.

16. *Official Records, Navies,* Ser. I, XIII, 622–623; James H. Tomb to the editor of the *Confederate Veteran* Magazine, n. d. (*Confederate Veteran* magazine File, Duke University Library).

17. D. W. Graply Diary (Historical Society of Pennsylvania, Philadelphia); Charles E. Clark, *My Fifty Years in the Navy,* 91–93.

LeRoy intended to ram. He stood directly for the *Chicora,* and as the distance rapidly closed, shots were exchanged. When they were within several hundred yards of each other (estimates vary from 200 to 500), a lucky shot from the Confederate vessel breeched the *Keystone State*'s port side, glanced off a knee supporting one of the main deck beams, passed over the dispensary, and entered both steam drums. Live steam at a pressure of twenty-five pounds instantly streamed through the berth deck, escaping in large volumes through the hatches. Engineer D. W. Graply wrote in his diary that night,

Many were suffocating including the wounded. . . . The doctor and his assistant were killed. . . . in the fire room most of the men escaped through the coal bunkers to the deck. One escaped strangely by quickly climbing one of the small pillars supporting [the] main shaft bearings, as the paddle wheel shaft was slowly revolving, the cross tail of the engine came within three inches of one side of him. . . . How he ever did it without injury was a miracle.

This shell was followed by others which exploded on the deck or crashed through the hull of the *Keystone State,* "spreading confusion and dismay." Water from the boilers and two holes below the waterline poured into her bilges and heeled her over to starboard. The situation was critical. LeRoy reported, "Our steam chimneys being destroyed, our motive power lost . . . two feet of water in the ship and leaking badly . . . the forehold on fire."[18] Graply wrote,

In a short time the escaping steam having steadily diminished . . . [I found myself] standing in company with the Captain and Executive officer alongside the rail at the rear end of the hurricane deck, looking at the [Confederate] Ram about 500 yards astern. Chief Engineer Meddows had just reported that the engine was still working and would continue so for several minutes on its vacuum. Captain LeRoy had given me the signal book and some manuscript to hold whilst he was tearing up some written papers. He was very nervous and excited. The flag had just been hauled down and Lieutenant [Thomas H.] Eastman [executive officer] had asked "Who hauled down the flag?" The Captain replied "I ordered it down. We are disabled and at the mercy of the Ram who can rake and sink us. It is a useless sacrifice of life to resist further." Lieutenant Eastman threw his sword upon the deck saying " God D——n it. I will have nothing to do with it." The Captain said "What would you do? Will you take the responsibility?" Eastman instantly replied "yes sir I'll take the responsibility," and picking up his sword sang out to the officer on the poop deck cooly and calmly, "Hoist up the flag. Resume firing."

The *Chicora* ceased firing and hove to when the flag on the Union vessel was hauled down. Tucker immediately ordered a boat to take pos-

18. *Official Records, Navies,* Ser. I, XIII, 581–582, 586; Samuel Jones, *The Siege of Charleston and Operations off the South Atlantic Coast,* 147–148.

session of the prize, but as it was being manned, he observed that the *Keystone State* was still moving. Tucker assumed that his intended victim was trying to escape, but refused to fire until he saw her flag hoisted again. What he did not know was that the starboard wheel had never stopped turning, because the engine continued working on its vacuum. Even on one wheel the *Keystone State* was able to widen the distance between the two vessels causing Tucker to write angrily later, "her commander by this faithless act [placed] . . . himself beyond the pale of civilized and honorable warfare." In this manner the *Chicora* was cheated of her prize and the *Keystone State* returned to Port Royal under tow.

While the *Mercedita* and *Keystone State* were becoming the victims of the Confederate attack, the remainder of the blockading squadron was either unaware of what was going on or found out about it too late. For some unexplained reason, neither vessel signaled that she was under attack. As a result, only four other Federal vessels entered the affray. The two ironclads engaged the *Memphis* shortly after the *Chicora* left the *Mercedita* "apparently sinking," and after the *Palmetto State* saw the *Keystone State* standing seaward with flames pouring out of her hold. After passing one of the rams and discovering she was an ironclad, the Union blockader steamed out of range to the eastward. The *Quaker City* blundered into the battle after the *Keystone State* was put out of action and received a shell in her engine room for her trouble. At half past six the *Augusta* and *Housatonic* got under way; both had heard the spasmodic firing, but assumed it involved blockade runners. A few shots were exchanged with the ironclads, but with the exception of a random shell demolishing the *Palmetto State*'s flagstaff, nothing was accomplished. Shortly after this, the two Confederate vessels steamed for the bar.[19]

The ironclad dropped anchor off Sullivan's Island, under the protective guns of army batteries there, to wait out the long day before the tide would be sufficient to carry them across the bar. Officers on the spar decks, with some apprehension, turned their glasses toward the calm waters of the outer harbor where they had been engaged only a short time before. Their fears were groundless, for the blockading squadron either remained out of sight or hull down on the horizon throughout the day. At 4:00 P.M. they crossed the bar and steamed slowly into the inner harbor. Salutes were fired by the forts and batteries, and hundreds of people lined the bank and wharves to cheer them as they berthed.

19. Edward D. Butler, "Personal experiences in the navy, 1862–65," in *Papers read before the Maine Commandery of the Loyal Legion of the United States*, II, 191; *Official Records, Navies*, Ser. I, XIII, 587–595.

The applause was appreciated, but after the excitement of the day had worn off, some began to have second thoughts about what had been accomplished. That night Engineer James H. Tombs of the *Chicora* wrote, "They say we raised the blockade, but we all felt we would have rather raised hell and sunk the ships."[20]

That same night General Beauregard wired Richmond: "Last night Confederate gunboats *Chicora* and *Palmetto State,* under Commodore Ingraham, sank . . . the steamer *Mercedita.* Enemy's whole fleet has dispersed north and south. I am going to proclaim the blockade of Charleston raised." The formal proclamation was signed by Ingraham and the general, and copies were sent to the various foreign consuls in the city. Later the Confederate government stood behind it, and when five of the captains commanding blockaders off Charleston on the thirty-first issued a joint denial, a controversy broke out as to whether the blockade had really been raised.

According to international law, if the blockade had been raised, even temporarily, the Union would have to go through the formality of issuing new notices of blockade before it could be re-established. Both Beauregard and Ingraham unquestionably believed that the blockade had been technically broken or breeched, even though Union vessels resumed their positions the following day. While the ironclads were anchored near Sullivan's Island, the French and Spanish consuls were taken by steamers on a tour of the area to witness the fact that the blockaders had disappeared from their stations. The British consul also went out in *HMS Petrel* for this purpose.

In the 1880s, Beauregard became involved in a renewal of the controversy with Captain William Rodgers Taylor, senior officer present and commander of the *Housatonic* the night of the raid. In an article in the *North American Review,* the general asserted again that the blockade had been broken, and when Taylor (then an admiral) wrote a denial, Beauregard replied, "I said that *for the time being* it was raised; and I maintain that my assertion was absolutely correct, notwithstanding the denial of Rear Admiral Taylor and others."[21] Lieutenant Parker also entered the letter-writing duel by saying that he considered the blockade broken, although the proclamation was "ill-advised, inasmuch as I did not believe the English government would recognize it."

Yet the two signers of the declaration knew that the blockaders would

20. *Ibid.,* 622–623; see also Parker, *Recollections of a Naval Officer,* 303–304.
21. P. G. T. Beauregard, "Defense of Charleston, South Carolina, South Carolina," *North American Review,* CXLVI (1886), 426; see also letters to the editor from Beauregard and William Rodgers Taylor in CXLIII, 97–99, 413–418; CXLIV, 308–312.

inevitably resume their positions when they realized that the rams had returned to Charleston. This probably explains Beauregard's haste in publishing his proclamation. He hoped to bluff (and it would be a bluff regardless of what the English and French naval commanders told him) foreign governments into recognizing that the blockade had been legally broken. Unfortunately, the bluff did not work: European nations ignored the announcement; Du Pont's squadron was back on station and the blockade was tighter than ever; and Gideon Welles ridiculed the proclamation.[22]

Although Du Pont was bitter over the northern newspapers' accounts of the affair, he salved his feelings with the belief that "good will come of it"; that the department would send on the additional monitors that had been promised. Other monitors did arrive in February and March, but along with these reinforcements came letters from Secretary of the Navy Welles urging Du Pont to use the ironclads to attack Charleston. As early as October 1862, Welles had ordered the flag officer to force Charleston into surrendering by running his vessels past the ports and threatening to bombard the city. Although Du Pont considered the monitors "failures" and was pessimistic about the success of such an attack, he made preparations to begin the operation early in April 1863.

On April 6, Du Pont, with his flag in the *New Ironside*, crossed the bar into Charleston Harbor, followed by the remainder of his ironclad squadron —seven monitors and the tower ironclad *Keokuk*. His initial objective was the reduction of Fort Sumter by bombardment. Foul weather, however, delayed the attack until the following day.

Beauregard, Du Pont's antagonist, reacted to the imminent attack with his customary vigor: his more than 30,000 troops in and around Charleston were alerted; his formidable batteries of heavy guns—seventy-seven of them —were manned and ready; and the Confederate naval squadron was ordered to take up its predetermined position between Forts Moultrie and Sumter.

The squadron was no longer under the command of Ingraham. On March 28 he had been relieved by Commander Tucker, captain of the *Chicora*. Tucker, called "handsome Jack" by the tars, was a member of a prominent Virginia family and a veteran of thirty-five years of naval service. The younger officers in the squadron were enthusiastic about the change. Lieutenant George H. Bier wrote, "Tucker is one of the most energetic and

22. Welles, *Diary*, I, 232–233; *Official Records, Navies*, Ser. I, XIII, 606; Ser. II, III, 703–704, 712; Bradlee, *Forgotten Chapters*, 24. See also Du Pont to his wife, February 7, 11, 1863, Journal Letters.

capable officers in the service. . . . In forty-eight hours after he [is] . . . given the command of the *vessels afloat* something creditable to the Navy [will] . . . be done."[23]

Bier must have been mildly disappointed, for Tucker's policy would vary little—if at all—from that of his predecessor. When the Union ironclads crossed the bar, the flag officer ordered his two armored vessels to engage the enemy only if necessary to protect the forts. Lieutenant John H. Rochelle, commander of the *Palmetto State* and later biographer of Tucker, wrote,

With his good judgment, [Tucker] held the *Chicora* and *Palmetto State,* aided by a number of rowboats armed with torpedoes, ready to make a desperate and final assault upon the Federal Squadron if it should succeed in passing the Confederate forts. . . . The Confederate naval forces afloat at Charleston did not possess either the strength or swiftness for an attack.[24]

Tucker's force was not required to perform any desperate deed; Du Pont's attack failed to get past the forts. The Union ironclads were subjected to more than two hours of terrific pounding from the forts before withdrawing, and although Du Pont planned to renew the action the following day, he dropped the idea after a conference with his captains. During the engagement, the two Confederate ironclads steamed in a circle between the forts but did not fire a shot.

Although Beauregard had expected little help from the Charleston vessels, he hoped for a strong feint from the Savannah ironclads. On April 5 he wired the naval commander at Savannah: "Ironclads have all left Port Royal [for Charleston]. . . . this would seem a proper time for a diversion against Port Royal."[25] The naval commander replied: "Cannot go to sea. . . . wish [I] . . . had the means of so doing." The general, not one to accept a simple no, fired telegrams to Richmond trying to pressure the navy into co-operating with him.[26] Beauregard's opinion of the sister service never was high, and the apparent inability of the ironclads to assist him against Du

23. To "George," January 29, 1863, Area file, Confederate Subject and Area File, National Archives Record Group 45; see also Grimball to his mother, April 1, 1863, Grimball Collection.

24. Rochelle, *Tucker,* 48–49; see also Tucker to Mitchell, April 1, 1863, Mitchell Papers.

25. To Commander Richard L. Page, Savannah Squadron Papers (Emory University Library, Atlanta).

26. Mallory to Page, April 6, 7, 1863, Savannah Squadron Papers; *Official Records, Navies,* Ser. I, XIII, 824; Page to Beauregard, April 5, 1863, Register of Letters Received, Department of South Carolina, Georgia, and Florida, National Archives Record Group 109.

Pont's attack did nothing to lessen this feeling. He later wrote, "None of these Confederate vessels or ironclads were [sic] . . . seaworthy, and, beyond river and harbor defense, none of them could render effectual service."[27] Yet, a diversion had been contemplated using the one ironclad in the Savannah Squadron that could have gone to sea and was considered by many to be the most powerful armored vessel in Confederate service. This was the *Atlanta*.

27. Roman, *Beauregard*, II, 421.

8

The *Atlanta*

IN NOVEMBER 1861, the *Fingal,* an iron-hulled merchant steamer built in England and purchased by the Confederate government, slipped through the blockade into Savannah with a valuable cargo of military supplies. It was December 20 before she was loaded with a return cargo of cotton and was ready to depart. She was unable to break out, however, and after languishing several months during the winter and spring of 1862, the vessel was turned over to Asa and Nelson Tift for conversion into an ironclad.

Despite the New Orleans disaster, Mallory still had confidence in his old friends the Tifts and allowed them unlimited authority in the project—a situation not at all appreciated by Flag Officer Josiah Tattnall, who had received command of the Savannah station and squadron after the destruction of the *Virginia.* Obviously irritated, he later said,

Mr. Tift, who was in charge of . . . construction, called at my office and showed me his authority . . . giving him the sole control of her [the *Atlanta*] construction, and, in reply to a question, he stated that it was intended that the commandant of the station should have nothing to do with her. I, of course, abstained from interfering in any shape whatever.[1]

"The *Fingal* was converted into the ironclad *Atlanta* . . . on the same plan, so far as practicable, as the ironclad *Mississippi,*" wrote Nelson Tift after the war. "The conversion . . . was a far more difficult, though not so extensive nor so formidable a work. . . . She was strongly and quickly built."[2] Edward C. Anderson, a Savannahian and a former naval officer, described how the *Fingal* was converted: "Her bulwarks were cut down, a heavy deck 3 feet in thickness laid over her own, and a shield of heavy timber plated with Rail Road iron erected."[3]

1. Quoted in Jones, *Tattnall,* 223.
2. To J. Thomas Scharf, June 9, 1890, folder on *Atlanta,* Confederate Subject and Area File, National Archives Record Group 45.
3. Edward C. Anderson Journal (MSS. in possession of Mrs. Florence Crane Schwalb, Savannah). For another description of the conversion see Bulloch, *Secret Service,* I, 144–145.

By the end of July, construction had progressed sufficiently to take her on a trial trip down the river with a crew borrowed from the various naval vessels in the squadron. On board the *Atlanta,* the Tifts, accompanied by Tattnall and other naval officers, observed her steaming qualities. Nelson Tift wrote later with pride that "her speed, her steering capacity and her guns were all tested and proven satisfactory." Tift may have been exaggerating some, but the *Atlanta* was certainly one of the most efficient Confederate ironclads.

Nonetheless, four months would pass before she was commissioned into service. Although some time is necessary to "shake down" for deficiencies and correct them in a new ship, four months was unusually long. The delay was probably a result of conditions which generally affected shipbuilding in the Confederacy, mostly the lack of skilled labor and essential materials. A local shipbuilder, Henry F. Willink, was requested to lend a number of carpenters to work on the *Atlanta.* Willink, who was under contract to build two ironclads for the Navy Department, refused sharply, saying that Mallory expected him to "use all possible diligence" in completing his vessels.[4] Tattnall emphasized that factors contributing to the delay were serious leaks in her sponsons and elsewhere (she was still leaking when captured) and the need for alterations to the machinery. On November 22, 1862, the *Atlanta* was finally commissioned, and awaited only her complement of officers and crew before becoming operational.

To the casual observer, the *Atlanta* appeared similar to other Confederate armored ships floating on the waters and lying on the ways throughout the South. The major distinctions were her iron hull and her machinery. She was 204 feet in length, 41 feet in beam, with a draft varying from 15 to 17 feet. Her machinery was relatively new, English built, and included probably the best propulsion unit in any Confederate ironclad. As the *Fingal* her speed had been approximately twelve miles per hour, but her increased weight and draft as an ironclad reduced it to half that. Her armament consisted of four guns (two 7-inch and two 6.4-inch Brooke rifles), a spar torpedo and a ram.[5]

Although she was adequately armed, armored, and powered, like most ironclads built within the Confederacy, she was nevertheless jerry-built. The Savannah *Morning News* reported that when the *Atlanta*'s bunkers were loaded with coal for the first time, increasing her draft slightly, water seeped

4. Willink to J. W. Brent, July 23, 1862, Brent to Willink, July 22, 1862, in Henry F. Willink Papers (Emory University Library, Atlanta).

5. For description of the vessel see Davis, *Rebel Ram,* 9–10; Philadelphia *Inquirer,* June 19, 1863; *Official Records, Navies,* Ser. I, XIV, 276; Ser. II, I, 248.

in so rapidly that the wardroom and berth deck were covered with nearly a foot of water. "The officers quarters are the most uncomfortable that I have ever seen," wrote a young midshipman. "There are no staterooms. . . . . the apartments are partitioned off with coarse . . . dirty canvas. . . . the only thing on board that we can call our own is a pair of hammock hooks, and a mess table."[6]

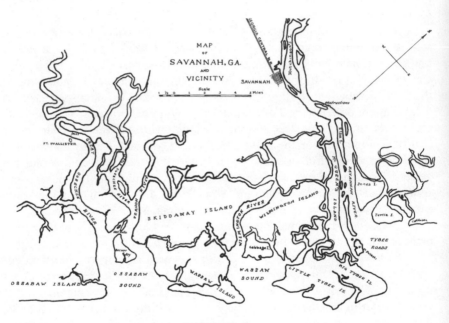

FIGURE 9

Leaks or no leaks, Commodore Tattnall was anxious to get to sea. He wanted to clear Wassaw and Ossabaw Sounds before the wooden blockaders on station there were reinforced by monitors. On January 5, 1863, the *Atlanta* got under way and steamed several miles down the Savannah River. Earlier in the war, Confederates had obstructed the main channel of the river by sinking huge wooden cribs filled with paving stones. The Navy Department had requested that a passage be cleared through the obstructions, and although army engineers assured Tattnall that a passage could be made in two hours, it was not ready when the ironclad arrived. In fact, it would take an additional month of steady labor to prepare the passage. The

6. Scales Diary.

Atlanta's crew was bitterly disappointed: "All on board had the mortification to see the anchor again dropped in Savannah River," Midshipman Dabney Scales recorded in his diary that night.

Flag Officer Du Pont had followed closely the progress of the Confederate ironclad; throughout the fall and early winter months of 1862, letters poured from his pen alerting Welles and Assistant Secretary of the Navy Fox to the possible danger from the vessel. His fears were also communicated to his wife: "The *Fingal* I think is likely to be formidable," he wrote in October, "but is not yet finished." As related in the previous chapter, the flag officer weighed the completion of the *Atlanta* against the potential danger of Confederate ironclads in Charleston harbor and decided to send the first of his monitors to the blockading force watching Savannah. On January 24, the monitor *Montauk* dropped anchor off Ossabaw Bar.

The presence of the *Atlanta* was not the only factor in Du Pont's decision. He wanted to test the performance of the new monitors against fortifications and also wanted to destroy the Confederate cruiser *Nashville*, aground in the Ogeechee River above Fort McAllister.[7] On January 27, a small flotilla of five vessels, including the monitor with her two powerful Dahlgren guns (a 15-inch and an 11-inch), engaged the fort. The result was indecisive; neither the sand works of the fort nor the monitor was damaged.

A few miles away the people of Savannah listened with alarm to the rumble of cannon fire. Tattnall was asked by the city council to go to the assistance of the fort. Although the council considered the Confederate armorclad to be "competent to almost any achievement," the commodore knew better. His experience with the *Virginia*, plus his knowledge of the *Atlanta*'s deficiencies, convinced him that she would not stand a chance. He later wrote, "I considered the *Atlanta* no match for the monitor class of vessel at close quarters, and in shoal waters particularly, as owing to the necessity of [lightening her in order] . . . to cross the flats and operate in the Sounds, at least two feet of her hull below the knuckle were exposed, covered with but two inches of iron."[8] Nevertheless, he reluctantly agreed to relieve the fort by attempting to run past the monitor, relying on superior speed to avoid an engagement, and attack the wooden vessels below. The operation never materialized, for on January 30 a second monitor, the *Passaic*, arrived from Port Royal. The *Atlanta* obviously could not slip by two monitors.

7. Samuel T. Browne, "First Cruise of the *Montauk*," in *Papers of the Soldiers and Sailors Historical Society of Rhode Island* (Providence, Rhode Island, 1879), 30–31; I. E. Vail, *Three Years on the Blockade*, 83–84.
8. To Mallory, April 23, 1863, quoted in Jones, *Tattnall*, 224.

In order to placate what the flag officer called an "angry and excited public," he agreed to General Hugh W. Mercer's suggestion to take up a position off a small sand fort at Causton's Bluff on Augustine Creek, a winding stream which linked Wassaw Sound with the Savannah River. The army wanted to shift several batteries, and the ironclad could provide support while this was being accomplished.

Even this operation was nearly denied by weather. A gap had finally been cleared through the obstructions, and soundings were made to determine when the water would be high enough for safe passage. The movement was set for February 3, 1863. The night before, after the *Atlanta*'s officers had returned from a party on the floating battery *Georgia*, a cold wind gradually developed out of the northwest and by four in the morning was "half a gale." The operation had to be canceled, for the wind prevented the tide from rising to a point where the ironclad could float safely through the obstructions. "So we were again disappointed," Midshipman Scales wrote in his diary,

and I fear we will be unable to get out on this spring tide. . . . of course we will be branded as cowards by the unthinking portion of the citizens of Savannah. . . . These people never stop to enquire into the cause [of] these delays; but stigmatize the navy generally, because we did not go down and *sink* the enemy's fleet even *before* the obstructions had been removed from the river. . . .

On March 19, Tattnall took the *Atlanta* through the obstructions. A reconnaissance the day before had established that Wilmington River was clear of enemy vessels. Intelligence also indicated that the monitors had returned to Port Royal in preparation for the attack on Charleston. This was the opportunity that the commodore had been waiting for; when the assault took place he was going to strike at Port Royal, "should the force left there justify it, or [if this was out of the question, sweep] . . . the Sounds to the south of the Savannah, [and] push on to Key West. . . ."[9]

While the *Atlanta* was at anchor waiting for high tide near the head of Wassaw Sound, an unfortunate incident occurred to ruin Tattnall's carefully laid plans. A small picket boat from the *Georgia*, commanded by a midshipman and rowed by four sailors, was in the mouth of the Savannah one night. The midshipman handed his jacket to one of the men to stow in the bow and cautioned him about the revolver in it. Unfortunately, he handed it to one of two disgruntled Irish conscripts in the boat. Within moments the Irishmen had the pistol and were in contról, and the boat was pointed toward Fort Pulaski. When the deserters were questioned, one of them informed his

9. *Ibid.*, 225–226.

examiners that he had overheard Tattnall outlining his plan of attack to several other officers.[10]

This information corresponded with what Du Pont expected Tattnall to do. The *Passaic* was promptly ordered back to Wassaw Sound, and two additional monitors were sent to reinforce the blockading force in the mouth of the Savannah.

Tattnall's plan was sound. Port Royal was the weak link in the blockading system, and Du Pont recognized this. After the failure of the ironclad assault on Charleston, Du Pont confided to his wife, "One thing more I could have done—I could have made a *second* attack with disabled vessels, have lost all or a greater portion of them. . . . We should have been driven from the coast and probably damaged the cause irretrievably. Beauregard sent an order for the Savannah rams to attack and make a raid on Port Royal during my absence."[11]

Port Royal, which had become a naval station almost overnight, was slightly more than twenty-five miles from Savannah by water and could be reached easily by Confederate ironclads. The reoccupation or destruction of Port Royal would have damaged seriously the effectiveness of the blockade along the eastern seaboard. Since provisioning and fueling a ship while under way was many decades in the future, a strategically located port was necessary for an effective blockading force. The importance of amphibious operations earlier in the war, which secured Port Royal and the other logistic bases, cannot be overestimated. A comment from Du Pont to his wife illustrates the precariousness of this support: "Danby made a very shrewd remark this morning—he says if the rebels now raiding in Pennsylvania knew it—they would destroy the Reading Railroad and cut off every squadron from its coal—which would virtually destroy them—we now live from hand to mouth for want of it."[12]

Some Confederate leaders recognized the importance of Port Royal to the Union cause. Commander John Taylor Wood, aide to President Davis and one of the most influential officers in the Confederate Navy, wrote on March 24, 1863: "With as many iron vessels in commission as the enemy,

10. Du Pont to his wife, March 21, 1863, Journal Letters; *Official Records, Navies,* Ser. I, XIII, 767–768; John F. Maguire, *The Irish in America,* 572; Ella Lonn, *Foreigners in the Confederate Army and Navy,* 294; R. M. Thompson and R. Wainwright (eds.), *Confidential Correspondence of Gustavus Vasa Fox, Assistant Secretary of the Navy 1861–1865, I,* 194.

11. April 13, 1863, Journal Letters.

12. June 29, 1863, Journal Letters. The "raid" was Lee's offensive which climaxed in the battle of Gettysburg.

we must be doing something. If they concentrate on Charleston, let us dash at Port Royal. If necessary, the vessels from Wilmington, Charleston, and Savannah might concentrate."[13] The idea, which was similar to Tattnall's plan, was first-rate strategy, even if Wood wishfully ignored the limitations of the ironclads. President Davis would urge essentially the same movement in the last months of the war.[14]

Wood also wrote in March: "There is quite a ferment just now in naval circles. . . . We want at Charleston, Savannah, and other points young men." The naval commander was not writing hearsay, for that same day Mallory relieved Tattnall of his command afloat. Within a week, a second distinguished officer, Flag Officer Ingraham, was dismissed from his command of the Charleston squadron. No reason was made public for their dismissals, although the secretary obviously preferred younger, more aggressive, officers for the squadrons. Even though these two were the only senior officers to lose command of their squadrons, Mallory continued his shake-up by recommending the creation of a "Provisional Confederate Navy"—a way of bypassing the promotional system based on seniority.[15]

Tattnall retained the naval station and served loyally as commandant until the city was evacuated, but the stubborn old hero was a broken man. After visiting him, a relative wrote, "Poor cousin Josiah is very much depressed."

Ironically, within two weeks Du Pont had recalled his monitors guarding Savannah and launched his attack on Fort Sumter. Tattnall's successor, Commander Richard L. Page, was in no position to take advantage of this, because the *Atlanta*'s steering gear was damaged while she was returning to Savannah for the change of command. Thus Beauregard's appeal for help went unheeded.

Page's flag flew slightly more than a month, for early in May the squadron received its third commanding officer in less than a year. There is little or nothing to indicate why Page was relieved except possibly the fact that Mallory was dissatisfied with the apparent continuing inactivity of the naval force at Savannah. Page was a senior officer, a personal friend of Tattnall, and like him probably realized that the *Atlanta*'s deep draft would not allow

13. *Official Records, Navies,* Ser. I, VIII, 862–863.
14. Davis to Beauregard, December 13, 1864, *Jefferson Davis,* VI, 415.
15. An Act of May 1863 established the "Provisional Confederate Navy." The aim of the measure, as explained later by Raphael Semmes, was, "without interfering with the rank of the officers in the Regular Navy, to cull out from the navy list younger and more active men, and put them in the Provisional Navy, with increased rank." Raphael Semmes, *Memoirs of Service Afloat during the War Between the States,* 368–369.

her to operate in confined waters against a monitor. Commander John K. Mitchell, in charge of the Bureau of Orders and Detail (technically responsible for all changes of command, although the naval secretary obviously made many, if not most, of them), received a letter dated April 22 from Lieutenant George T. Sinclair, commanding the *Atlanta*. He requested a transfer, stating dejectedly, "nothing would induce me to leave here so long as there is the *slightest* prospect of a fight, which by the way, I now think is very remote, more probably never."[16] Whether Mallory was even aware of this communication is not known, but Page was transferred to a shore billet less than two weeks later. He became commanding officer of the Charlotte (North Carolina) Naval Station. When he failed to get more active duty, he resigned his commission and received an appointment as a brigadier general in the army. He later fought at Fort Morgan during and after the battle of Mobile Bay.

The new squadron commander at Savannah was Commander William A. Webb, a Virginian who in the battle of Hampton Roads was captain of the little *Teaser,* a converted tugboat. He had a reputation with his fellow officers as "a very reckless young officer," who received his appointment because he would "at once do something." A former shipmate wrote in his journal, "Webb . . . [had] orders to assume offensive operations against the enemy. . . . He was specially promoted in order to give him rank enough to assume his new position. Webb accordingly came down here very much elated at his advancement. He was boastful and disinclined to listen to the counsel of older and wiser heads."[17]

Webb's aggressiveness was evident. Within a week of taking the command, he informed the naval secretary that he planned to strike at the enemy on the next spring tide "at such places as circumstances may determine." His luck, however, seemed to be little better than that of his predecessors. On May 30, after coaling and provisioning ship, he got under way in the *Atlanta*. She passed through the obstructions safely, but while steaming down the narrow south channel of the Savannah River, the forward engine broke down, forcing her aground. The sortie was off, for it took more than twenty-four hours to pull her free. Webb was disappointed but still confident. When Mallory suggested that he delay his attack until the ironclad *Savannah* could co-operate, Webb grandiloquently replied, "I assure you the whole abolition fleet has no terror for me, though the co-operation of the *Savannah* would be of great assistance."[18] His plan was nearly as inflated as his self-confidence.

16. Mitchell Papers.
17. Journal of E. C. Anderson.
18. June 10, 1863, William A. Webb Letterbook, National Archives Record Group 45. The *Savannah* was completed but lacked her battery. Charles C. Jones to

He planned to take advantage of the next full tide, "raise the blockade between here and Charleston, attack Port Royal, and then blockade Fort Pulaski." After this, if there was still time to kill until the tide was full again, he would cruise southward. No mention is made of what he planned to do about the various monitors that he would probably encounter during this operation. In fact, while the *Atlanta*'s engine was being repaired, Webb received word that two monitors were in Wassaw Sound—in position to challenge the Confederate armorclad if she attempted to come out.

Du Pont's intelligence concerning the Confederate ironclads was uncanny. On the day that Webb was wiring his proposed plan of attack to Mallory, the Union flag officer was writing, "We have a ram fever on again— *Fingal* [*Atlanta*] ready to pounce on the *Cimarron* at Wassaw, and *Dawn* at Ossabaw. . . . Sending off *Weehawken* . . . immediately. Sending up to Edisto for *Nahant* and *Montauk*." Webb's zeal gave way to circumspection; he decided to attack the monitors but wait for the *Savannah* before taking on the remainder of the fleet.

The night of June 16 was humid; the sailors perspired heavily as they filled the *Atlanta*'s bunkers with coal, increasing her already deep draft. Before dawn she weighed anchor and stood down the dark river, hoping to surprise the enemy vessels shortly after sunrise. Webb planned to ram his spar torpedo into the nearest monitor and attack the second one with his battery.

At 4:10 A.M., a lookout on the *Weehawken* observed the approaching ironclad in the Wilmington River and gave an alarm.[19] The *Weehawken* was commanded by Captain John Rodgers, a member of one of the most illustrious families in American naval history. Rodgers himself had gained the admiration of Union (and many Confederate) naval officers for his conduct during the first battle of Drewery's Bluff in May 1862. His crew were veterans; when the Confederate vessel was sighted, they quickly came to quarters, cleared for action, and took the *Weehawken* downstream, raising full steam while under way. The second monitor, *Nahant,* commanded by John

father, March 5, 1863, Charles C. Jones Papers (University of Georgia Library, Athens).

19. For accounts of the engagement see *Official Records, Navies,* Ser. I, XIV, 265–267, 290–292; Rodgers to Davis, June 25, 1863, quoted in Davis, *Charles Henry Davis,* 286–287; Log of *Weehawken,* National Archives Record Group 45; Charleston *Daily Courier,* December 29, 1863; Savannah *Republican,* July 9, 1863; Savannah *Morning News,* June 27, 29, July 9, 1863; *Federal Circuit and District Court Reports. Case No. 619; 3 Wallace 425* (1866); *The Atlanta* (District Court, Mass., 1864), *2 Federal Cases,* 116–121; Malcolm MacClean, "The Short Cruise of the *C.S.S. Atlanta,*" *Georgia Historical Quarterly,* XL (1956), 130–143.

Downes, followed in the wake of the *Weehawken*.[20] After ten minutes, Rodgers turned about and closed with the *Atlanta*. When the range had dropped to approximately a mile and a half, the Confederate ship fired a shot which passed over the *Weehawken* and struck near the *Nahant*. Rodgers was puzzled, for it looked as if the ironclad had stopped and was lying cross channel awaiting his attack; it was certainly not a tactic expected from a vessel evidently trying to reach the sea.

To Webb the position was unexpected also: his ship was aground. Upon entering the mouth of the Wilmington River, he had sighted the monitors and ordered full steam toward them. Webb's enthusiasm may have caused him to leave the channel to attack the monitors; one of his officers was later quoted by a newspaper as saying the pilots informed him that there was sufficient water to accommodate the *Atlanta*'s sixteen-foot draft.[21] In any case, this calculated risk failed, for within minutes the ironclad ran onto a sandbar. She was backed free, but because of the shallow water she failed to respond to her helm and gradually was forced aground again, listing slightly as she grounded.

In the meantime the *Weehawken* continued her approach. At 300 yards range, Rodgers opened fire. The monitor with her 11- and 15-inch Dahlgrens fired only five times, but four scored with devastating results. The first hit from the 15-inch struck the starboard side of the *Atlanta*'s casemate, and although it failed to penetrate, fragments of iron from the armor and splinters from the wood backing spewed across the gun deck, wounding a number of men. Between forty and fifty were laid out from concussion by this shot. The second hit slightly damaged the knuckle, while the third one glanced off the porthole shutter of the starboard battery, just as the crew had the gun loaded and were in the act of raising the shutter. Over half of the gun crew were wounded by this shot. The fourth and last shot carried away the top of the pilot house and wounded two of the pilots.

The *Atlanta* was able to fire only seven shots, none of them effective because her list prevented proper aiming. After only fifteen minutes of battle, Webb surrendered. He clearly had no choice. Commander James D. Bulloch later wrote, "It can hardly be said that he was fighting his ship—he was simply enduring the fire of his adversary."[22]

The capture of the *Atlanta* was a profound shock to the Confederacy. When news of her misfortune first reached Richmond, John B. Jones remarked in his diary, "there is a rumor that the Secretary of the Navy sent an ironclad out yesterday, at Savannah, to fight two of the enemy's blockading

20. Only the *Weehawken* had a pilot.
21. Savannah *Morning News,* July 9, 1863.
22. Bulloch, *Secret Service,* I, 147–148. See also *Official Records, Navies,* Ser. I,

squadron, and . . . our ship struck her colors. If this be so, the people will wish that the Secretary had been on the boat that surrendered." He added the following day that Mallory was "in bad odor" for the *Atlanta* affair. For some time newspapers had been gloating about the ironclad until the public came to consider her practically invincible. In fact, public pressure played no small part in the Confederate ironclad's mischance. When she not only failed to accomplishing anything, but evidently surrendered after a brief fight, they reacted angrily: "nothing but treachery or incompetency would [have prevented] her from vanquishing the monitors." Two wooden steamers had accompanied the *Atlanta* down river at a discreet distance. Some say they were loaded with sightseers including women, and that the spectators returned carrying tales of a possible mutiny among the crew. Exactly where they got this information is not recorded—the crew was demoralized but not mutinous.

The *Atlanta* was simply no match for one monitor, much less two. Tattnall, and probably Page, realized this. If Webb could have put the *Weehawken* out of action with a spar torpedo, he planned to close with the *Nahant*. Confederate tactics called for concentrating fire on the base of the turret—where it joined the deck—hoping to jam the turret and keep it from revolving. The chances are very slim, however, that the *Atlanta* could have closed enough to accomplish it with her 6.4- and 7-inch rifles. Both monitors were evidently firing their guns with more than thirty pounds of powder, and it was only a matter of time before an 11- or 15-inch gun would have penetrated the *Atlanta*'s armor.

While all was gloom in the South, the North was jubilant. Rodgers received a vote of thanks from Congress and advancement to commodore; Welles believed that the monitor type had finally been vindicated; and Du Pont could turn over the South Atlantic Blockading Squadron to Rear Admiral John A. Dahlgren with more contentment.

On July 4, 1863, Dahlgren broke his flag for the first time as commanding officer of the squadron; that same day Commander Isaac N. Brown, CSN, formerly commander of Confederate naval activities on Western Waters, was on his way to assume command of a newly launched ironclad at Charleston.

XIV, 290. One crew member said that two shots from the *Atlanta* failed because the cartridges did not fit. Savannah *Morning News,* July 9, 1863. A number of newspaper accounts and at least one authority, H. W. Wilson, *Ironclads in Action* (2 vols., London, 1896), I, 98, emphasized the lack of training of the crew. This was not true. The diary of Midshipman Scales clearly indicates that training at the guns was carried on continually.

9

Ironclads and the Defense of the West, 1862-64

THE LOSS of the *Arkansas* had been a disaster to Confederate efforts in the West; in fact, it was the climax to a series of disasters involving the navy. General Josiah Gorgas observed, "with her dies all hope of re-conquering the Mississippi."[1] The ordnance chief was exaggerating some, but the Confederate ironclad was the last serious threat to Union control of the river. The capture of New Orleans and Memphis, along with the elimination of the Confederate fleets at these cities and the capture of the unfinished *Eastport*, opened the rivers to invasion. The Confederate armies were left with their river flanks exposed for, with the exception of a few miscellaneous wooden vessels, there was no longer a Confederate navy in the West.

Mallory, aware of the seriousness of the situation, assured Secretary of War George W. Randolph and others that immediate steps were being taken to construct additional ironclads in the West.[2] Even before the *Arkansas* was destroyed, the wooden gunboat *Mobile* had been ordered to Yazoo City for conversion into an armorclad. Then early in September naval agents were told to contract for the construction of a large sidewheel ironclad there. They had an initial appropriation of $300,000 for labor and materials, but Mallory cautioned them "to act in the premises generally as if you were building for yourselves and had to pay the money out of your pocket."[3]

---

1. Frank E. Vandiver (ed.), *The Civil War Diary of General Josiah Gorgas,* 13.
2. *Official Records, Navies* Ser. I, XIX, 788–89; Mallory to J. D. B. De Bow, August 19, 1862, J. D. B. De Bow Papers (Duke University Library, Durham).
3. To Weldon & McFarland, September 16, 1862, Area file, Confederate Subject and Area File, National Archives Record Group 45. See also Mallory to Taylor, September 19, 1862, and to Baker, July 28, 1863, in Area file, Confederate Subject and Area File, National Archives Record Group 45. The *Mobile* was a small steamer used at the beginning of the war to patrol the Gulf of Mexico from Louisiana to Sabine Pass. After the fall of New Orleans she performed similar duties in the Yazoo River. George C. Waterman, "Notable Naval Events of the War," *Confederate Veteran,* VI (1898), 170; Sheppard to Nixon, October 11, 1862, folder on repairs to Confederate vessels,

Isaac Brown, who had returned to Yazoo City after the destruction of the
Arkansas, was directed to superintend construction of the sidewheel armorclad. In his orders the naval secretary wrote, "I know that you fully appreciate the importance of having iron clad vessels built for the defense of the
Mississsippi. This vessel designed by the Naval Constructor [John Porter]
will I think be formidable and serviceable. You are clothed with a large discretion, and your judgment is confided in to exercise it for the best interest
of the country. You are a long ways from Richmond and must not hesitate
to take responsibility. . . . Your . . . labors will be onerous. The collection of
railroad iron, its transportation and preparation, the collection of machinery,
ordnance stores, must all be entered upon at once."[4]

The decision to complete the *Arkansas* at Yazoo City had resulted in
the establishment there of the most extensive Confederate shipbuilding
center in the West. Shipways, saw and planing mills, machine shops, carpenter shops, and blacksmith shops had been built.

Mallory was also trying to contract for warships at other points in the
West. On October 2, Captain Samuel Barron, CSN, received orders to
supervise the building of armored sidewheel gunboats on the Tennessee and
Cumberland Rivers, and the following day Lieutenant Jonathan H. Carter
was instructed to contract for the building of "one or more iron clad vessels
of war" on the Red River.

Barron's efforts were unsuccessful. Before the month of October was
out, he had reported that "the repulse of . . . General Van Dorn and the
retreat of General Bragg render it altogether inexpedient to attempt at
this time the construction of gunboats on either of the rivers."[5] The Confederate government was never able to outfit war vessels on these rivers, and
their control was lost for the remainder of the war. Carter, however, was
more successful, and on November 1 he signed a contract for the building of
an ironclad gunboat at Shreveport, Louisiana.

By December 1862, two new ironclads had been laid down, and a third
was under conversion on tributaries of the Mississippi. Whether they would
be operational in time to contribute to the Confederate defense was the
important question. A month earlier, General Ulysses S. Grant set in motion

National Archives Record Group 45; Fiske to Comstock, July 24, 1862, John H.
Comstock Papers (Southern Historical Collection, University of North Carolina Library, Chapel Hill).

4. September 23, 1862, Area file, Confederate Subject and Area File, National
Archives Record Group 45.

5. *Official Records, Navies,* Ser. I, XXIII, 703–705.

what was designed to be a two-pronged thrust at Vicksburg by moving 30,-000 troops along the Mississippi Central Railroad from Corinth to Holly Springs. On December 20, the second prong, his right wing under General William T. Sherman, embarked on board a large flotilla of transports for the mouth of the Yazoo River on the northern flank of the city. Sherman was escorted by the gunboats of Acting Rear Admiral David D. Porter, who had just recently assumed command of the naval squadron on the Mississippi.

On Christmas Day they reached the mouth of the Yazoo and moved up the river. Sherman planned to seize the high ground along the left bank and then attack Vicksburg in co-operation with Grant, who was coming up from behind the city. Grant failed to appear, however, and on the 29th the Federal assault was bloodily repulsed at Chickasaw Bluffs. The thrust was stalled and forced back, but no one doubted they would come again, perhaps from the south where General Nathaniel Banks had reached Baton Rouge with a large body of troops.

Brown at Yazoo City and Carter at Shreveport were trying desperately to complete their armored ships before the trap closed on Vicksburg and completely severed the Trans-Mississippi West from the remainder of the Confederacy. But the problems facing them were nearly insurmountable.

Even if the Confederacy had been fortunate enough to have had adequate shipbuilding facilities and materials, a chronic shortage of labor, both skilled and unskilled, would have severely curtailed ironclad construction. Throughout the war, agriculture, transportation, and industry were constantly struggling with the military authorities for the rapidly decreasing labor supply. There were probably enough skilled mechanics in the South at the beginning of the war to have provided a nucleus labor force, but the Confederacy, facing total war, was never able to solve the complex manpower problems it encountered.

The Navy Department did not lack labor throughout 1861. Most ship construction then occurred in localities with adequate labor, particularly ports such as Norfolk and New Orleans. Nevertheless, even then Mallory was concerned over obtaining skilled labor. The trouble stemmed from over-mobilization at the beginning of the conflict, which had swept most of the skilled workers into the army. As shipbuilding expanded, and as the ordnance works and other related naval facilities began operating, the need for machanics and carpenters increased.

In August 1861, Mallory began a long and frustrating correspondence with the War Department concerning shipwrights and mechanics in the army.

He requested that designated ship carpenters, "as may be willing to receive discharge . . ." be released to work for the navy.[6] The secretary of war ordered commanding officers to discharge these men, but from the beginning opposition developed. John Shirley, constructor of the two Memphis iron-clads (*Arkansas* and *Tennessee*), sent a list of thirty or more carpenters and their regiments to General Leonidas Polk with the request that they be released for naval service. The request was denied. Similar occurrences took place throughout the Confederacy. This opposition led to the modification of the original order. In December, Mallory was told that all requests for mechanics and carpenters would be refused unless "the parties interested will furnish substitutes" to serve in the ranks in place of the workmen.[7]

The continual refusal of the War Department to provide workmen without substitutes prompted Mallory, in January 1862, to urge the President to take action to secure the services of carpenters, shipwrights, and joiners in the army who would volunteer to work on the construction of ships for the navy. Although Davis refused to agree to this, he did go along with the idea of detailing or temporarily assigning men from the army to work on ships and in various naval facilities. In January this policy was put into effect and was gradually expanded until it encompassed all types of manufacturing in the Confederacy. The War Department seemingly co-operated fully in this system, but there was one factor which ruined its effectiveness— the allocation of men was left to the discretion of commanding officers of various units. This applied to all levels from generals in command of armies to company commanders. Military commanders, also faced with a man-power shortage, were generally reluctant to part with their men.

On December 10, 1862, the secretary of war replied to Mallory that a request for men to work on gunboats was declined because various commanding officers unanimously opposed it. Carter, trying to complete the ironclad at Shreveport, complained that with few exceptions military officers had refused to assign men to work on the vessels. In February 1863, Franklin Buchanan at Mobile applied for carpenters, but was turned down because "the Commander of armies from which these details are requested report that they can not spare the men. . . ."[8]

Contractors encountered similar opposition and red tape. On Septem-

6. Quoted in a letter from Secretary of War Leroy P. Walker to Mallory, August 30, 1861, War Department Papers, National Archives Record Group 109.
7. A. T. Bledsoe to Mallory, December 19, 28, 1861, War Department Papers, National Archives Record Group 109.
8. Seddon to Mallory, February 24, 1863, War Department Papers, National Archives Record Group 109.

ber 10, 1862, Colin J. McRae, under contract to establish an ordnance works and rolling mill at Selma, Alabama, wrote Lieutenant George Minor,

When I made the contract with the Secretaries of War and Navy it was understood between you, Colonel Gorgas [chief of ordnance] & myself that the Departments were to give me all the aid they could in procuring both materials and mechanics. Though I have applied for the detail of a good many mechanics from the army I have never succeeded in getting but one and now a cancellation of his detachment by the army has deprived me of his services. . . .[9]

In Yazoo City, Brown, Flag Officer William F. Lynch (in command of naval forces in the West), and the builders tried in various ways to persuade the army to provide carpenters, caulkers, and mechanics. Letters and telegrams as well as agents were sent to various military commands in Mississippi and Alabama, but, with the exception of a few furnished by General John C. Pemberton at Vicksburg, no men were obtained. They were more successful with Governor John J. Pettus of Mississippi, who canvassed the state military units under his control and detailed as many "ship carpenters and other mechanics as could be found."[10] Many—perhaps most— army officers agreed with General George E. Pickett, who said that not only should all such requests be refused, but all of those already detailed should be ordered back to their units.

Congressional action was tried also, but here the matter became involved in conscription legislation. On March 20, 1862, a bill entitled "an act to provide for ascertaining and detailing artizans and mechanics from the Confederate Army" was passed by the Senate and sent to the House. But there the bill was delayed and finally killed when Davis, on March 29, asked for the conscription of all men between the ages of eighteen and thirty-five. (Six months later, a second conscription act extended the upper military age from thirty-five to forty-five.) This first selective service program in American history also established the system of excusing various classes of persons from military service. (The first exemption law was passed on April 21; it was repealed in October 1862, and a more detailed one was enacted.)

9. Colin J. McRae Collection (Department of Archives and History, Montgomery, Alabama).

10. Weldon to Pettus, October 14, 15, 1862, January 26, and February 25, 1863, Mississippi Governor's Papers (Department of Archives and History, Jackson, Mississippi); Weldon to Breckinridge, August 3, 1862, Citizen File, Weldon, National Archives Record Group 109; Lynch to Wyatt, October 7, 1862, Area file, Confederate Subject and Area File, National Archives Record Group 45; Ware to Nixon, August 26, 1862, Paymaster Thomas H. Ware Letterbooks, National Archives Record Group 45; Pettus to Pemberton, n.d., Pemberton Papers, National Archives Record Group 109.

These laws apparently worked well for a time in protecting the labor already employed in the manufacturing facilities, including naval construction, but the core of the matter as far as the navy was concerned was still unsolved, namely, the acquisition of workers from the army. No provisions were included for releasing or transferring carpenters and mechanics to work for the navy, and no legislation pertaining to this matter passed Congress.

The materials needed to construct ironclads in the West were practically nonexistent by the fall of 1862, with the exception of timber—and that was green. Nails, so ordinary but so essential, had disappeared from the market. One of the naval agents at Yazoo City wrote to Governor Pettus pointing out that "It is impossible to buy nails for the use of the gun boat," and asking that "a quantity of nails belonging to the [state] government at Meridian" be turned over to him.[11] Some materials could not be located; the vessels at both Yazoo City and Shreveport had to be caulked with cotton because oakum was not available.

The most difficult material to acquire—not only in the West but throughout the Confederacy—was iron, particularly iron plate for armor. Four out of every five ships built in the Confederacy after the spring of 1862 were ironclads, and there simply was not enough iron, or enough mills to roll the iron into plate.

At the outset of the war there were no rolling mills in the South capable of producing two-inch plate, and by the fall of 1862 only two—Tredegar Iron Works in Richmond and the Scofield & Markham Iron Works in Atlanta—had developed that capacity. When the ironclads in the West were laid down late in 1862, these two facilities were already months behind in trying to provide armor for the ironclads under construction along the eastern seaboard. Carter gave up on plate and decided to cover his vessel with railroad T-rails.

Flag Officer Lynch, however, continued to seek plate and wrote to the Scofield & Markham works about iron for the two Yazoo ironclads; when that inquiry produced nothing, he wrote to the president of a small concern—the Shelby Iron Company in Columbiana, Alabama—about rolling plate for the navy. Albert T. Jones, the president, agreed to do so, although he was under contract with the War Department at that time "to deliver the entire proceeds of the work [sic] up to 12,000 tons per year."[12] Rolled plate, however, was more profitable than pig or bar iron, and Jones apparently believed

11. McFarland to Pettus, October 23, 1862, Mississippi Governor's Papers.
12. Jones to Lynch, September 4, 1862, Shelby Iron Company Papers.

that he could fulfill a naval order without breaking his contract with the ordnance bureau of the War Department. Discussions were held in Richmond, and on September 27 Jones received a contract for 400 tons of two-inch plate to be delivered on or before December 1, 1862.[13]

The company then found itself in difficulty. In the first place, because Shelby was not prepared to roll two-inch plate, additional machinery had to be installed. Jones promised to obtain the necessary equipment and to begin operations by the middle of December—a two-week delay at the outset. He also became involved in a dispute with the Confederate iron agent for Alabama, Colin J. McRae. McRae was not informed of the order Lynch had negotiated and found out about it only when his requisitions for iron were not filled. On November 5 he wrote to Jones, "You are not the proper party to decide the necessity of the government. If such authority rests anywhere outside of the Department charged with making the contracts, it would in this instance be with me as I have been appointed by the proper authority."[14] Two days later he wrote to Colonel Gorgas, "I have been made to play a most ridiculous part in the business and I again ask to be relieved from acting as the agent of the Department."[15] Evidently, the trouble was cleared, for the Lynch order retained its priority and McRae continued as iron agent until early in 1863 when he left on a mission to Europe.

Nonetheless, the sixteen hundred tons of plate ordered for the Yazoo City vessels were never delivered. Two days after Christmas, Commander Ebenezer Farrand, superintending the building of two ironclads at Selma, informed an agent of the company that the Selma vessels were nearly ready for armor and that they would have priority over the Yazoo ships. The first plates were rolled early in March, and on the 13th Major William R. Hunt of the Nitre and Mining Bureau ordered all orders suspended until the plate for the Selma boats was completed. The suspension order abrogated the Lynch contract.[16] Brown, who had replaced Lynch as ranking naval officer in the West, refused to stop trying. He sent his naval constructor to Columbiana to try to obtain enough iron to complete only the *Mobile;* when this failed, he tried to locate T-rails as a last resort. By the middle of April he had

13. George Minor to Jones, September 27, 1862, Shelby Iron Company Papers. On September 30 the amount was extended to sixteen hundred tons.

14. McRae to Jones, Shelby Iron Company Collection.

15. McRae Collection.

16. Hunt to J. A. Wall, March 14, 1863, in Shelby Iron Company Papers; Frank E. Vandiver, "The Shelby Iron Works in the Civil War: A Study of Confederate Industry," *Alabama Review,* I (1948), 121–122.

apparently given up; despondently he wrote, "We cannot get it before the dry season will close for six months the navigation of our now besieged gunboats."[17]

Brown realized that Yazoo City was open to attack at any time that strong Federal forces should venture up the river. Defenses were weak; although the stream was obstructed at Haynes Bluff, and torpedoes were scattered in the channel (one had already claimed the Union ironclad *Cairo*), the army provided only a few batteries and troops to protect the valley. Brown appealed to General Pemberton (in command of the Vicksburg defenses, which included the Yazoo valley as far up as Yazoo City) to strengthen the defenses. When his appeals were ignored, the department gave him permission to discontinue work on the ironclads.[18]

The rains were heavy in the late winter and early spring of 1863, flooding the Yazoo River and adding to the difficulties of the builders at the shipyard. The waters swirled around the stocks where the large ironclad lay, caving in the ground and causing the vessel to careen.

The flood not only handicapped naval construction but also threatened to seal the fate of Vicksburg. Union amphibious expeditions were launched through Yazoo Pass and Steele's Bayou in an attempt to reach the city from the rear. In response to Pemberton's urgent appeals, Brown tried to gather a naval force together, but with the exception of a few "cotton clads" no warships were available. Pemberton sent several telegrams inquiring about the *Mobile,* but the naval officer could report only that he had been unable to acquire iron to armor her. Early in May, Union gunboats moved once again up the Yazoo. Grant by this time had begun his audacious attack at Vicksburg, moving below the city and cutting his communications, with the intention of striking at the landward side of the city. Pemberton reacted by withdrawing the scattered troops and batteries from the forifications along the Yazoo, thereby enabling the Union gunboats to move on Yazoo City. They reached Haynes Bluff, fifty miles by water from Yazoo City, by May 20. When the Confederates abandoned the fort at the Bluff, the obstructions across the river were cleared, and several of Porter's river gunboats began steaming toward Yazoo City.

The citizens began evacuating. A local correspondent reported,

Thursday, the 21, our town presented a scene of bustle and confusion. . . . Squads of gold laced gentlemen with their staffs and dependents might be seen

17. Brown to Jones, April 17, 1863, Shelby Iron Company Papers; see also Buchanan to Brown, February 13, 1863, Buchanan Letterbook.
18. *Official Records,* Ser. I, XVII, pt. 2, 788; LII, pt. 2, 382; Moseley, "The Naval Career of Henry Kennedy Stevens," 326–327.

hurrying to and fro making ready to leave our 'dear, damned, deserted town.' The rumbling of ambulances and wagons and rattling of hoofs told our people that they would soon be left to the mercy of a dreaded foe. . . . At half past eleven o'clock scouts reported the hostile fleet at Session's plantation, five miles below, leisurely steaming up. Soon after this, two vast colums of black smoke were ascending—one from the navy yard, and the other from the wharf . . .[19]

Under Brown's orders, workmen and sailors had begun preparations the day before to destroy the yard and vessels. Portable tools and equipment were sent to Selma, Alabama, and by the time the first gunboats hove in sight, little remained. The Federals finished the job of destruction.[20]

The spring floods of 1863 were also an important consideration to those in charge of naval construction on the Red River. An ironclad's keel had been laid down there in December 1862, and by the following February, Carter, the naval officer superintending, was able to report that "the entire shield deck and most of the frames of the vessel . . . are up and the planking will soon commence. The drilling of the iron has commenced. . . ."[21] He also recommended "Caddo" as the vessel's name, after the name of the parish the yard was in. Mallory, however, ignored his suggestion and named her the *Missouri*. By the end of February, the framework was finished, planking of the bottom and sides was nearly completed, and the spar and gundecks were being laid. Carter hoped to launch the vessel early in March without armor and armament, but the machinery, taken from a wrecked riverboat, had to be overhauled and reassembled. She was finally launched on April 14.

Carter was worried about the condition of the river. "Red River is falling," he wrote to the naval secretary, "and it may be necessary to go below the falls at Alexandria before completion." A week after launching, the river began rising, and the vessel had to remain at Shreveport. Work progressed rapidly, and on April 29 Carter wrote, "The cladding below the knuckle is nearly complete and the cladding of the shield will commence at once. The boilers are in position and the remainder of the machinery will be put in place as rapidly as possible."

There was one discordant note in this otherwise encouraging report— "no guns have yet been received," Carter noted. As early as February 1, the department had been urged to provide the ironclad's battery soon, for, as

19. Charleston *Daily Courier,* June 20, 1863.
20. Statement of Constructor William M. Hope, June 17, 1863, Area file, Confederate Subject and Area File, National Archives Record Group 45; David D. Porter to Welles, May 24, 1863, David D. Porter Papers (Library of Congress, Washington, D.C.).
21. Carter to Mallory, February 15, 1863, Correspondence Book of Lieutenant J. H. Carter, National Archives Record Group 45.

Carter pointed out, the guns and carriages ought to be installed before the shield is closed up. This, however, was not to be; guns destined for the *Missouri* were seized at Grand Gulf by Pemberton for use there. The secretary of war gently reprimanded the general, but Pemberton kept the guns.[22] Eventually Carter obtained three guns—an eleven- and a nine-inch Dahlgren from the captured *Indianola*'s battery and an old thirty-two-pound siege gun from the army. In spite of further appeals—the vessel was supposed to have a battery of six heavy guns—this remained her armament.

On June 17, the *Missouri* had her first trial run. She reached a speed of six miles per hour, four miles per hour below that which the contractors guaranteed. Modifications in the ironclad's hull and machinery failed to increase her speed. By the end of August the vessel was as ready for service as she could be, and on September 12, 1863, she was officially turned over to Commander Thomas W. Brent, senior naval officer west of the Mississippi.

The *Missouri* was especially designed for river operations. She was 183 feet in length with a beam of 53 feet and 8 inches. Her casemate was similar to those on other Confederate armorclads, but it was longer—130 feet. Perhaps the ship's most unusual feature was her power plant; she was propelled by a single wheel contained in a recess in the after end of the shield. Nearly eight feet of the wheel's 22-foot diameter were exposed. Machinery consisted of two engines and four boilers connected to a single smokestack. She steered by three balanced rudders beneath the fantail, with the steering wheel located on the gundeck forward under the pilothouse.[23]

The *Missouri* was apparently not much of a ship by anyone's standards. Lieutenant Commander Charles M. Fauntleroy, her first commanding officer, was so "shaken" by his new command that he told Carter, "he hoped the damned boat would sink. . . . that he never intended to serve on her if he could help it."[24] The disgruntled officer later told General Magruder in Galveston that the vessel was worthless. Magruder then brazenly wrote Carter asking for the return of the seamen that he had sent him, for "I hear the *Missouri* can never be of any use."[25]

Fauntleroy may have been somewhat prejudiced because of his disappointment at being transferred to the West, but there were unquestionably an

22. Carter to Mallory, April 1, 1863, Carter Correspondence Book, National Archives Record Group 45; Musgrave to R. D. Minor, March 13, 1863, and Minor to Mallory, March 12, 1863, in Minor Papers.
23. *Official Records, Navies,* Ser. I, XXVII, 242; *Official Records,* Ser. I, XLVIII, pt. 2, 93.
24. Carter to Mallory, October 24, 1863, Carter Correspondence Book. See also *Official Records, Navies,* Ser. I, XXV, 295.
25. *Official Records,* Ser. I, XXVI, pt. 2, 261.

unusual number of defects and weaknesses in the vessel, some of them serious. She was built of green timber, caulked with cotton, armored with T-rails that were not flush with each other, and riddled with leaks. The single stern wheel made her difficult to steer, and her speed was so slow she could hardly stem the current. Carter blamed her defects on the design. Most of her troubles, however, were a result of poor material and poor workmanship. Nevertheless, the *Missouri* and the small wooden steamer *Webb* were the only Confederate warships in Louisiana. Under the command of Carter, who replaced Brent, they would soon be needed.

On January 4, 1864, General Henry W. Halleck wrote General Nathaniel P. Banks, "Generals Sherman and Steele agree with me in opinion that the Red River is the shortest and best line of defense for Louisiana and Arkansas and a base of operations against Texas." Banks was ordered to "operate in that direction" as soon as there was "sufficient water." Coincidentally, Confederate General Kirby Smith was in complete agreement with Halleck; writing to General Richard Taylor, his subordinate in the Louisiana military district, he shrewdly observed: "I still think the Red and Washita Rivers. . . . are the true lines of operation for an invading column, and that we may expect an attempt to be made by the enemy in force before the river falls."

Taylor was also informed that the ironclad *Missouri* would take advantage of the first rise in the river and move down to Alexandria in order to co-operate with his forces.[26] Unfortunately, before the river reached a level sufficient to move the vessel, Alexandria was taken by the advancing forces of General Banks and Admiral Porter. On April 2, thirteen Union gunboats passed through the rapids above Alexandria with considerable difficulty and started toward Shreveport. Banks's main column followed roads parallel to the river. Carter was under pressure from Kirby Smith and Mallory to operate against the approaching force, but exactly what they expected him to accomplish with his two vessels is hard to say. The river never rose high enough for his ships to move down river and co-operate with Taylor's troops. (It was discoverd later that a bayou below Shreveport was draining off much of the water.)

But the ships were not needed; on April 8 and 9, 1864, Banks was defeated and turned back in the battles of Mansfield and Pleasant Hill. The retreat which ensued did not stop until the Union vessels were back in the Mississippi River and Banks was in New Orleans. The *Missouri* remained stranded at Shreveport, although Carter optimistically pointed out that the river usually rose in the summer, "and I may have a chance."

26. *Ibid.*, XXXIV, pt. 2, 325.

10

Wilmington and the Sounds

ON JANUARY 2, 1864, General Robert E. Lee wrote to Jefferson Davis, "The time is at hand when if an attempt can be made to capture the enemy's forces at New Bern it should be done. I can now spare troops for the purpose, which will not be the case as spring approaches. . . . A bold party could descend the Neuse in boats at night, capture the gunboats and drive the enemy by their aid from the works. . . . the gunboats, aided by the iron clads building on the Neuse and Roanoke, would clear the waters of the enemy."[1] The President approved the details of the plan except for the use of ironclads: "progress . . . is slow and too uncertain to fix a date for completion." Even by Confederate standards, Davis's observation was an understatement, for efforts to build armored vessels in North Carolina had been characterized by inefficiency, incompetency, and discord, compounded by the usual problems of shipbuilding in the South.

In the spring of 1862, two 150-foot ironclads were laid down at Wilmington and an undetermined number of shallow-draft vessels capable of navigating in the shoal waters of the sounds were started at Norfolk. The Norfolk vessels were destroyed, however, when the city was abandoned to the enemy.[2] In early fall, contracts were made with two North Carolina firms to build three ironclads to replace those destroyed on the stocks at Norfolk. Howard & Ellis, shipbuilders of New Bern, agreed to construct the hull of one at Whitehall, a small town on the Neuse River. Martin & Elliott contracted for a second one to be laid down at Edward's Ferry on the Roanoke River and a third at Tarboro on the Tar River.

Flag Officer William F. Lynch was transferred from Mississippi and given command of naval forces in North Carolina with the immediate responsibility of completing the ironclads.[3] The choice was unfortunate.

1. *Official Records,* Ser. I, XXXIII, 1061, 1064.
2. *Official Records, Navies,* Ser. II, II, 803; Lee to Porter, March 27, 1862, copy in Forrest Papers; Mallory to Harrison, April 3, 1862, construction at Norfolk folder, Confederate Subject and Area File, National Archives Record Group 45.
3. Mallory to Lynch, October 2, 1862, Forrest to Lynch, October 28, 1862, in William F. Lynch folder, BZ File.

Although Lynch had many good qualities, they were of little use in his new command. He had reached the rank of captain in the United States Navy before resigning his commission in 1861 and had gained fame for his exploration of the Jordan River and Dead Sea. (He later published an account of this expedition /*Narrative of the United States Expedition to the River Jordan and the Dead Sea/*, followed by a second book, *Naval Life; or, Observations Afloat and on Shore.*)

Other qualities, if not representative of the typical naval officer, certainly were those of a gentleman. In the afternoons during warm weather he enjoyed picnics and excursions on the river. Once he had a foot race with a young Wilmington belle along the beach. In the evenings he was fond of discussing literature and poetry with his officers and his secretary, James R. Randall, the celebrated author of "Maryland, My Maryland." He was a devout Episcopalian. His first wife was described as a beauty, the daughter of a senior officer; his second was "sensible but quite plain if not ugly."[4]

Commanding a naval station in the Confederacy was a difficult responsibility. Constructing and fitting out naval vessels, recruiting and training seamen, and making preparations for defending his area of command were some of the more important duties. The nature of the war, particularly along the coast and inland rivers, made co-operation between the army and navy essential. Unfortunately, the division of command was vaguely defined, if at all. Some generals, such as Beauregard and Van Dorn, attempted to control naval operations within their districts; others emphasized collaboration with varying degrees of success. But inevitably friction appeared which hampered Confederate war efforts. This was true in North Carolina.

During the first year of the war, Lynch saw considerable action. He commanded the Aquia Creek batteries on the Potomac during their bombardment by Union gunboats May-June 1861 and afterwards fought the small flotilla of wooden gunboats during the engagement off Roanoke Island and Elizabeth City. Courageous, daring, and as a young officer, adventurous, Lynch was a good combat commander. But he lacked the administrative ability and tact necessary to make him a successful station commander; and his hypersensitivity over the navy and his authority produced continuing dissension. Gilbert Elliott, one of the contractors and the builder of the *Albemarle,* became so embittered toward the flag officer that he wrote to Governor Zebulon Vance, "Lynch is universally looked upon in this State as incompetent, inefficient and almost imbecile. . . ."[5]

4. Randall to Katie, February 10, 26, 1864, James Randall Papers (Southern Historical Collection, University of North Carolina Library, Chapel Hill); Parker, *Recollections of a Naval Officer,* 228.
5. Elliott to Vance, January 24, 1864, Vance Collection.

Elliott was angry because the first carload of iron plate was sent to the ironclad building on the Neuse rather than to his vessel, the *Albemarle,* on the Roanoke, although his ship was further along. Lynch later became apprehensive for the safety of the *Albemarle* and ordered her towed upstream to Halifax. Elliott refused because he felt the move would delay completion for at least two months; the flag officer then seized the vessel, along with the materials and tools. A strong protest to Mallory resulted in the chief naval constructor's hurrying down to try to smooth over the difficulty. Commander James W. Cooke was also ordered to the Roanoke. He was to superintend the ship's completion, and "that your judgment may be untrammeled, you are relieved from duty under Flag Officer Lynch, and will correspond directly with the Department."[6] A few weeks later, the vessel on the Neuse was also taken out of the flag officer's hands. Governor Vance agreed with Elliott's sentiments as to the ability of Lynch. "I am satisfied of his total and utter incapacity for the duties of his position," he wrote to the naval secretary.

The governor was a strong proponent of states' rights and a vigorous opponent of the Davis administration. He had been unusually co-operative in aiding the navy in acquiring railroad iron to be rolled into armor—that is, as long as it was for vessels under construction in North Carolina and for the protection of North Carolina. Mallory found out (probably from Elliott, who had tried to obtain the rails himself) that the Atlantic and North Carolina Railroad Company, of which the state was a principal stockholder, had control of a large quantity of T-rails. The secretary requested the iron, and Vance agreed, specifying that it be used on the *Neuse* (ironclad under construction on the Neuse River). He added, "in regard to the other boat in the Tar or Roanoke, I think you ought to furnish with iron from the Seaboard and Roanoke Road, which is . . . principally the property, as I am informed of an alien enemy."[7]

The Seaboard iron could not be obtained, and Commander Cooke recommended to Mallory that "if no iron can be obtained to clad these boats . . . the entire work ought to be abandoned." A copy of this letter was forwarded to Vance with the notation that "the vessels would not have been undertaken had the Department not had good reason to believe the Rail Road iron could be obtained in North Carolina." Mallory's prodding was somewhat successful, for the governor was able to persuade a reluctant

6. *Official Records, Navies,* Ser. I, IX, 799–800.
7. *Ibid.,* VIII, 849–850. See also Martin to Martin & Elliott, October 30, 1862, North Carolina Adjutant Department Letterbooks, 1861–65 (Department of Archives and History, Raleigh); *Official Records,* Ser. I, XVIII, 777–778.

railroad company to part with a large number of rails. By the summer of 1863, 400 tons of iron had been obtained, but it would be nearly a year before the metal could be rolled into plate and transported back to the building sites.[8]

In March 1864, the naval officer supervising the *Neuse* wrote, "The *Neuse* floats not—the first course of iron is complete—the second fairly begun. . . . the *stop* is at Wilmington, where there are several car loads of iron waiting transportation." When Mallory reminded the War Department of the disaster that might befall the vessels if transportation were not provided for the iron, the quartermaster general replied coldly, "at present forage and food necessary for our armies in the field demand our entire transportation." Quartermaster General A. R. Lawton was not completely ignoring the navy; there simply were not enough cars available. On March 21, 1864, Lawton reported to Lee, "we are feeding the soldiers and horses of [your] . . . army to a large extent from Georgia." On April 7, Lieutenant Benjamin P. Loyall, who was to command the *Neuse,* wrote, "you have no idea of the delay in forwarding iron to this place—it may be unavoidable, but I don't believe it. At one time *twenty-one days* passed without my receiving a piece. . . . Every time I telegraphed to Lynch he replies, 'Army monopolizing cars.' It is all exceedingly mortifying to me."[9]

Lynch was not to blame for the transportation problem, but Vance attributed it to him. On the other hand, the flag officer cannot be completely exonerated. His relations with the military commander in Wilmington, Major General William Henry Chase Whiting, were notoriously bad, a situation that certainly did nothing to help the transportation problem. Whiting's attitude toward the navy can perhaps best be illustrated by the following quote: "So far the gunboats have caused more trouble, interferred more with government business and transportation, been bound up more and accomplished less than any other part of the service. Here I do not permit them to interfere any longer."[10]

Differences between military and naval leaders are not unusual, to say the least, but the antagonism between the Wilmington commanders reached the point where a serious breach between the two service branches was a distinct possibility. In the spring of 1863, Lynch wrote to Senator George

8. William N. Still Jr., "The Career of the Confederate Ironclad *Neuse,*" *North Carolina Historical Review,* XLIII (1966), 5.
9. To Robert Minor, Minor Papers; Whiting to Lynch, February 6, 1864, District of Cape Fear and North Carolina Letterbooks, National Archives Record Group 109.
10. *Official Records,* Ser. I, XXIX, pt. 2, 676–277.

Davis of North Carolina criticizing the defenses of Wilmington. A copy of this letter found its way to the desk of Whiting. Shortly after this, the flag officer (who may have been angered because Whiting telegraphed directly to the naval secretary for permission to use the *Raleigh*'s guns until she was finished) accused the military commander of interfering in naval matters by ordering machinists to work on a blockade-runner. In the exchange of notes that followed, Lynch became so abusive that the general reprovingly wrote, "I could not have supposed that a gentleman of your character and station would have adopted such a tone and such language in addressing me either officially or socially. I trust in reply that I shall not do likewise, both from respect to you and respect to myself." Whiting assured him that he claimed no "authority over the Navy or any part of it," but added, "when in the legitimate exercise of my authority I do give orders, I respectfully recommend you to refer them should they not happen to suit your ideas." This statement did nothing to lessen the flag officer's suspicions that Whiting was determined to control naval activities as well as army in his district. Relations did not improve, and they refused to associate with each other—officially or otherwise—unless "duty demanded."[11]

One of the obvious areas of conflict over authority concerned regulation of blockade-runners. The army, in the person of Whiting, had control at Wilmington. Because of the requirement that every steamer leaving port must carry a certain amount of government cotton, however, both the War and Navy Departments had cotton agents in the city. In the spring of 1864, Mallory ordered his agent to direct two ships planning to run the blockade, the *Hansa* and the *Alice,* to carry cotton for the navy. This was apparently done without notifying the War Department or Whiting. Upon appeals from the private shippers, the Secretary of War ordered one of the vessels detained in order to take on the navy cotton, but the other was allowed to proceed. Mallory was not informed of this decision, and when his agent telegraphed, the *Hansa* was preparing to get under way: Lynch was then ordered to stop her. The flag officer promptly placed a marine guard on board and anchored the vessel under the guns of the ironclad *North Carolina.*

What probably started as a lapse in communication became a personal vendetta between the two military commanders at Wilmington. "Little Billy," as Whiting's troops affectionately called him, was a brilliant young engineering officer who was responsible for the construction of Fort Fisher, the

11. May 26, 1863, District of Cape Fear and North Carolina letterbooks, letters received, National Archives Record Group 109. See also *Official Records, Navies,* Ser. I, XVIII, 867–868.

powerful fortress guarding the mouth of the Cape Fear River. He was also noted for his quick temper, and Lynch's seizure of the *Hansa* caused him to simmer. Whiting sent a note to the flag officer demanding withdrawal of the guard. The naval commander refused, and according to his secretary wrote, "[I know of] no authority paramount to that of the Secretary of the Navy except that of the President and [will] . . . sink the *Hansa* if she attempt[s] to put to sea." The following morning, naval officers reporting for duty were prevented from going on board the various vessels by a battalion of infantry and a battery of artillery drawn up along the water front. Soldiers also boarded the *Hansa,* removed the marine guard, and took the steamer to the army quartermaster's wharf.

Later that morning, Lynch attempted to leave his flagship and was challenged by a guard as he mounted the landing. According to eyewitnesses, the flag officer used his cane to brush aside a bayonet pointed at him and in silence marched on to his headquarters.[12]

The crisis ended when the Secretary of War ordered Whiting not to "interfere with measures ordered by the Navy Department." This so infuriated the general that he came close to insubordination: "I command here, and can permit no interference by the Navy in my legitimate duty . . . I have received no order from the President specially assigning a portion of my duties to any other authority."[13] He had earlier asked that Lynch be removed: "I have often thought it due to myself personally to report him and request his removal. . . . If I have refrained heretofore, it has been because his course here has convinced me that with his opportunities, if he could do no good for his country's defense, he might perhaps do no harm." Davis, as might be expected, was extremely displeased over this affair and ordered both commanders to Richmond immediately. Speculation was rife that one or the other would be relieved of his command, but neither was.

Whiting fought with courage in the final assault on Fort Fisher, suffered

12. Accounts of this incident are conflicting. Lynch's personal secretary reported that he was attempting to board his flagship, but his "Flag Midshipman," who was with him, said that he was going ashore. Randall to Kate, March 10, 1864, Randall Papers; William F. Clayton, *A Narrative of the Confederate States Navy,* 68–70. A soldier stationed in Wilmington wrote his father about the incident: "General Whiting and Commodore Lynch . . . fell out abou [*sic*] some cotton. . . . So the land forces were in arms a day and night. Lynch brant [*sic*] up the iron cladd *North Carolina* abrest with her gunns run out and loaded. . . . our own men going to fight. I was glad they [didn't]. . . ." E. Burginns to father, March 13, 1864, CSA Army Archives, Officers and Soldiers Miscellaneous letters (Duke University Library, Durham, North Carolina).

13. *Official Records,* Ser. I, LI, pt. 2, 883.

a critical wound, and died shortly afterward. Lynch survived the war by only a few months, dying in October 1865.

The affair might be considered ludicrous, except for the fact that it contributed to the already strained relations between the army and navy at Wilmington and in turn affected the ironclad program, which was so dependent upon the army for success. This discord was only one of the impediments to completing the ironclads, however. Inadequate facilities, materials, and labor played their usual discouraging roles. At one time carpenters working on the *Raleigh* went on strike because the Navy Department had insufficient funds to pay them. In the summer and fall of 1862, and again in 1863, yellow fever epidemics swept through Wilmington; the workmen in the shipyards were forced to flee from the city until the dread peril disappeared. Later one of the yards was partly destroyed by fire.[14]

Private contractors had their problems also. The *Albemarle* was damaged when launched, and the chief naval constructor had to be sent from Richmond to supervise repairs. The *Neuse* was shelled and damaged by a Union force which attacked Whitehall in December 1862; the shell-scarred hull was repaired, turned over to the navy, and towed to Kinston to be completed. The ironclad laid down at Tarboro, still only a skeleton, was destroyed in July 1863 by the Federals.

Four of the ironclads originally laid down in North Carolina were still in various stages of construction when General Lee proposed his attack on New Bern. The attack was carried out and failed; as Lee feared, the ironclads were not available. "I think every effort should be made now to get them into service as soon as possible," he advised the President after the New Bern attack. "Without them maintenance of the command of the waters in North Carolina is uncertain. . . ."[15]

Commander John Taylor Wood, naval aide to the President, had led the boat force in the New Bern expedition, and upon returning to Richmond he reported to Davis and his naval secretary on the slow progress of the ironclads. The President did not normally occupy himself with naval matters, but in this instance he took notice because any serious attempt to recover the North Carolina Sounds would require a considerable number of troops.

14. *Ibid.*, 680–681; XVIII, 416, 829–830. See also Clayton, *Confederate Navy*, 67.

15. *Official Records*, Ser. I, XXXIII, 1101. See also John Peck to Henry K. Davenport, n.d., Area Seven File, National Archives Record Group 45. General George Pickett suggested to the War Department, "I would not advise a movement against New Berne or Washington again till the iron-clads are done." February 15, 1864, *Official Records*, Ser. I, XXXIII, 94.

Since Grant's movement against Richmond was imminent (as soon as the roads became passable), such an operation would have to be undertaken immediately. Lieutenant Robert D. Minor, CSN, was ordered to proceed to North Carolina, inspect the *Neuse* and *Albemarle,* and make any recommendation that would hasten their completion. (Minor had acted as a departmental trouble-shooter earlier in the war when he went on a similar mission to examine vessels under construction at Mobile and New Orleans.) He arrived in Kinston on February 14. Two days later he reported to Mallory that the *Neuse* was partially armored with all of her machinery in and should be completed in a month, "if the material is delivered here as rapidly as I hope it will be."[16]

Minor then went to Scotland Neck to inspect the *Albemarle*. He found her nearly finished; mechanics were at work bolting the last layer of iron on her shield. Minor wrote to Mallory that she should be ready early in March if the last of the armor plate for the shield and the two guns for the vessel's battery arrived on schedule. But the iron did not arrive on time, and days wasted while the workers passed their time in marching and drilling. An officer commanding one of the units detailed to provide labor complained in his journal, "I furnish good ship carpenters—the navy keep[s] the workmen waiting for material."[17]

April drew near, and General Lee's anxiety increased; time was running out. The original plan called for a co-ordinated movement against both New Bern and Plymouth. The *Neuse* was to co-operate with General George E. Pickett against New Bern, while the *Albemarle* was to render similar aid to General Robert F. Hoke in attacking Plymouth. The two ironclads would then clear the Sounds of Union gunboats. Lee, however, was ready to call off the operation; the vessels were not completed—nor could he find out when they would be—and he believed that the campaign in Virginia would begin before the one in North Carolina was successfully concluded. Pickett had already moved his troops to Petersburg, Virginia, leaving Hoke in command in eastern North Carolina. In early April, Lee urged the War Department to order the return of Hoke.

On April 9, Pickett proposed that Hoke be allowed to carry out his part of the operation—the attack on Plymouth—with or without the ironclads.

16. Minor Papers. See also Minor to his wife, February 14, 1864, Minor Papers, and John Taylor Wood to Catesby ap R. Jones, February 26, 1864, Area File, Confederate Subject and Area File, National Archives Record Group 45.
17. "Descriptive Journal of Company B, 10th North Carolina Artillery Regiment," in William Alexander Hoke Papers (Southern Historical Collection, University of North Carolina Library, Chapel Hill).

Lee reluctantly agreed, but he insisted that Hoke's brigade should be relieved by one from Whiting's command as soon as the town was secured. The President, however, still hoped to recapture all of eastern North Carolina. General Braxton Bragg, at that time acting as his military advisor, telegraphed Hoke, "Should you succeed . . . in capturing Plymouth and opening the river, then your attention should be immediately directed to Washington and New Berne. . . ."[18] Bragg had some encouragement that the ironclads would be finished in time.

The *Albemarle* was nearly ready. On the 16th Hoke visited Commander Cooke and received Cooke's assurance that the ship would cooperate. Less than twenty-four hours later the battle for Plymouth began; at 4:00 P.M. his grey-clad soldiers assaulted the Federal lines surrounding the town. Coincidentally, the *Albemarle* was commissioned and started down river at approximately the same time. She was not completed, however; mechanics were still working on her as she steamed slowly downstream. Cooke not only was sailing with an unfinished, untried ironclad, but his "salty crew" was made up from Hoke's brigade—"long, lank, Tar Heels . . . from the Piney woods," with no experience as seamen. But Cooke's courage was rewarded.

That night while the crew was repairing the ship's machinery, which as usual on a Confederate ironclad had broken down on the first venture, a small steamer arrived with a detachment of twenty veteran seamen and an officer from Charleston. When dawn broke on the 18th, the *Albemarle* once again steamed toward Plymouth. During the day the decks of the ironclad presented a picture of utter confusion: gun crews exercising their weapons and drilling together for the first time; workmen bolting the last iron plates to the shield and forward deck. A farmer observed this spectacle and later wrote, "I never conceived of anything more perfectly ridiculous than the appearance of the critter as she slowly passed by my landing."[19]

That afternoon the echo of cannon fire could be heard downstream. Hoke had attacked the small but strategically important town of Plymouth with 7,000 men, divided into three small brigades, plus several batteries of artillery. The town was heavily fortified. General Henry W. Wessells had nearly 3,000 infantry and artillery distributed in the various earthworks and forts, while on the river floated a small flotilla under Commander Charles W. Flusser, including the flagship *Miami* (eight guns), the converted ferryboat *Southfield* (six guns), and two small gunboats, the *Ceres* and *Whitehead*.

18. *Official Records,* Ser. I, LI, pt. 2, 857–858; XXXIII, 1278, 1273–1274.
19. Quoted in a letter from James Cooke to Scharf, n. d., Scharf Papers.

On the 18th the Confederate attack continued, but with only moderate success. Fort Wessells was stormed and captured by Hoke's troops, but infantry assaults upon the lines in the vicinity of Fort Williams were repulsed. Flusser's gunboats supported the ground forces effectively, firing directly over the Union ranks into the oncoming Confederates.

Although Hoke achieved some degree of surprise, his attack was not totally unexpected. On April 13, Wessells reported the concentration of a large Confederate force at Hamilton, "designing in conjunction with an iron clad boat, to make an attack on Plymouth *this week*" (author's italics).[20] This report, however, was ignored; "nothing can be done by the rebels while the weather continues as it has been for many days," General John Peck, Wessells' superior at New Bern, wrote. Earlier he said, "I feel entirely sanguine that the iron clad in the Roanoke will be destroyed if she attacks Plymouth." Wessells could have been reinforced, but Peck was convinced that New Bern was to be attacked; he had reliable information on the two-pronged attack originally planned.[21]

Nevertheless, Hoke probably could not have taken the town without the *Albemarle*. Many Confederates blamed the failure of the 18th on the absence of the vessel. A few days after the battle, one young officer wrote how "bitterly disappointed [we were] at our gunboat not making its appearance." On the evening of the 18th, Flusser wrote, "the ram will be down to-night or tomorrow. I fear for the protection of the town."

The *Albemarle* was in position. At 10:00 P.M. she had anchored approximately three miles above Plymouth, near Thoroughfare Gap, but Hoke was apparently unaware that the ironclad had arrived. Cooke does not mention in his report whether liaison was attempted; he was more concerned about the obstructions and batteries between the ship and the town. A lieutenant, after a reconnaissance of the river below, reported that torpedoes, sunken vessels, and obstructions made the river impassable at night. The fires were then banked, and the ironclad's crew tried to grab a few hours of needed sleep. Gilbert Elliott, the young builder and volunteer, made a second examination and discovered "to [my] great joy" that there were ten

20. *Official Records,* Ser. I, XXXIII, 281.
21. General Benjamin Butler, at that time in command of Federal troops in southern Virginia and North Carolina, with his usual perception about military affairs, ignored the warnings from various subordinates, and not only refused to send reinforcements, but withdrew some troops. He was equally knowledgeable about the *Albemarle*: "I don't believe in the iron clad," he wrote. William M. Smith, "The Siege and Capture of Plymouth," in *Personal Recollections of the War of the Rebellion. Addresses Delivered before the New York Commandery of the Loyal Legion of the United States,* I, 322–343; *Official Records,* Ser. I, XXXIII, 748.

feet of water over the obstructions—the result of unusually heavy spring rains. When Cooke was informed of this, he immediately ordered steam raised, and within a few minutes the ironclad started slowly down the dark stream. Shortly before 3:00 A.M. she passed Fort Gray, receiving a few desultory shots without firing back. After passing the obstructions safely, she proceeded toward Plymouth, but within minutes lookouts observed two steamers converging on her out of the darkness.

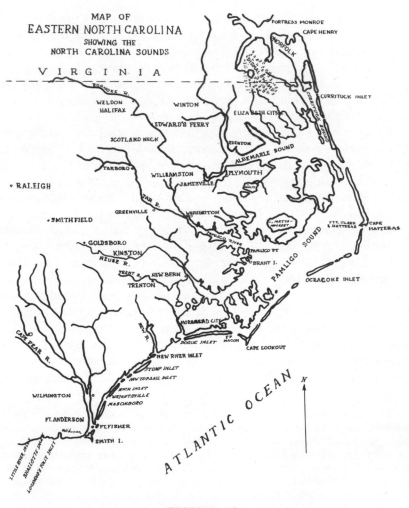

FIGURE 10

Shortly after 12:00 noon the steamer *Whitehead* had warned Flusser of the ram's approach.[22] The *Miami* then dropped down near the river's mouth where she joined the *Southfield* and prepared for battle. Flusser had planned to lash these two vessels (his most powerful) together by chains, and then force the ironclad between them where she could be battered into submission. This was done, but the ships were parted when the fighting occurred on the 17th. They were linked together again at the mouth, but because of the need of haste, hawsers rather than chains were used. (this may have saved the *Miami* later.) The two vessels then proceeded upstream.[23]

Cooke evidently spotted what he thought were chains, for he conned his vessel in close to the south shore of the river and then swung with throttles wide open toward the two Union gunboats. The *Albemarle* glanced off the port bow of the *Miami,* leaving superficial damage, and ploughed into the *Southfield,* tearing an immense hole "clear through to the boilers." The mortally wounded ship sank almost immediately, carrying with her many members of her crew. The *Albemarle* nearly followed her victim, for her ram was caught in the side of the sinking vessel. As the *Southfield* plunged to the bottom, the ship's bow was pulled under until water poured into the forward portholes. After what seemed like eternity to the *Albemarle's* apprehensive crew, her prow wrenched free.

Meanwhile the *Miami* was firing point blank at the ironclad. The gallant Flusser was killed when one of the shots rebounded from the slanted side of the *Albemarle's* shield and exploded on the gunboat's deck. Lieutentant Charles A. French, commanding officer of the sunken *Southfield,* assumed command of the *Miami* and withdrew downstream. The two smaller Union vessels had not engaged the ram and retired with the *Miami.* One seaman on the flagship wrote, "When Captain Flusser fell, the men seemed to lose heart, and we ran away from the ram into the Sound."[24] French rightly felt, however, that it was senseless to remain in the river, "being fully convinced that had we closed with this vessel it would have resulted in her loss."

With the departure of the Union vessels from the river, the ironclad turned her attention to Wessell's entrenched forces in and around Plymouth. Throughout the day and into the night, the *Albemarle's* two 8-inch Brooke rifles bombarded the enemy positions. At daybreak on the 20th one brigade assaulted Plymouth from the east while the other two demonstrated on the

22. Official reports of the naval battle at Plymouth, April 19–20, 1864, can be found in *Official Records, Navies,* Ser. I, IX, 634–658. This includes Cooke's report.
23. Frank W. Hackett, *Deck and Field,* 131–132; Roy Nichols, "Fighting in North Carolina Waters," *The North Carolina Historical Review,* XL (1963), 80–82.
24. Nichols, "Fighting in North Carolina Waters," 79–80.

western side of the town. As the Confederate soldiers charged, the ironclad steamed along on their flank and raked the Union lines. A Union officer recalled after the war, "A heavy force of Confederates was pressing on the front of the works; the rebel ram had possession of the river, thus enfilading the intrenchments upon the right and left, and exposing the rear of the devoted garrison to its merciless broadsides."[25] At 10:00 A.M. Wessels surrendered Plymouth. Thus ended one of the most successful combined operations conducted by Confederate forces during the war. Without question the decisive factor was the presence of the *Albemarle*. "But for the powerful assistance of the rebel ironclad ram . . . Plymouth would still have been in our hands," General Peck later testified.

Hoke's victory at Plymouth cleared the way for the attempt to retake the Sounds. The Confederate general planned to move on Washington first and then New Bern. On April 30, Washington was captured after a brief siege.[26]

In the meantime the *Neuse* was finally completed. Her commanding officer received orders to take her down river for the proposed attack on New Bern. The ship's crew made final preparations, confident that they would "take the city and sink the gunboats without much trouble . . . and have a fine time afterwards."[27] There was concern about the obstructions and the depth of the water in the river, which had been falling since early in March; despite heavy rains, the water was still low.

On April 27 the *Neuse* got under way. The ironclad, however, had steamed about a half mile from her anchorage when a crunching sound was heard. She had grounded on a sand bar. The crew tried frantically to get her afloat again, but without success. By nightfall the bow was four feet out of the water. One bitterly disappointed officer wrote, "We will have to wait for a freshet again and that will probably take place in July or August."

The news was telegraphed to Beauregard, who on April 23 had assumed command of the newly-created Department of North Carolina. Beauregard wanted to call off the offensive, but President Davis advised him to wait and see whether the vessel could not be freed. By the first of May it was obvious

25. Smith, "The Siege and Capture of Plymouth," 322–343; see also William A. Graham to father, April 24, 1864, William A. Graham Papers (Southern Historical Collection, University of North Carolina Library, Chapel Hill); *Official Records, Navies, Ser.* I, IX, 657–658.

26. The *Albemarle* was not present, although Hoke had apparently planned to use her. Beauregard to Bragg, April 25, 1864, quoted in Roman, *Beauregard*, II, 542.

27. Richard H. Bacot to Sis, March 19, 1864, Richard H. Bacot Papers (Department of Archives and History, Raleigh, North Carolina).

that she was "hard aground" and could not participate in the operation. Nonetheless, Beauregard decided to allow Hoke to continue preparations to attack. He became convinced (or someone convinced him) that the *Albemarle* could be used in place of the *Neuse:* "With its assistance I consider capture of New Berne easy," he telegraphed Bragg.[28]

Without question the presence of an ironclad would be an important factor in determining the fate of the town. With the *Neuse* it had been a matter of steaming down the river and passing the obstructions. However, for the *Albemarle* to participate in the attack, she would have to leave the Roanoke River, cross the Albemarle, Croatan, and Pamlico Sounds, and then steam up the obstructed Neuse River. The fact that nearly every Union gunboat in the Sounds was expecting the ironclad to come out at any moment made such an operation quite hazardous. Cooke must have been aware of this, but the ease with which he had sunk the *Southfield* and dispersed the remainder of Flusser's small force encouraged him. He was also aware that there were no monitors in the Sounds.

Cooke, "a quaint little North Carolinian," as a young middy had fought a duel over the "honor" of the Queen Dowager of Prussia. Because of the anachronistic promotion system in the prewar navy, Cooke (who entered in 1828) was still a lieutenant in 1861. In fact, he was frequently derided by his fellow officers as the "patriarch of the lieutenants."[29] In the Confederate Navy he gained recognition early as an able and aggressive officer.

At noon on May 5, the *Albemarle* steamed down the Roanoke, followed by the steamers *Bombshell* and *Cotton Plant*.[30] The *Bombshell,* sunk in the battle of Plymouth, had been raised and armed with three guns; the *Cotton Plant* had a detachment of sharpshooters on board. Three hours later the Confederate vessels were observed by picket boats stationed near the mouth

28. Roman, *Beauregard*, II, 544.

29. Daniel Ammen, *The Old Navy and the New*, 291; see also Albert Gleaves, *Life and Letters of Rear Admiral Stephen B. Luce*, 16; Scharf, *Confederate States Navy*, 408–409; Maffitt after the war said that Cooke should have been promoted to admiral. To George Davis, August 17, 1874, George Davis Papers (Duke University Library, Durham, North Carolina).

30. The writer has found no Confederate description of the May 5 engagement except for the statement of a deserter. See *Official Records, Navies*, Ser. I, IX, 968–969. The account is taken primarily from reports of the various Union commanders engaged. See *Ibid.*, 732–759. See also Samuel P. Boyer, *Naval Surgeon: Blockading the South* ed. by Elinor Barnes and James A. Barnes, 290–292; Edger Holden, "The *Albemarle* and the *Sassacus,*" *Battles and Leaders*, IV, 628–633; Henry Phelon to Josephine, May 3, 1864, Henry Phelon Papers (Southern Historical Collection, University of North Carolina Library, Chapel Hill).

of the river, and the alarm was given. Within minutes the Union squadron under Captain Melancton Smith stood up Albemarle Sound toward the approaching ram. The squadron consisted of four double-enders (designed especially for river fighting with a rudder at either end) and three small wooden steamers.

Smith's tactics called for the double-enders to close in line astern, and in this order they attacked, the *Mattabesett* leading.[31] At 500 yards the Union vessels opened fire. Cooke had already commenced bombarding the rapidly converging ships with his bow pivot—the first shot destroyed the *Mattabesett's* launch and wounded several men, while the second one cut away the rigging. The *Albemarle* then tried to ram the lead vessel, but the deep-draft ironclad was sluggish in answering her helm and missed her target. The *Mattabesett,* shadowed by the *Sassacus* and *Wyalusing,* rounded her bow, each firing a salvo at one hundred and fifty yards as they did so. The *Albemarle* then found herself surrounded by the four Union vessels, pouring broadside after broadside at her iron shield. They all proved futile, however, for as one officer on the *Sassacus* noted, "the guns might as well have fired blank cartridges, for the shot skimmed off into the air. . . ."[32]

The *Sassacus* then turned on the *Bombshell,* forcing the Confederate vessel to haul down her flag within a few minutes. This left only the ironclad to face Smith's gunboats, for the *Cotton Plant* had already returned up river. Lieutenant Commander Francis A. Roe, commanding the *Sassacus,* made for the *Albemarle,* determined to ram her as she lay broadside on about four hundred yards distant. As the *Sassacus* bore down on her adversary, Roe shouted: "All hands, lie down." Assistant Surgeon Holden recalled, "with a crash that shook the ship like an earthquake, we struck full and square on the iron hull, careening it over and tearing away our own bow." On the *Albemarle,* the shock knocked some men off their feet, but they recovered quickly and fired into the Union vessel. One shell exploded in the starboard boiler, filling the ship with steam and scalding a number of men. The vessels then drifted apart.

Although the fight continued for nearly two hours, until nightfall, no other Union vessels closed with the ironclad. The double-ended *Miami* had been fitted with a spar torpedo but was unable to maneuver into position to use it. She was punished for her efforts, however. One of the *Albemarle's* shots demolished the captain's cabin; miraculously, the paymaster, who was

31. The smaller vessels were to destroy the launches supposedly coming out. The launches never appeared, however.
32. Holden, "The Albemarle and the Sassacus," 628.

lying on the couch, was not injured. Other hits destroyed her small boats, holed her smokestacks, and penetrated the wheelhouse smashing the signal lanterns. Although the *Miami* suffered no casualties, the *Sassacus* was not so fortunate. She had fifteen men scalded, of whom four died later. A shell swept along the deck of the *Mattabesett* and decapitated three men. The *Albemarle* was seriously damaged, but only one man was killed. The stern gun's muzzle was knocked off, several iron plates were torn away from the wood backing, her steering mechanism was crippled, and her stack was so damaged that bacon, lard, and butter had to be thrown into the boiler fires to enable her to limp back to Plymouth.

The May 5 engagement was tactically a draw, but strategically it was a Confederate defeat, for the *Albemarle* was unable to help Hoke in the New Bern attack.

Twenty-four hours after the guns fell silent in Albemarle Sound, Union naval forces in North Carolina waters were again under assault by a Confederate ironclad. Early in the evening of May 6, the CSS *Raleigh,* Pembroke Jones commanding, crossed the bar at New Inlet and attacked the blockading squadron off Cape Fear.[33]

The *Raleigh* and her sister ship the *North Carolina* were built at Wilmington, the largest town and principal port in North Carolina before the war. By the beginning of 1863, Wilmington had become the most important center for blockade-running in the Confederacy, primarily because the Union navy found it most difficult to close. There were two navigable entrances to the Cape Fear River, which connected the port with the Atlantic. New Inlet and Old Inlet were separated by Smith's Island, about ten miles long and located directly in front of the river mouth. Jutting out into the Atlantic about twenty-five miles from the southeast corner of the island were Frying Pan Shoals. One authority estimated that as many as four hundred steamers slipped in and out of Wilmington during the war. The city became a beehive of maritime activity—docks, wharfs, yards, warehouses, and foundries were taxed to their limits. With these facilities available, it is somewhat puzzling that the two ironclads built at Wilmington have been described as the most decrepit of those constructed within the Confederacy.

33. For the engagement see the Wilmington *Journal,* May 7, August 18, 1864; Wilmington *Weekly Journal,* May 12, 1864; James G. Albright Diary, Soldiers Collection (Southern Historical Collection, University of North Carolina Library, Chapel Hill); Charleston *Daily Courier,* May 11, 1864; Henry M. Doak Memoirs (Tennessee State Archives, Nashville); James Sprunt, *Chronicles of the Cape Fear River 1660–1916,* 481–482; *Official Records, Navies,* Ser. I, X, 18–23. No official Confederate reports have been located by the writer.

Both vessels were commissioned in the spring of 1864. The *North Carolina* was completed first, but because of serious imperfections—primarily her unreliable machinery taken from an old tugboat—she was used mainly as a floating battery. She was anchored most of the time off Smithville, a small village three miles up the Cape Fear from Old Inlet, and protected the anchorage of inbound and outbound blockade runners. The *North Carolina* had a most inglorious ending, sinking at her moorings as a result of a worm-eaten bottom.

During the afternoon of May 6, the *Raleigh* and two small wooden steamers, *Yadkin* and *Equator,* anchored just inside of New Inlet waiting for high tide. They were observed by the Union gunboat *Mount Vernon,* but either the senior officer present, Captain Benjamin F. Sands, was not notified or he did not see cause for alarm. At any rate, the two blockaders, *Britannia* and *Nansemond,* both converted merchantmen, were stationed off the bar, while five additional vessels were at various points nearby. Shortly after 8:00 P.M. the Confederate force slipped across the bar—the *Raleigh* in the lead to drive off the nearest blockaders. The *Britannia* detected the ram coming in her direction, fired off alarm rockets, opened on the approaching ship with her thirty-pounder Parrott and, when this failed to stop the ram, fled seaward. Lieutenant Samuel Huse, her commanding officer, probably was not sure whether the vessel was an ironclad, blockade-runner, or even another blockader at first; identification at night is difficult under the best conditions. The *Raleigh* gave chase, but in the dark the *Britannia* disappeared. What happened for the next two and a half hours is uncertain. Evidently, the ironclad, steaming around blindly in the night, failed to sight a Union vessel until 11:45 when she exchanged shots with the *Nansemond.* But within moments this vessel also disappeared into the darkness.

Daybreak found the Confederate ironclad several miles off the bar with the *Yadkin* and *Equator* inshore of her. The blockading squadron was scattered, with only four ships visible. The *Raleigh* closed with the nearest, the screw steamer *Howquah,* armed with five light guns, and put a shot through her stack before she could steam clear. The *Nansemond* then came within range and let go with her twenty-four pounder, followed by the gunboat *Kansas* with a battery of eight guns including two 9-inch Dahlgren smoothbores and a 150-pounder Parrott rifle, and the *Mount Vernon* with a 100-pounder Parrott rifle plus two 9-inch Dahlgrens and two lighter guns. The firing was inaccurate, and no vessel was hit. At approximately 7:00 A.M. the *Raleigh* disengaged and followed her consorts back over the bar. No attempt was made to pursue her. A newspaper reporter later wrote that she retired because her steering chains became entangled with her propeller.

This may have been true, but her commanding officer probably would not have remained in open water until the next tide anyway.

The ironclad passed safely over the bar, but while steaming back to Smithville, she grounded. All efforts to refloat her failed, and she later broke her back. A court of inquiry held a few months afterwards blamed her destruction on faulty construction. Lynch's poetic secretary, writing in the summer of 1864, said that she "had the appearance of a monstrous turtle, stranded and forlorn. . . ."[34]

What was the objective in the *Raleigh's* attack? Lieutenant William H. Parker, CSN, wrote in an essay on the Confederate States Navy that, "What [she] . . . went out for has never been ascertained."[35] This is true as far as official records are concerned. At the same time one wonders whether it was mere coincidence that the engagement took place at exactly the time the New Bern operation was in progress. Perhaps the attack was to create a diversion. If so, it was futile. On May 5, the day the *Albemarle* clashed with the Union naval force in Albemarle Sound, Hoke received orders to call off his attack immediately and entrain his troops for Virginia: Grant's offensive had finally begun. On that day the Army of the Potomac was fighting Lee's troops in the wooded area known as the Wilderness.

34. Randall to Kate, June 3, 1864, Randall Papers. See also W. Calder to mother, June 7, 1864, William Calder Papers (Southern Historical Collection, University of North Carolina Library, Chapel Hill); Sprunt, *Chronicles*, 481–482; Wilmington *Journal*, August 18, 1864; *Official Records, Navies*, Ser. I, X, 24.

35. C. A. Evans (ed.), *Confederate Military History*, XII, 85.

11

The James River

UNION GRAND strategy as decided upon in the spring of 1864 included a vast turning movement by Sherman through the heartland of the South and a campaign for the destruction of Lee's army in Virginia. Ulysses S. Grant, who was appointed supreme commander of all Federal armies in March 1864, would conduct the campaign against Lee with General George C. Meade's Army of the Potomac as the principal weapon. At the same time there were to be subsidiary operations in Virginia. Benjamin Butler, in command of the Army of the James at Fortress Monroe, was to move up the south side of the James River, threatening Petersburg and Richmond. By cutting the Petersburg and Richmond Railroad he could seriously hurt Lee's logistic support. This combined operation would call for the co-operation of a Union naval force powerful enough to stop any threat by Confederate naval units in the James.[1]

The Union Navy had maintained control of the rivers flowing into Chesapeake Bay since McClellan's Peninsula campaign early in 1862. Although this control was generally nominal until 1864, Confederate forces had made no serious effort to challenge it. Admittedly, the Confederate navy was weak, consisting of only a few wooden gunboats until the ironclad *Richmond* was finished, but gradually a "fleet in being" was built in shipyards in the capital. By the spring of 1864, three ironclads formed the nucleus of the James River Squadron.

Shortly before Norfolk was evacuated in the spring of 1862, the wooden hull of an unfinished ironclad was towed to Richmond.[2] Six months later the

---

1. For naval operations on the James River see John D. Hayes, "Sea Power in the Civil War," *United States Naval Institute Proceedings*, LXXVII (1961), 60–69; Julius W. Pratt, "Naval Operations on the Virginia Rivers in the Civil War," *United States Naval Institute Proceedings*, LXXI (1919), 185–195; James R. Soley, "Closing operations in the James River," *Battles and Leaders*, IV, 705–707.

2. She was launched on May 6, 1862, and towed to Richmond the following day by the gunboats *Patrick Henry* and *Jamestown*. Mallory had requested tugboats from the army (apparently the navy did not have any), but none was available. Mallory to

vessel was completed and commissioned as the CSS *Richmond*. Until 1864 the *Richmond* operated with the wooden gunboats between the capital and the obstruction at Drewry's Bluff, six miles below the city.

Drewry's Bluff had been the scene of a sharp engagement between Confederate military forces and a Union naval squadron under Commander John Rodgers in May 1862. The Union assault was hurled back; Confederate engineers then proceeded to strengthen the barrier and supporting works, effectively blocking the river door to Richmond.

Although Lee and others recognized the strategic importance of re-taking the Peninsula and closing what was probably the most vulnerable approach to the Confederate capital, the naval co-operation essential to such an operation was not available. Mallory wanted to help, but his vessels were blocked by the obstruction at Drewry's Bluff until 1864; as early as July 1862 the naval secretary had recommended to the War Department that a channel be cut through the barrier, but nothing was done. In September, Lee told General Gustavus W. Smith, in command of Confederate forces in the Richmond area, that he believed the Maryland invasion would divert Federal troops and suggested that he take advantage of the situation to retake Suffolk and Norfolk, using the ironclad *Richmond* to clear the lower James of Union gunboats. The movement, however, was not carried out; on September 17 and 18, Lee was checked at Antietam, the *Richmond* was not operational, and Davis refused to permit a passage to be cut through the obstructions until the ironclad was completed and "tested."[3]

In the spring of 1863, General James Longstreet proposed an advance along the south side of the James in the direction of Suffolk and Norfolk. His immediate objective would be to secure control of the area east of the Black-water River in order to obtain provisions and quartermaster stores. He also suggested that Suffolk could probably be retaken, "if the navy department can co-operate with us."[4] To Lee he pointed out that naval support was essential in order to protect his left flank, which would be resting upon the James. In a later note he added, "I do not expect aid from the Navy unless you can get it for me." Longstreet's skepticism that he would receive naval co-operation was well founded, but it was not the navy that turned him down.

Randolph, April 29, 1862, War Department Papers, National Archives Record Group 109. John Taylor Wood to his wife, May 7, 1862, Wood Papers.

3. *Official Records,* Ser. I, XIX, 599. Army engineers strongly opposed opening a passage then and later. *Ibid.,* LI, pt. 2, 616–617; Randolph to Rives, September 18, 1862, War Department Papers, National Archives Record Group 109.

4. *Official Records,* Ser. I, XVIII, 910, 944, 950, 959; James Longstreet, *From Manassas to Appomattox,* 324.

Mallory was ready to order the *Richmond* and at least one wooden gunboat to assist him, but once again efforts to cut a passage through the barrier were successfully blocked by engineers and by congressmen, the latter frightened by the possibility of endangering the capital from Union gunboats that might slip through an opening.[5]

Longstreet refused to give up. On April 17 he again appealed to the Secretary of War

to take [Suffolk] by assault would cost us 3,000 . . . there is but one other means —that of turning it. This cannot be done by the river in consequence of the gunboats in the river. On the right it could be done by taking Norfolk, but we cannot hold Norfolk twenty-four hours without the aid of the Navy. . . . I do not think that we should have much trouble getting both places with the aid of the *Richmond*.[6]

This appeal, too, was fruitless. A few days later, Davis approved a recommendation from Colonel Jeremy F. Gilmer, chief of the bureau of engineers, to the effect that the passage through the obstructions be delayed until a second ironclad was completed.

More than a year passed before another ironclad, the *Virginia II,* one of the "ladies gunboats," was ready for commissioning. In June 1863, a large crowd had witnessed her launching, but the vessel remained moored to a wharf at Rocketts for months before she could be tested. The story was the same as elsewhere in the Confederacy—no iron for armor. On May 31, a few days before the *Virginia II* was launched, the president of Tredegar informed Mallory that the company was immediately having to "suspend the operation of making gun boat iron for want of material."[7] It was March 1864 before her guns were mounted and her complement of officers and men reported on board. That same month, a third ironclad, the *Fredericksburg,* was commissioned and would be ready to join the squadron in six weeks.

While these vessels were approaching completion, Mallory once again began urging the War Department to open a passage through the obstructions. This time approval was given, and the engineers agreed to have it ready at least two weeks before the squadron prepared to go down the James.[8]

5. *Official Records, Navies,* Ser. I, XVIII, 866; *Official Records,* Ser. I, 967–968; Robert C. Kean, *Inside the Confederate Government.* ed. Edward Younger, 49–50.

6. *Official Records,* Ser. I, XVIII, 996–997.

7. Anderson to Mallory, 1863–1864 letterbook, Tredegar Rolling Mill and Foundry Collection.

8. *Official Records, Navies,* Ser. I, IX, 809; Williams to Mason, March 1, 1864, Charles T. Mason Papers (Virginia Historical Society, Richmond); Stevens to Mason,

On May 5, the *Fredericksburg, Richmond,* and several wooden vessels were anchored above Drewery's Bluff, while the *Virginia II* was in the yard being fitted out. Engineers were still at work removing rubble and pile from the river bed to clear a passageway. At two o'clock in the afternoon, Major Frank Smith, commanding the detachment of marines at the Bluff, boarded the temporary flagship, the training vessel *Patrick Henry,* with the news that a large number of gunboats had been sighted ascending the river. While he was conversing with Commander William A. Parker, senior officer afloat of the vessels above the Bluff, a messenger arrived with a signal dispatch that troops were landing at Bermuda Hundred and City Point, twelve miles below Bermuda Hundred.

These troops were the vanguard of General Butler's Army of the James, completing the first step in Grant's spring offensive. The transports carrying Butler's 22,000 men were convoyed by units of the North Atlantic Blockading Squadron, commanded by Acting Rear Admiral S. P. Lee. Four monitors and the captured ironclad *Atlanta,* each towed by two gunboats or tugs, were preceded by seven wooden steamers dragging the river for torpedoes. By 1863 Union commanders had lost much of their fear of the Confederate ironclads; it was commonly believed that they were built for the purpose of defending Richmond and would not venture below Drewry's Bluff. Nonetheless, Admiral Lee was taking no chances; the wooden mine-sweepers were ordered to drop below the monitors in case the ironclads appeared.[9]

During the next few days, as Butler moved timidly toward Petersburg, Lee's vessels moved from City Point through the bends and shallows of the James, probing for torpedoes while protecting the army's right flank. Although no Confederate ironclad challenged the Union vessels, torpedoes sank the *Commodore Jones* and shore batteries destroyed the *Shawsheen.* By May 13, Lee had arrived at Trent's Reach; here his snail-like advance came to a halt, despite the fact that his vessels were needed to co-operate in an attack against the strong Confederate defenses at the Bluff. The admiral

---

March 27, 1864, Mason Papers. Captain Charles T. Mason was the engineer in charge of preparing the passage.

9. General Order, May 5, 1864, Area 7, File, National Archives Record Group 45; See also Lee to Fox, April 4, 1864, *Fox Correspondence,* II, 280; James I. Heslin (ed.), "Two New Yorkers in the Union Navy: Narrative Based on Letters of the Collins Brothers," *New York Historical Society Quarterly,* XLIII (1959), 191. For the anxiety caused by the Confederate "fleet in being" earlier in the war on the James River see William W. Jefferies, "The Civil War Career of Charles Wilkes," *Journal of Southern History,* XI (1945), 324–348; and Thomas O. Selfridge, Jr., *Memoirs of Thomas O. Selfridge, Jr.: Rear Admiral, U.S.N.,* 68.

informed Butler that the shoal waters, draft of the monitors, torpedoes, and "occupation by the enemy of the high left bank," made it impractical, if not impossible, to go any farther.[10] Three days later in the fog of early morning, Confederate troops commanded by Beauregard poured out of the entrenchments at Drewry's Bluff, and by nightfall Union troops were retiring to a fortified line that stretched from Bermuda Hundred to Trent's Reach. Butler, who probably had the strength to drive to the outskirts of Richmond, was neatly penned up by Beauregard's attack, and there he remained.

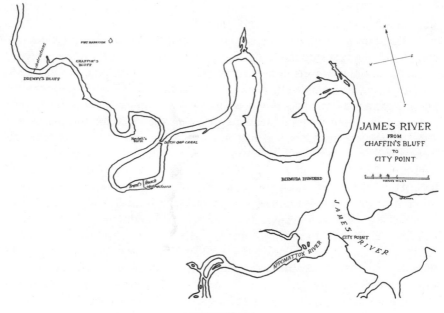

FIGURE 11

It was a period of crisis. The Confederate capital seemed threatened from three sides: General Lee's ragged veterans were fighting in the Wilderness, Spotsylvania, and the "Bloody Angle"; J. E. B. Stuart was making his last gallant try to block Sheridan's cavalry raid on the outskirts of the city; and Beauregard was successfully checking Butler's thrust from the East.

During this period the James River Squadron remained inactive, anchored above the obstructions. Commander John K. Mitchell, who assumed command of the squadron the first week in May, later said that he had

10. *Official Records, Navies,* Ser. I, X, 51–52.

not been informed of Beauregard's plan to attack but decided on his own initiative to place "one or more of the ironclads below the obstructions the moment the passage was found practicable."[11] Every effort was made to complete the channel—even marines from Drewry's Bluff were ordered to aid the engineers—and by May 16 it was apparently ready. Mitchell had planned to pass through the obstructions at high tide that day, but several hours before—in the early afternoon—soundings were made by several naval officers who reported that the passage was not deep enough for the ironclads to steam through safely. The *Virginia's* draft was nearly fourteen feet, and the water's depth was only a few inches more.

Mallory's patience was rapidly coming to an end. For months he had requested repeatedly that a passage be cut and had been promised it would be ready in time. On May 19, he wrote sharply to Secretary of War James Seddon,

Without special reference to my correspondence on the subject, you are aware of the earnest desire I have evinced to have a passage made through the obstructions, to permit our iron-clads . . . to go below them, a measure deemed by me important to the defenses of Richmond. . . . Up to this hour I am not advised that a practicable passage for the iron clads has been completed. . . . Had a practicable passage even for the *Fredericksburg,* the lighter iron clad, been made in time, she could have arrested the operations of the enemy [wooden gun] boats and checked his advance. He would have been compelled to explore the river in his iron clads, against which our torpedoes were designed to act. . . . I regard the failure [to complete the channel] as prejudicial to the interests of the country, and especially to the naval service, which has thus far been prevented from rendering important service.[12]

The naval secretary's disappointment was apparent to those working around him. John B. Jones, the War Department's clerk recalled, "Mr. Mallory's usual [sic] red face turned purple. He has not yet got out the iron-clad *Richmond,* etc., which might have sunk General Butler's transports."[13]

Five days after Mallory's protest, engineers using gunpowder blasted the channel deep enough for the squadron to steam through easily. During this period, however, the naval secretary's enthusiasm for a movement below the obstructions had cooled considerably. When Mitchell proposed a secret

11. *Ibid.,* 639.

12. *Official Records,* Ser. I, LI, 946–947. See also Seddon to Mallory, May 20, 1864, Secretary of War letterbook, National Archives Record Group 109; H. Hamilton to father, May 19, 1864, H. Hamilton Papers (Southern Historical Collection, University of North Carolina Library, Chapel Hill); Mason to Stevens, May 17, 18, 1864, Mason Papers.

13. Jones, *Diary,* II, 2–5.

night attack on the Union vessels in Trent's Reach, he urged caution: "In view of the importance of the fleet you command to the defenses of Richmond and of the superior force of the enemy, it would seem proper so to conduct your operation as to reserve the option of fighting."[14]

Mallory's about-face may be attributed to several factors. In the first place he had originally planned to use the ironclads to attack the minesweepers, not the more formidable monitors. But by the 24th, the wooden steamers had retired below the monitors in Trent's Reach, and Mallory had no illusions about challenging the monitors with his three ironclads. In the second place, President Davis still feared the possible consequence of a naval defeat and the loss of the squadron. Forgetting, or ignoring, the fact that it was his decision to delay the channel until all of the ironclads were completed, Davis wrote on May 20, "There has been great delay in opening the obstructions at Drewry's Bluff . . . for our gun boats to go out. There have been opportunities when they might have been used with great effect. Whether they could be at this junction or not is doubtful." Third, a number of officers in the fleet were unhappy about the contemplated operation. Lieutenant Robert Minor, who had become flag lieutenant in the squadron, gloomily wrote his wife, "There is an insane desire among the public to get the ironclads down the river and [I] am afraid that some of our higher public authorities are yielding to the pressure. . . . but *I for one am not* and in the Squadron we know too much of the interest at stake to act against our judgment. . . ."[15]

Nevertheless, on May 24, the three ironclads passed safely through the obstructions and anchored at Chaffin's Bluff. Mitchell and Beauregard held a meeting to consider a joint attack; the general strongly suggested delaying the operation until he could move several batteries of heavy artillery into position to aid the naval vessels. The flag officer drafted a revised plan of attack calling for fire ships and wooden gunboats armed with torpedoes to attack in a night engagement, followed by the ironclads when there was "sufficient light for the pilots to see the way." When he asked his officers for suggestions they recommended that the ironclads lead the attack followed by the wooden gunboats. Fireships, they said, should not be used because of the unpredictable current and wind. Further delays occurred while torpedoes were fitted on all of the vessels, when the *Fredericksburg* had engine trouble, and when the batteries that Beauregard promised were not forthcoming.

14. *Official Records, Navies,* Ser. I, X, 651–52.
15. May 15, 1864, Minor Papers. See also Parker, *Recollections of a Naval Officer,* 331.

Mitchell also expected the monitors to change position or drop below in the river, but daily reconnaissance reports indicated that three of them remained anchored abreast at the upper entrance to Trent's Reach. Finally, on June 8, he submitted the entire question of offensive action to a council-of-war composed of the various commanding officers. They concluded that the attack was inadvisable "under existing circumstances"—meaning the strength and disposition of opposing force, low water, and narrow channel.[16]

Minor, in a later letter to his wife, clearly placed the blame on Beauregard for discouraging the attack by agreeing at first to co-operate and later withdrawing his offer of co-operation. A conference between the general and Mitchell was held on May 27 resulting in Beauregard's offer being withdrawn. After the meeting was over and the officers informed of this decision, Minor wrote, "without land co-operation . . . our battle would be but a grand spectacle, with heavy injury to both sides, and but an inadequate result to our cause. So [it] will not, in all common sense, be made. . . ."[17]

Beauregard's decision to drop the idea of a combined attack may have been dictated by his increasing concern over Grant's next move. In fact, he correctly divined what the Union commander-in-chief was going to do. On June 9 he wrote to Bragg that Grant would shift his forces around Lee's left flank to the James River. "He may," Beauregard suggested, "continue his rotary motion around Richmond and attack by concentrating the whole of his army on the South side of the James River, using the fortified position at Bermuda Hundred Neck as a base for operations."[18]

Beauregard's actions, in light of his perception of the enemy's strategy, are puzzling. He certainly realized the importance of gaining "command of the navigation of the James"; on June 9 he pointed out to Bragg that an ironclad could "prevent the crossing of the river between [Howlett's] . . . battery and Chaffin's Bluff."[19] On the 13th he wrote to Mitchell promising him that a battery of heavy guns would be located at Howlett's immediately, but "as I have already informed you, I am unable to furnish a permanent support to the land battery. . . ." A few days later the battery was in position, but by then it was too late. Beauregard had little confidence in the navy, including the ironclads; his criticism of these vessels were well known. Reports of the

16. *Official Records, Navies,* Ser. I, X, 691–692; Minor to wife, June 5, 1864, Minor Papers.

17. May 30, 1864, Minor Papers.

18. *Official Records,* Ser. I, XXXVI, pt. 3, 886; see also Williams, *Beauregard,* 78.

19. Beauregard to Mitchell, June 13, 1864, Mitchell Papers; *Official Records,* Ser. I, XXXVI, pt. 3, 886.

"Councils-of-War" held by the naval officers and passed on to him by Mitchell did nothing to change his opinion. In any case, Grant would be safely across the James before the ironclads moved.

Between June 12 and 14, Grant shifted his army with incredible secrecy and rapidity from north of Richmond to south of the James. On the 17th he reported to General Halleck,

Our forces drew out from within fifty yards of the enemy's entrenchments at Cold Harbor, made a flank movement of an average of about 50 miles march, crossing the Chickahominy and James Rivers, the latter 2,000 feet wide and 84 feet deep at point of crossing, and surprised the enemy's rear at Petersburg. This was done without the loss of a wagon or piece of artillery and with the loss of only about 150 stragglers.

By taking Petersburg, an important transportation center, Grant hoped to force Lee to come out of Richmond and attack his entrenched forces. The Petersburg campaign ultimately resulted in the fall of Richmond and the end of the war.

Union commanders had been worried that Confederate ironclads might attack while the Army of the Potomac was involved in crossing the river. On June 3, Admiral Lee mentioned in his correspondence with Butler the "necessity . . . of holding this river beyond a peradventure for the great military purposes of General Grant and yourself." Butler's chief-of-staff warned one of his corps commanders on June 13, "we have just received word that the enemy's gun boats have made their appearance. . . . General Butler thinks that we may be attacked tonight or in the morning." Grant was also concerned about these vessels. He later wrote in his *Memoirs,* "It was known that the enemy had some gun boats at Richmond. These might run down at night and inflict great damage upon us before they could be sunk or captured by our navy." Toward the end of May, Butler had consulted with Lee about obstructing the James above Trent's Reach. The admiral was reluctant to do so; "The Navy is not accustomed to putting down obstructions before it, and the act might be construed as implying an admission of superiority of resources on the part of the enemy."[20] Although Lee delayed, Grant did not. He ordered Butler to sink stone-laden vessels to block the stream. Butler, however, was slow to obey the order, and the vessels were not sunk until the army was halfway across the river.

Now that there was little chance of a clash between the ironclads and monitors, Mitchell took his squadron downstream, "to enable the forces under my command to move at any moment that they may be required to act

20. *Official Records, Navies,* Ser. I, X, 129.

against the enemy in Trent's Reach." On June 19, the Confederate vessels came to anchor above Trent's Reach, approximately 3,000 yards from the monitors. A steep bluff on the right bank of the river prevented the Confederates from seeing the Union vessels, but the Union sailors could watch their enemy from a tower or "crow's nest" in the upper branches of a tall pine tree.[21] The *Richmond*'s commanding officer later recounted that he was reclining in a chair on the hurricane deck reading a book when a shell exploded near the bow and wounded several men. "While we were wondering at this, another shell came and exploded just after it had passed."[22] The Confederate vessels, unable to elevate their guns to return the fire, retired out of range.

Two days later the squadron again dropped down river to a point near the obstructions. Mitchell had agreed to co-operate with a land battery at Howlett's in bombarding the Union vessels. Exactly what they hoped to accomplish is not clear; the ironclads obviously could not get within effective range of the monitors, and there was no general assault planned for that day.[23] Fog hugging the water delayed the bombardment until shortly after noon when a brisk fire was opened on the nearest monitors. The two fleets fired at each other throughout the afternoon, but no vessel was hit. A bend in the river prevented direct observation, and the gunners fired blind, on information provided by signalmen. Lieutenant Parker wrote later that "the whole affair . . . was a fiasco."[24]

During the remainder of the summer and fall, Lee and Grant continued to face each other along the Richmond-Petersburg front. Butler's troops, bottled up in Bermuda Hundred, "engaged in using spades and shovels— little skirmishes, repelling false attacks at night, all of which were magnified into desperate combats by the hoards of newspaper correspondents which infested his camp and were his guests."[25] In early August, Butler decided to construct a canal at Dutch Gap, where the meandering river, shaped like a horseshoe, formed a neck of land one hundred and seventy-four yards wide.

21. James S. Barnes, "My Egotistography" (MS. in New York Historical Society, New York City); *Official Records, Navies,* Ser. I, X, 704–05.

22. Parker, *Recollections of a Naval Officer,* 336–337.

23. General Lee, who had reached Petersburg on the nineteenth, was concerned about a Union movement toward Weldon and the Richmond & Danville Railroad. The only attack ordered for the 21st was to repulse this movement. Douglas S. Freeman, *Lee's Lieutenants,* III, 450–453; *Official Records,* Ser. I, XL, pt. 2, 678.

24. Parker, *Recollections of a Naval Officer,* 337–338. For Mitchell's report see *Official Records, Navies,* Ser. I, X, 186–188. See also *Ibid.,* 176; and the *Beaumont* diary, National Archives Record Group 45.

25. Barnes, "My Egotistography."

A canal would permit the Union gunboats to get above and behind not only the obstructions at Trent's Reach, but also the Confederate batteries at Howlett's on the outer curve of the horseshoe. The Union vessels would then be in position to attack Chaffin's and Drewry's Bluffs, as well as to aid any movement Butler's troops made. Digging started on what one newspaper reporter called "Butler's gut," on August 9. Lee, somewhat perplexed by the digging, ordered an immediate bombardment. "What use they will make of it I do not see," he wrote. "Perhaps it is thought the James River can be so reduced as to prevent the navigation of our naval boats."

On August 13, the three ironclads, along with the gunboats *Hampton*, *Nansemond*, and *Drewry*, shelled the enemy working parties. Union land batteries and gunboats replied. Firing began at 6:00 A.M. and continued until sunset, with light damages and casualties on both sides. The *Fredericksburg* was struck several times; one shot went through her stack. Two Union wooden gunboats were slightly damaged by land batteries, and Butler's digging parties suffered thirty killed and wounded. Mitchell correctly assessed the attack as "unsuccessful" in his report to Mallory.[26]

In the following days heavy skirmishing took place along the north side of the James. Grant was putting pressure on Lee's forces in order to prevent Confederate troops in the Richmond area from being sent to the Shenandoah Valley.[27] On August 16, a small Union force of 1,200 men advanced from Dutch Gap and Deep Bottom in the direction of Chaffin's Bluff and the New Market Road. By nightfall they had nearly reached the road and had occupied Signal Hill approximately two and one half miles from the Bluff. The following morning Confederates counterattacked, retaking everything lost the previous day but Signal Hill. At 10:30 A.M., Commander Thomas R. Rootes, temporarily in command of the James River Squadron in the absence of Mitchell, was requested to bombard the hill. At 3:00 the three iron clads opened fire and continued shelling the enemy positions throughout the night.

One officer on the *Fredericksburg* wrote that when the ironclads arrived

26. For Confederate accounts of the action see *Official Records, Navies,* Ser. I, X, 352–358; *Official Records,* Ser. I, XLII, pt. 2, 1173; Rootes to Minor, August 16, 1864, Minor Papers; Richmond *Daily Dispatch,* August 15, 1864. For Union accounts see *Official Records, Navies,* Ser. I, X, 348–351; *Official Records,* Ser. I, XLII, pt. 2, 145–147, 650, 158; *Beaumont* diary, National Archives Record Group 45.

27. In order to relieve the pressure on Richmond, Lee sent Lieutenant General Jubal A. Early to the Shenandoah Valley to threaten Washington. Early had some initial success, but Grant sent a cavalry force numerically much superior to Early's under General Phillip Sheridan. By the end of September, Early had been badly defeated and was no longer a threat to Washington.

and anchored in position, the men were given dinner, a signal gun was then fired, and

at it we went. Not more than ten minutes had elapsed before whiz, bang, bang, came the 100 pdr, Parrott shells over us, and so accurately did they fire that the water was splashed against our starboard side, and as the huge missiles would plunge into the river within a few yards of us, great jets of water would be thrown up, and this with the screaming noise of the shells made the scene rather a novel one. . . . *our fire was elegant*—the shells exploded right in among them, and when the beggers [sic] tried to get out of the way of [the *Virginia's*] fire, they fell into the range of our guns and the *Richmond*'s.[28]

The bombardment went on throughout the night, and when Confederate troops advanced the following morning they found the hill evacuated. After more than eighteen hours of steady firing, the ironclads retired upstream to Chaffin's Bluff. Rootes reported that the squadron was "exhausted from the heat . . . everything being closed down to prevent the enemy's shot from passing below."[29]

On September 28, the Army of the James attacked Confederate forces on the north side of the James. Butler had orders to drive all the way to Richmond if possible, but Grant more realistically hoped that the attack would force Lee to weaken his defenses at Petersburg. The advance was initially successful; Union troops under General E. O. C. Ord took Signal Hill and Fort Harrison and threatened Chaffin's Bluff—all key positions in the outer defense line of the Confederate capital. The capture of Chaffin's Bluff could collapse the defense line and open a path to Richmond. Lee reacted by telegraphing for reinforcements from the south side of the river (as Grant had hoped he would do), and ordering an immediate counterattack.

The *Virginia* and her two consorts were "protecting" a bridge across the James above Chaffin's Bluff when a courier arrived from Lee requesting aid. The squadron, still under the temporary command of "Old Tom" Rootes, steamed down below the bluff and opened fire on Fort Harrison with shell and shrapnel. A signal officer on shore directed the bombardment: "He informed me," Rootes reported, "that the enemy were in line of battle in larger numbers to the right of the fort and some distance beyond and that our shells were falling short." Rootes ordered heavier charges: "he [then] . . . made signal that the enemy had broken and were retreating across the field to the

28. Minor to wife, August 19, 1864, Minor Papers.
29. Rootes to Mallory, August 19, 1864, copy in the Robert E. Lee Papers (Virginia Historical Society, Richmond).

woods. . . ."[30] Confederate defenses at Chaffin's Bluff held, but every attempt to recover Fort Harrison was repulsed with heavy loss.

Throughout the cool months of October and November an uneasy stalemate prevailed along the Chaffin's Bluff front, punctuated by picket clashes and artillery bombardments. The Confederate squadron continued to drop below the bluff and pound Union lines with harrassing fire, despite Mitchell's increasing concern for the safety of his vessels. They were constantly under fire from masked batteries, and the flag officer expected daily to be attacked by torpedo boats or mines laid in his rear by parties operating from the south bank of the river. On October 22 the ironclads were surprised by a nearby battery and the *Fredericksburg* was slightly damaged. After that the vessels only went down at night, moving upstream again before daybreak. When Mitchell wrote to Lee about withdrawing his squadron farther up the river, the general strongly urged him not to: "I can foresee no state of circumstances in which the fleet can render more important aid than . . . at present by guarding the river below Chaffin's Bluff."[31]

Lee feared a new attack along the north side of the river, and the uninterrupted digging going on twenty-four hours a day at Dutch Gap did nothing to relieve his anxiety. Early in November, when the weather began to turn cold and rainy, the Confederate Navy added to the misery of the diggers by bombarding the canal at brief intervals. On November 3, Jones in Richmond recorded in his diary, "During this damp weather the deep and sullen sounds of cannon can be heard at all hours, day and night. The firing is mostly from our ironclads." A few days later he wrote, "All quiet below, save the booming of bombs every night from our iron clads, thrown at the workmen in the canal." The officer in charge of the naval ordnance works at Charlotte, North Carolina, wrote, "We are working day and night trying to keep the gunboats on the James supplied with projectiles. They are now firing nearly constantly. . . ."[32] Despite Confederate efforts to prevent it, the canal was eventually completed, although it was never used.

30. To Mitchell, October 4, 1864, in Lee Papers; see also Brooke to Jones, October 3, 1864, Area File, Confederate Subject and Area File, National Archives Record Group 45; Lee to Mitchell, September 29, 1864, in Douglas S. Freeman (ed.), *A Calendar of Confederate Papers,* 327.

31. *Official Records,* Ser. I, XLII, pt. 3, 1174–1176; Douglas S. Freeman, *R. E. Lee: A Biography,* III, 512; Jones, *Diary,* II, 317; *Official Records, Navies,* Ser. I, X, 750–751.

32. Ramsay to Jones, October 18, 1864, Area File, Confederate Subject and Area File, National Archives Record Group 45. See also McLaurin to uncle, November 29, 1864, Duncan McLaurin Papers (Duke University Library, Durham, North Carolina).

The Union Navy had little part in the operations above Trent's Reach during the fall of 1864; in fact, the monitors were gradually withdrawn until only the *Onondaga* remained in the river below the obstructions by the beginning of the new year. Fear that the Confederate ironclads might get through the obstructions gradually subsided. Grant realized that the success of his campaign depended upon naval control of the river and warned Admiral Lee that

whilst I believe we will never require the armored vessels to meet those of the enemy, I think it would be imprudent to withdraw them. . . . There is no disquieting the fact that if the enemy should take the offensive on the water— although we probably would destroy his whole James river navy—such damage would be done our shipping and stores . . . that our victory would be dearly bought.[33]

Grant's fears were correct.

New Year's Day, 1865, was a foretaste of what was to come in that last winter of the war. A heavy driving snowstorm blanketed the state of Virginia, adding to the misery of the Confederate soldiers huddled in the trenches at Drewry's Bluff, along the Williamsburg Road, and at Hatcher's Run. Misery was compounded by the wind of despair penetrating the ranks of the Army of Northern Virginia. Morale which had held up magnificently during the summer months deteriorated noticeably during the fall; drinking and drunkenness became worse, and the rate of desertion increased significantly. Because of the severity of the winter, there were no large-scale actions along the Richmond-Petersburg front from the end of November through February 1865, although bombardments, sharpshooting, and raids were daily occurrences.

The hard winter had little effect on the routing activities of the James River Squadron. Mitchell had become so obsessed with the danger from torpedo boats, particularly after Cushing successfully attacked the *Albemarle* on October 27, 1864, that he ordered his ironclads surrounded by protective nets and booms. They became so nearly immobile that, as one of his commanding officers sarcastically wrote, "when the iron clads are wanted they will be so securely fixed . . . that we shall be able to do with them but little. . . ."[34] The vessels were anchored near Chaffin's Bluff most of the time with picket boats on guard farther downstream every night. Although the Confederate bluejackets were generally much better off than their land-bound compatriots, they complained just as intensely. One young sailor pleaded

33. *Official Records*, Ser. I, XLII, pt. 3, 951.
34. Rootes to Minor, November 21, 1864, Minor Papers.

with an influential relative to aid him in obtaining a transfer: "please do not fail to do what you can for me, to get me away from here. . . . the weather is cloudy and cold."

Mitchell, whose career as flag officer of the James River Squadron was certainly not notably aggressive, became even more circumspect. On January 4, he admonished Brigadier General W. H. Stevens, Chief Engineer of the Army of Northern Virginia, to build more permanent obstructions similar to those at Drewry's Bluff on the James River. "We can never hope to encounter [the enemy] . . . on anything like equal terms, except by accident," he observed; "it behooves us, therefore, to bring to our aid all the means in our power to oppose his monitors. . . . Our own ironclads will be expected to take a part. . . ."[35] The "accident" that Mitchell spoke of, however, occurred in the middle of that month.

Several days of heavy rain caused the James to rise rapidly. Lieutenant Charles "Savez" Read, who served on the *Arkansas* and was in command of a naval battery overlooking Trent's Reach, observed a large amount of ice floating down the river. He concluded that a portion of the obstructions had washed away; a reconnaissance confirmed it. Read immediately informed Mallory, and on January 16, Mitchell was ordered to move down the river. "I deem the opportunity a favorable one for striking a blow at the enemy, if we are able to do so. . . . If we can block the river at or below City Point, Grant might be compelled to evacuate his position."[36]

Although the flag officer was still reluctant to carry his squadron beyond the protection of the obstructions, he nonetheless decided on a rather ambitious plan. One of his officers later wrote,

Our object [was] . . . nothing less than the division of Grant's army into three parts and the destruction of his water base at City Point. We were to go through their obstructions and after running through the pontoon bridge some fifteen miles below would have left one ironclad to cruise up and down the river and prevent them from communicating with each other. The other two would have gone down to City Point . . . and there obstructed the channel with sunken vessels so that it would have been impossible for them to have remained there under the fire of the ironclad that would have been left . . . while the other ironclad would have been free to run up the Appomattox. . . .[37]

Rapid movement was necessary if the various components of the plan were to be carried out, but Mitchell stalled. After nearly a week the naval

35. *Official Records, Navies*, Ser. I, XI, 791–792.
36. *Ibid.*, 797–798. See also Scharf, *Confederate States Navy*, 740.
37. Eggleston to R. J. Downes, February 27, 1865, Area File, Confederate Subject and Area File, National Archives Record Group 45.

secretary tried to prod him into action: "Your movement is being delayed fatally, I fear. Unless you act at once action will be useless. . . . I expect you to move tomorrow." In a second note, forwarded later that day (January 21), Mallory further rebuked him for his procrastination: "I deplore that you did not start immediately after the freshet, and have deplored the loss of every day since. . . ."[38] Because of heavy fog, however, it was not until shortly after dark on January 23 that the squadron finally got underway.

The night was ideal—for several nights the moon had been rather bright (which may account for the delay); it was "dark and very cold" as the vessels approached the obstructions. The *Fredericksburg,* the lightest of the ironclads, led the way followed by the other ironclads and wooden gunboats in the squadron. Several small vessels and two torpedo boats were lashed to the sides of the ironclads, but they were cut free at the obstructions.

Union authorities were well informed about the proposed attack. All batteries and pickets along the river were alerted, and Commander William A. Parker, senior officer afloat and commander of the Fifth Division of the North Atlantic Blockading Squadron, was warned. Normally the Fifth Division consisted of five armorclads and approximately twenty-five gunboats, but in January four monitors and a number of the gunboats were detached to participate in the second attack on Fort Fisher. Parker had only the double-turreted monitor *Onondaga* and seven gunboats with which to guard the sunken hulks that made up the obstructions at Trent's Reach and the pontoon crossings of the James and Appomattox Rivers. He asked for reinforcements, but his request failed to imply urgency. Evidently, the senior naval officer did not consider an attack by Confederate ironclads to be imminent, despite the warnings.

Upon arriving at Trent's Reach the squadron, excepting the *Fredericksburg,* anchored about a half mile above the barrier. The *Fredericksburg* came to just short of the sunken hulks, while the torpedo boat *Scorpion* with Mitchell on board searched for a passageway. While sounding, a Union picket boat discovered the Confederates and gave the alarm. Immediately a barrage descended upon the river from both banks. The firing was blind, however, and sounding continued until a channel suitable for the ironclads was chartered. At 1:00 A.M. Mitchell maneuvered the *Fredericksburg* through the gap, but when he returned for the *Virginia* he found her aground. To add to his "inexpressible mortification," the *Richmond* and two of the small vessels were also aground. Because the tide was ebbing rapidly, the *Fredericksburg* was recalled to provide cover for the helpless vessels.

38. *Official Records, Navies,* Ser. I, XI, 803–804.

The squadron remained under heavy fire throughout the night, but no damage was done. Daybreak, however, revealed the stranded ships to Union gunners, and their accuracy increased rapidly. The *Richmond* was straddled, and at 7:10 A.M. a mortar shell plunged into the *Drewry,* exploding her magazine. She simply disintegrated; "the shock on board the *Richmond* was terrific," her commanding officer, John McIntosh Kell, wrote. Fortunately, Mitchell had ordered the *Drewry's* crew removed to one of the ironclads beforehand. Shore batteries continued to pound the Confederate squadron, concentrating their fire on the two ironclads. "The ship was struck so constantly by shot and shell that it was impossible to keep account of the number," the *Richmond's* captain later recounted.

At 10:30 A.M., black smoke was seen below the obstructions, and within a few minutes the powerful double-turreted monitor *Onondaga,* followed by a small wooden steamer, appeared in view. Weary Confederate gunners, expecting the Union vessels to penetrate the barrier and attack, braced themselves for a ship-to-ship encounter. Just within range, but short of the barrier, the monitor hove to and added her massive 15-inch guns to the fray. Confederate officers had known that the *Onondaga* was in Trent's Reach and had expected to be engaged by her, but when daylight came, the river below was empty of enemy vessels.

What had happened to the *Onondaga* from the time Mitchell's squadron first reached the obstructions and her appearance the following morning (eleven hours later)? Upon their initial approach Parker ordered the monitor to retire downstream. Explaining this move later, he wrote, "I thought [that] there would be more room to maneuver the vessel and to avoid the batteries bearing on Dutch Gap." This reasoning was rather flimsy since Confederate land batteries fired only briefly during the night, and the vessel obviously had less room for "maneuvering" in the narrow neck below than in the Reach—but the move was sound. Each Confederate vessel supposedly carried a spar torpedo capable of sinking or damaging the monitor—the only Union ironclad in the river at that time. By retiring and waiting for daylight he would be in position either to keep them at a distance with his heavy guns or possibly to avoid them. This, however, does not explain why he delayed his attack until nearly eleven o'clock in the morning. By then, of course, it was too late.[39]

Within minutes after the monitor's first shells plunged into the river, the stranded ironclads, aided by the rising tide, slipped into deep water. Although the *Onondaga* could get away only seven shots before the Con-

39. For Parker's report to Porter see *Ibid.,* 627–628.

federate vessels steamed out of range, two of them registered on the *Virginia*. One struck squarely above the after port of the flagship, shattering her six-inch armor plate, crushing and splintering the inner woodwork. One man was killed and two wounded by the concussion and splinters. The second shot glanced off the fantail and exploded near the stack. None of the other vessels was hit by the monitor, nor was she touched by the weak and ineffective fire from the retreating Confederates.

At nine o'clock that night, when the tide was full, the Confederate squadron minus the *Drewry* (blown up), the *Scorpion* (abandoned), and the *Wasp* (seriously damaged) moved down the river for a second attempt. Within a few minutes, however, the *Virginia* rounded to; the exhaust pipe and smokestack had been so damaged that steam was billowing throughout the gundeck and main deck. Although she could still make headway, her pilots maintained that they could not see because of the escaping steam. Mitchell then signaled for his captains to come on board the flagship, and after a brief conference the attack was called off. The reasons given were damage to the *Virginia,* loss of the three wooden vessels, loss of surprise, and presence of a powerful calcium light at the entrance to Trent's Reach exposing the river at that point.[40] Mitchell and his officers had never been enthusiastic about going down the river, and damage to the *Virginia* provided them with the pretext they needed to abandon the attack. The flag officer could have gone on with his two remaining ironclads but chose not to. Although strong naval reinforcements were hurrying up the river, other than the *Onondaga,* there were only lightly armed wooden steamers between the obstructions and City Point. The Confederates certainly had a passing chance of success, and the rewards would have more than justified the odds. The destruction of the enormous supply depot at City Point could have seriously affected Grant's campaign.

Grant was well aware of this and was furious with Parker for his withdrawal on the 24th. Admiral Porter was just as incensed: "No man ever had a better chance than you had to make yourself known to the world. . . . It must have been as mortifying to [the Navy Department] . . . as it was to me to see such an opportunity lost . . . to say nothing of the odium brought upon the Navy. . . ."[41]

Mallory was just as displeased with Mitchell; within three weeks he was

40. *Ibid.,* 671.
41. *Ibid.,* 658. For Grant's correspondence see *Official Records,* Ser. I, XLVI, pt. 2, 224–225. Parker was relieved of his command and later tried and convicted by a court martial. Welles dismissed the sentence on a technicality and put him on the retired list.

186

replaced in command of the James River Squadron by Rear Admiral Raphael Semmes, who had just returned to the beleaguered Confederacy from aboard. Semmes would have no opportunity to repeat the "attack" of January 24, for in February the Fifth Division was reinforced by the *Atlanta* and *New Ironsides*. The squadron could only wait for the end.[42]

42. Grant and Porter expected Semmes to attack. See Radford to Porter, February 23, 1865, Area 7 File, National Archives Record Group 45; Grant to Radford, February 25, 1865; Area 7 File, National Archives Record Group 45; *Official Records,* Ser. I, XLVI, pt. 2, 686–701, 929.

12

Buchanan and the Mobile Squadron

FOR YEARS the city of Mobile, at the head of the Alabama-Tombigbee river system, had been second to New Orleans in the Gulf trade, but Farragut's monumental victory in the spring of 1862 changed that, at least for the Confederacy. Until the Battle of Mobile Bay in late summer of 1864, Mobile was one of the most important centers of blockade-running on the Gulf. Farragut, in command of the West Gulf Blockading Squadron, was determined to end this trade by gaining control of the bay, and Franklin Buchanan, in command of the Confederate naval forces, was determined to hold onto the bay and end the threat by forcing the Union blockading forces to retire. The battle in August 1864 decided the issue and closed the port.

The city was on the northern shore of Mobile Bay, about thirty miles from the Gulf itself. The channel between the bay and the Gulf was guarded by two forts: Morgan, with forty-five guns, on a long tongue of land extending out from the mainland on the eastern side, and Gaines, with twenty-six guns, about three miles west of Morgan on Dauphin Island. Submerged pilings extended across the channel from near Fort Gaines to form an obstruction almost two miles long. A triple line of moored torpedoes further lengthened the barrier to within a quarter of a mile of Fort Morgan. Buoys marked the dividing line between the minefield and the narrow ship channel. There was also an entrance into the bay from Mississippi Sound by way of Grant's Pass, located between Dauphin Island and the mainland. Unfinished Fort Powell guarded this channel.

Although Farragut wanted to attack Mobile immediately after the fall of New Orleans, no attempt was made to run the forts and enter the bay until August 1864. Opening the lower Mississippi delayed him until the summer of 1863, and then he became convinced that ironclads as well as troops were needed for the attack. None was immediately forthcoming, however, and by 1864 Confederate defenses had been considerably strengthened and included a respectable naval force with ironclads.

During the early months of the war, Mobile was generally ignored by the Confederate Navy Department. Naval affairs were left in the hands of

Lieutenant James D. Johnston, CSN, with the title of "Keeper of the Light House," and Colin J. McRae, who acted as civilian agent for the department. Fortunately, both were men of ability and realized the urgency of creating a naval force for the defense of the bay. By the fall of 1861 two vessels, the *Alert* and *Florida,*[1] had been converted into gunboats, and contracts were signed for the construction of two light-draft warships. Johnston and McRae were also instrumental in persuading the state of Alabama to build an ironclad, the *Baltic,* and the Navy Department to negotiate for two more ironclads to be built at Selma, Alabama.[2]

In February 1862, Captain Victor Randolph, CSN, assumed command of the Mobile Station with Johnston as his executive officer. Randolph was described by one of his officers as "a charming old gentleman in the parlor, very amiable and very kind and polite in his manners and you cannot help liking him, but he is sixty-five years old and hasn't all the fire of youth . . . and at best [is] never remarkable for energy or decision. . . . We are without a head, there is no controlling spirit."[3] He was the first naval officer of flag rank to resign his commission in the United States Navy to join the South, but his Confederate career was jeopardized from the beginning because of animosity between him and the secretary of the navy. He tried, in fact, to block Mallory's appointment through correspondence with members of the provisional Congress and later attempted to pressure the naval committee of the first regular Congress into investigating Mallory. He refused to divulge his reasons, although later he confided to a fellow officer, "I have made no statement of the Hon. Secretary's disloyalty which I did not hold myself prepared to prove." Nevertheless, the matter was dropped when Mallory gave Randolph command of the naval batteries on York River.[4]

Strained relations between the two continued, and later when Buchanan,

1. The *Florida's* name changed to *Selma* in September 1862.

2. For the *Baltic* see above, pp. 80–81. For Johnston's role in building naval vessels in Alabama see Johnston to Wright, February 11, 1881, in James D. Johnston folder, ZB File; Governor Shorter to Mallory, October 15, 1862, Governors' Letterbooks, 1861–65 (Alabama Department of Archives and History, Montgomery); Johnston to Mitchell, May 22, 1863, Mitchell Papers. For McRae see various letters from September 1861 to June 1862 in the McRae Collection; Edwin Layton, "Colin J. McRae and the Selma Arsenal," *Alabama Review,* XVIII (1966), 129–130; Charles S. Davis, *Colin J. McRae: Confederate Financial Agent.* Johnston actually superintended the construction of the *Baltic, Morgan,* and *Gaines,* and commanded the *Baltic* before receiving command of the *Tennessee.*

3. Charles Graves to cousin, May 1, 1862, Graves Papers.

4. The appointment was made eight months after he first entered the Confederate naval service.

Randolph's junior, was appointed admiral, the embittered captain wrote to several congressmen complaining of this "slight." "Mr. Mallory would never employ me, or allow me to be placed in a position by which I might be brought honorably before the country, or where I would distinguish myself in my profession," he lamented to one congressman.[5] But as commander of the Mobile Station and Squadron from February until September, 1862, Randolph certainly had every opportunity to "distinguish" himself.

Randolph was ordered to open communications and to convoy ships between Mobile and New Orleans by way of Grant's Pass and Mississippi Sound. Flag Officer George N. Hollins was to co-operate with his Lake Pontchartrain flotilla. The plan was never carried out because the army refused to remove the obstructions placed in Grant's Pass by the Confederates, and Hollins had all he could handle in the Mississippi River.[6]

The Mobile commander was also to disperse the Federal forces blockading the main entrance to the bay as soon as the gunboats under construction were completed. By the beginning of April, the *Morgan* and *Gaines* were ready, and on the night of the third, these vessels, along with the *Florida* and *Alert,* made a half-hearted attack against the blockaders. After firing for several hours in their general direction, the Mobile Squadron withdrew. Scharf called this affair a "reconnaissance," but the executive officer of the flagship *Morgan* wrote that it was a planned attack and called Randolph an "old coward" for not pushing it.[7] This was the only attempt to strike at the Union blockading force off Mobile in 1862, despite the weakness of the Union force there. The flag officer contented himself with guarding the passes while urging the department to provide ironclads. He called his wooden gunboats "cockle shells," almost worthless as fighting ships because "one well directed shot would cripple [any of them]."[8]

5. Randolph to Drepe (?), August 18, 1862, construction at Mobile file, Confederate Subject and Area File, National Archives Record Group 45; see also to Yancy, August 18, 1862, construction at Mobile file, National Archives Record Group 45.

6. Graves to Maggie, April 21, 1862, Graves Papers; Randolph to Buchanan, February 15, 1862, construction at Mobile file, Confederate Subject and Area File, Record Group 45.

7. Graves to cousin, April 6, 1862, Graves Papers; Scharf, *Confederate States Navy,* 536; see also Johnston to Mitchell, June 19, 1863, Mitchell Papers.

8. The *Morgan's* first commanding officer agreed as to her weakness: "Her steam pipes are entirely above the water line, and her boilers and magazines partly above it, so we have the comfortable appearance of being blown up or scalded by any chance shot that may not take off our heads." C. H. Kennedy to Charles Ellis, n. d., Charles Ellis Papers (Duke University Library, Durham, North Carolina). The blockade off

In August 1862, Mallory relieved Randolph of his command and ordered him to Jackson, Mississippi, to stand trial by court martial. What the charges were and whether or not he was actually tried have not been ascertained, but he never held an active command in the Confederate navy again.

Admiral Buchanan, the new flag officer, was at that time the most respected officer in Confederate naval service. When the crusty old warrior, limping from wounds received while commanding the *Virginia,* arrived in Mobile, one officer wrote, "Buchanan is a *man* and a *Commander.*" Another noted, "warm work is expected in a few days."

Though aggressive and anxious to challenge his adversary beyond the bay, Buchanan was not imprudent. Shortly after reaching Mobile, the new flag officer reported that he found the squadron "in a state of efficiency, highly creditable to their officers and the service." But he also cautioned the naval secretary that the squadron would be no match in an engagement with Union ironclads.[9] All that he could hope for was that the expected attack would be delayed long enough to allow completion of the two ironclads under construction.

On May 1, 1862, Henry D. Bassett, a Mobile shipbuilder, signed a contract to construct two ironclad floating batteries for $100,000 each. The *Tuscaloosa* was to be completed by July 1, 1862, and the *Huntsville,* thirty days later. The small city of Selma, about 150 miles up the Alabama River from Mobile, was chosen as the construction site, probably because of the influence of Colin McRae. An iron foundry and arsenal were being developed at Selma by McRae, and he promised to provide the guns, boilers, and armor plate for the vessels.

Commander Ebenezer Farrand was engaged in selecting defensive sites on the Alabama and Tombigbee Rivers. In August, he was ordered to obtain suitable locations for shipyards and to initiate the building of additional ironclads.[10] On August 19, he contracted for one large sidewheel ironclad and two 150-foot propeller ironclads to be built at Oven Bluff on the Tombigbee River. Early in September he negotiated for another sidewheel vessel to be built at Montgomery and for a powerful ram to be built at Selma. By the

---

Mobile was practically ineffective during most of 1863. Most of the blockaders were sailing vessels unable to stop steamers. *Official Records, Navies,* Ser. I, XIX, 102–103; Charles L. Lewis, *David Glasgow Farragut,* II, 136.

9. To Forrest, September 12, 1862, Buchanan Letterbook.

10. Farrand was placed in charge of all shipbuilding in the state, but he was evidently subordinate to Buchanan. Mallory to Farrand, August 1, 1862, Ebenezer Farrand folder, BZ File; Mallory to Farrand, September 2, 1862, Area file, Confederate Subject and Area File, National Archives Record Group 45.

time Buchanan arrived in Alabama, seven ironclads were either under construction or about to be laid down. When these vessels were completed and commissioned, he would have eight armored warships, counting the *Baltic,* to defend the bay and to challenge Union control of the Gulf and the Mississippi River. For the next eighteen months the task of finishing and manning them absorbed most of his time.

The two ironclads building at Selma were behind schedule—three fifths completed at the end of the stipulated time—but Farrand reported to Buchanan at the end of September that the first one would be ready in about six weeks. Within two weeks, however, his optimism had decreased considerably: "I cannot write with the least encouragement with regard to the completion of the floating batteries here. They are at almost a dead stand still waiting for iron plating and machinery. . . . not a particle of machinery for either and only the boiler for one has been received." In passing on this information to the naval secretary, Buchanan wrote, "this deprives me of the use of these boats for at least two months, which I regret, as I relied principally upon them to prevent the passage of the enemy through the obstructions in the Bay."[11]

The power plants for the several Alabama ironclads were originally to have been built at the naval iron works in Columbus, Georgia, but the Columbus establishment lacked the facilities to equip all the ships. In October 1862, McRae wrote to the Shelby Iron Company to forward twenty-five tons of pig iron to Columbus. When two thirds of this order was held up at Selma because of inadequate transportation facilities, McRae sent an urgent message to the army quartermaster to ship the iron immediately, as "this iron . . . is required to complete the engines and machinery for the floating batteries at this place [Selma]. . . ."[12] By January 1863, the machinery for the *Tuscaloosa* was installed, but the *Huntsville*'s boilers and engine failed to arrive before the vessel was towed to Mobile. The Tombigbee vessels received their power plants in the latter part of 1863 and early 1864.

Machinery for the *Tennessee,* the large ram being built at Selma, and the *Nashville,* the sidewheel ironclad on the stocks at Montgomery, was obtained from Mississippi riverboats stranded up the Yazoo River.[13]

11. October 15, 1862, Buchanan Letterbook.

12. McRae to Harris, October 31, 1862, McRae Collection.

13. The detailed survey of the *Tennessee* made by a board of Union naval officers after she was captured indicated that her machinery came from the riverboat *Alonzo Child.* This is apparently a mistake, for the machinery from this boat was not removed until December 1863 to be transported to Selma, probably to be installed in a fourth ironclad under construction there. The *Tennessee's* machinery was being installed in

The inadequate supply of iron also retarded the armoring of the vessels. When Selma was selected for a navy yard, one of its supposed advantages was the availability of iron and of the facilities to manufacture it into plate. McRae was under contract with the Navy Department to erect a rolling mill and foundry, while the Shelby Iron Company was rapidly converting its facilities in order to roll plate. By the fall of 1862 this situation had changed considerably. McRae's rolling mill was delayed indefinitely, and although Shelby had begun to turn out armor plate, pig iron was becoming increasingly scarce. A sufficient quantity of plate to cover the *Tuscaloosa* arrived in December 1862 and January 1863 from the Scofield and Markham works in Atlanta. Both the Atlanta and Shelby works supplied armor for the *Huntsville* and *Tennessee*. But the three Tombigbee vessels were never finished because of lack of plate, and the *Nashville* was only partly clad with armor taken from the *Baltic*.[14]

On February 7, 1863, Farrand wired Governor John Gill Shorter of Alabama that the *Tuscaloosa* and *Huntsville* had been successfully launched, "amid enthusiastic cheering." Three weeks later the hull of the much larger *Tennessee* slid into the muddy waters of the Alabama River. Lieutenant Johnston, who was in Selma to take the vessel to Mobile for completion, gives this account of her launching:

About midday there was heard the sound of a gun, and immediately afterwards the *Tennessee* was shot into the swift current like an arrow, and the water had risen to such a height that she struck in her course the corner of a brick warehouse, situated on an adjoining bluff and demolished it. This was her first and only experience as a ram.[15]

---

the summer and fall of 1863—at the time the *Alonzo Child* was being stripped of her power plant. On December 15, 1863, Buchanan wrote, "will try the machinery tomorrow or the next day." *Official Records, Navies,* Ser. I, xx, 856; see also Farrand to Engineer G. W. Fisher, March 6, April 13, and June 1, 1863, construction at Selma file, National Archives Record Group 45; Farrand to DeHaven, December 30, 1863, in *Alonzo Child* folder, Vessel File, National Archives Record Group 109; Farrand to Whitesides, December 30, 1863, Confederate Navy Brigade Personal Papers, National Archives Record Group 109; Savannah *Morning News,* December 23, 1863.

14. *Official Records, Navies,* Ser. I, XXI, 600; Simms to Jones, July 5, 1864, Area file, Confederate Subject and Area File, National Archives Record Group 45; Farrand to Myers, December 1862, construction at Selma file, Confederate Subject and Area File, National Archives Record Group 45; Farrand to Jones, December 23, 1862, Shelby Iron Company Papers; McCarrick to Kennan, January 12, 1863, Shelby Iron Company Papers, Farrand to Hunt, January 25, 1863, copy in Shelby Iron Company Papers.

15. From an address delivered by James D. Johnston before the Georgia Historical Society. Copy in National Archives Record Group 45.

The *Tennessee* and *Huntsville* were launched before completion in order to take advantage of the prevailing high water. Buchanan ordered the vessels to Mobile immediately, by tow if necessary, because of the "danger of the river falling so much that [they] . . . cannot cross the shoals. . . ." The *Tuscaloosa* steamed to the port city under her own power, but the other two had to be towed by the pride of the Alabama River, the magnificent steamboat *Southern Republic*. The trip down the twisting river with its steep banks took more than a week. Because of snags and the difficulty of towing, the boat and her charges tied up at a landing during the night. The appearance of the *Southern Republic* with her calliope shrilling "Dixie" always drew a crowd of curious people, and the presence of the strange-looking craft under tow added to the interest.[16]

Once the vessels reached Mobile, Buchanan, with his driving energy, tackled the job of getting them fitted out and ready for action. "I have neither flag-captain nor flag-lieutenant, nor midshipmen for aides; consequently, I have all the various duties to attend to from the grade of midshipman up. My office duties increase daily, which keeps me in the office until 3 o'clock, and then in the afternoon I visit the navy yard, navy store, ordnance, etc. . . ." he confided to Catesby Jones. Fearful of being attacked before his squadron was ready, Buchanan was reluctant to delegate responsibility and hypercritical of everything and everyone connected with the ships under construction. On June 13 he wrote, "The idleness of the workmen has caused remarks by citizens and others and I have been obliged to make a short speech but a *strong one* to the men, and have also stirred up Mr. [Joseph] Pierce and Engineer [George W.] Fisher. . . . I spare no one if he is delinquent." On July 5: "Old Pierce the constructor can plan work, perhaps, but he cannot control men. He is a perfect old woman. I have gone on much further since he left here. . . . Pierce delayed the work [on the *Tennessee*] by putting on the wrong iron."

Old Buck was just as hard on the civilians, both workers and contractors. When a number of carpenters struck at Selma and traveled to Mobile looking for work, marines met their boat, arrested them, and hauled them off to the guard house. When the admiral threatened to turn them over to

16. Montgomery *Daily Advertiser,* March 8, 1863; Ware to Pierce, May 7, 1863, Ware Letterbooks, National Archives Record Group 45; Buchanan to Comstock, February 12, 1863, Area file, Confederate Subject and Area File, National Archives Record Group 45; Memorandum from deserter in the Gustavus Fox Papers, February 24, 1863 (New York Historical Society, New York City). For a description of the *Southern Republic* see Thomas C. DeLeon, *Four Years in Rebel Capitals,* 57–63; and William N. Russell, *My Diary North and South.* ed. Fletcher Pratt, 103–107.

the conscription officer, they agreed to return to work. Pep talks and threats apparently did not motivate the workers enough, at least as far as Buchanan was concerned, for in August he had all of them conscripted and detailed to work under his orders.[17] The contractors, too, came in for their share of his criticism. After the *Nashville* reached Mobile in June, Buchanan complained frequently of their absence. In August, two months after the sidewheel ironclad reached the city, he reported to Mallory, "Great delay on the *Nashville* is caused for want of material, which could be procured without difficulty if either of the contractors were here to attend to it; only one of them, Mr. Montgomery, has been here, and then only *one day. . . .*"

Buchanan was also displeased with the builders at the Tombigbee River yard. The site had been ill chosen; its location near a swamp resulted in a great deal of sickness and dissension among the workmen. On October 1, 1863, Buchanan informed the naval secretary that one of the contractors was unpopular with the workmen and the other "a hard drinker [who] . . . spends much of his time in Mobile." With the department's approval, the flag officer took the vessels out of the contractors' hands, appointed a naval officer to supervise the shipyard, and commissioned Sidney Porter as a naval constructor. Porter was the former contractor who drank and was absent much of the time, and Buchanan hoped to control his negligence by subjecting him to naval discipline. Considering these problems and remembering that Buchanan, like many professional military officers, found working with civilians disagreeable, it is not surprising that he wrote in January 1864, "I have lost all confidence in *all* contractors."[18]

Under the flag officer's constant surveillance, the vessels as they arrived in Mobile received their armor, guns, and crews; after a shakedown cruise they were commissioned. The *Tuscaloosa* made her trial run early in April 1863, followed two weeks later by the *Huntsville*. By summer, both of these floating batteries were operational, although Buchanan decided not to send them into the bay because of their slowness. With 125 pounds of steam pressure, the *Tuscaloosa* made only two and a half knots.

On June 18, 1863, the hull of the *Nashville* arrived from Montgomery

17. Buchanan to Mallory, September 20, 1863, Buchanan Letterbook; Buchanan to Mitchell, June 13, 1863, Mitchell Papers.

18. to Mitchell, January 26, 1864, Mitchell Papers; see also Buchanan to Mallory, October 1, 1863, Buchanan Letterbook; Buchanan to Farrand, December 1, 1863, Area file, Confederate Subject and Area File, National Archives Record Group 45; Farrand to Buchanan, April 5, 1864, Ebenezer Farrand folder, Citizens File, National Archives Record Group 109; Voucher, November 19, 1863, construction at Selma file, Confederate Subject and Area File, National Archives Record Group 45.

and was towed to the navy yard for completion. Her 270-foot length and 62-foot beam gave her an impressive appearance—one officer after visiting the vessel wrote that he was "perfectly delighted with her. Never was so much pleased in my life. She is a tremendous monster. . . . The *Tennessee* is insignificant along side of her. . . ."[19]

Buchanan hoped that the *Nashville* and *Tennessee* would be ready by the end of the summer, but the *Tennessee* would not be commissioned until February of 1864 and the *Nashville* more than six months afterward. Because of the problem of acquiring sufficient plate for armor, the flag officer determined to complete one vessel at a time. The *Nashville,* naked without her covering of iron armor, lay moored to a wharf, while the *Tennessee* was completed. In September, Buchanan reported, "The work on the *Tennessee* has progressed for some weeks past. . . . There is much delay for want of plate and bolt iron; it was impossible to iron both sponsons at the same time, as the vessels had to be careened several feet to enable them to put the iron on; even then several of the workman were waist deep in the water to accomplish it. . . . The work has been carried on night and day when it could be done advantageously. . . . The first course of iron and part of the second are on one side of the *Tennessee* and nearly all the first course on the opposite side." By December 1863 she was ready, and Buchanan wrote wistfully, "if I only had her guns and crew, and had her across the short water on the bar, I would be satisfied it would not be long before she should try her strength."[20] But guns were not available and would not be for some time.

Originally, the ordnance for the Mobile vessels was to be supplied by the iron works Colin McRae had acquired at Selma. The contract for the casting of cannon signed between representatives of the War and Navy Departments with McRae in February 1862 stipulated that the first guns were to be delivered by September 1 of that year. The first piece was not forwarded to Mobile, however, until January 1864. In June 1863 the foundry had come under exclusive naval control with the former executive officer of the *Virginia,* Catesby ap R. Jones, as its commanding officer. From the casting of the first experimental gun a month after he took charge until the spring of 1865 nearly two hundred guns were manufactured.

Because the Selma foundry was unable to provide the *Huntsville* and *Tuscaloosa* with guns, other means had to be found. Six (two 42-pounders, two 32-pounder smoothbores, and two 32-pounder rifles) were obtained

19. Gift to Ellen, June 19, 1863, Gift Papers.
20. To Mitchell, December 11, 1863, Mitchell Papers.

from the army as temporary batteries, and later two 7-inch Brooke guns were sent from Tredegar and two more from Charleston.[21]

The origin of the *Tennessee's* battery of six guns is uncertain. Presumably part of it came from the Selma foundry, which shipped its first two 7-inch Brooke rifles to Mobile early in January 1864. But it is highly unlikely —as some historians state—that her entire battery came from the Selma works, at least not at first. On January 26, Buchanan wrote that her battery was complete, and records of the naval iron works do not indicate that additional guns were shipped to Mobile during January. More than likely the other four guns (6.4-inch Brooke rifles) came from two stationary floating batteries in the harbor, for that is what Buchanan proposed to the Navy Department.[22]

The *Nashville's* armament was unusual for a Confederate ironclad. Because her builders increased the forward inclination of the shield to twenty-nine degrees, more than the specifications called for, the 7-inch bow gun had to be lengthened several inches. The *Nashville* was also one of the first Confederate ironclads to use 7-inch guns in her broadside. The standard broadside gun was the 6.4-inch Brooke, but the introduction of a new type of carriage enabled the side-wheel armored ship to carry 7-inch guns.[23]

Finding seamen to man the ships was probably the most irksome problem Buchanan encountered. He wrote dozens of letters to Mallory and to the various officers that headed the Office of Orders and Detail requesting men. He complained frequently of his inability to obtain men from the army. For example, on April 6, 1863, he wrote, "I am much in want of men and unless the Secretary of War and the Generals are more liberal toward the Navy in permitting transfers from the army to the Navy we cannot man either the Gun boats or floating batteries." He told Augusta J. Evans, a well-known writer in Mobile, that of 650 applications to the War Department for seamen

21. The latter two brought on a controversy between the Navy Department and Beauregard that went all the way to the President before being decided in favor of the navy. Roman, *Beauregard,* II, 41; Tredegar Foundry Sale Book, December 3, 1862, Tredegar Rolling Mill and Foundry Collection; Buchanan to Minor, October 9, 1862, Buchanan Letterbook.

22. Buchanan to Mitchell, October 7, 1863, Mitchell Papers; Buchanan to Mallory, October 1, 1863, Buchanan Letterbook; Walter Stephens, "The Brooke Guns from Selma," *Alabama Historical Quarterly,* XX (1958), 465. Johnston states that her battery came from Selma. James D. Johnston, "The Ram *Tennessee* at Mobile Bay," *Battles and Leaders,* IV, 401.

23. Brooke to Catesby Jones, January 15, 1864; Jones to McCorkle, January 28, 1864; McCorkle to Jones, February 1, 27, 1864; Brooke to Buchanan, January 21, 1864, all in the Selma Foundry Papers, National Archives Record Group 45.

in the army to be detailed for naval service, only twenty had been approved.[24] He did receive a sufficient number of men from the army to fill his ship complements, and contrary to his complaints, most military commanders, particularly General D. H. Maury at Mobile, were co-operative. Perhaps they were impressed by the admiral's rank and reputation or by his pugnacious stubbornness, for military commanders elsewhere were notoriously unco-operative in detailing men to the navy. On December 12, 1863, Maury asked the Adjutant General, "Please call the attention of the Secretary of War to the importance of affording every aid to the naval commander here in procuring the transfer of men from the Army to the Navy."[25] In March 1864 he offered Buchanan artillery details to man the guns in the naval vessels if the flag officer decided on an attack before his crews were completed. Eventually about 150 men were detailed from a Tennessee unit to serve on the *Tennessee.*

Although these Tennesseeans were praised during and after the war by Buchanan as well as Johnston, the admiral was not entirely pleased with the personnel of the squadron. "There are on board . . . these vessels some of the greatest vagabonds you will ever read of," he related to Mitchell. "One or two such hung during this time would have a wonderful effect." Buchanan's opinion was probably inevitable considering the fact that a large percentage of men who manned his ships (as well as those throughout the Confederate navy) were not seamen; they had never been to sea or experienced the life of a jack tar in a ship-of-war in the old navy. Only a well-disciplined ship was a good ship to a naval officer steeped in the tradition of Stephen Decatur and Oliver Hazard Perry. Buchanan was a disciplinarian. "If we could use the lash we should have no trials for desertion or thefts—I never knew solitary confinement to have any effect upon a crew."[26] Buchanan strongly disapproved of the regulations against corporal punishment in the Confederate Navy and so informed Secretary Mallory.

The flag officer was not alone in his censorious opinion of the enlisted personnel in the Mobile Squadron. An officer reporting on board the *Morgan* for the first time was shocked at her crew. "To call the *Morgan*'s crew sailors would be disgracing the name," he wrote with a touch of xenophobia,

Out of a hundred and fifty not one is even *American,* much less a Southerner. We have Irish, Dutch, Norwegian, Danes, French, Spanish, Italian, Mexican, Indians, and Mutezos [*sic*]—a set of desperate cut throats. But worst of all their

24. Quoted in Clement Eaton, *A History of the Southern Confederacy,* 325.
25. War Department Papers, National Archives Record Group 109.
26. To Mitchell, June 22, 1863, Mitchell Papers.

loyalty is doubtful. . . . I could go into the country and get *ten Southerners* and teach them more in one week about seamanship and gunnery than these fellows will learn in twelve months.[27]

A similar description was given of the *Selma's* crew by one of her officers. By June 1864 there were more than 800 enlisted men and 133 officers in the squadron, enough to man the vessels and station.

Buchanan appealed almost as frequently for officers as for enlisted men, and, characteristically, he was constantly deriding the officers' competence. Many officers he wrote, "appear to think that the Navy was made for their *pleasure* and *accommodation,* and I take good care to assure to them that such is not the case." Buchanan could be intemperate and vituperative in his remarks about individual officers. Rank, age, or experience meant little to him. "——— is a very nice gentleman, but is not enough of a *navy officer* for me. He has never felt much interest in the life." "Why did you send me old ———. I don't think I ever had an officer of so little force. *He is of no earthly use to me."* "I am obliged to ask a court of Inquiry on ——— you are aware that he never was worth anything in the old Navy." ". . . Lieutenants and officers are dissatisfied with him. . . . he makes enemies of nearly all [of them]." "——— is nothing—not worth his salt." "——— is here on board the *Huntsville*—wish he was anywhere else."

Although to his officers he was much more free with his criticisms, he could give compliments. Farrand was "respected," Lieutenant George W. Gift a "fine officer," Lieutenant John R. Eggleston "a clever man." "I cannot get along here without [Johnston] . . . he is never idle; he is constantly employed with matters connected with the vessels of the Squadron . . . a thousand things which I cannot ennumerate." He was so impressed with the abilities of Johnston that he persuaded the department to advance him over a number of senior officers to the rank of commander in command of the *Tennessee.*[28]

Any attempt to generalize about the attitude of the personnel in the Mobile Squadron toward Buchanan would be at best haphazard. There are no known records or diaries of enlisted men who served in the squadron, and personal papers from officers are scanty. Buchanan, however, was the type of personality that a young officer would write home about, and we gain some impressions from these letters. He was universally admired and

27. Graves to cousin, March 2, 1862, Graves Papers.
28. For remarks about various officers, see Buchanan to Mitchell, December 1, 3, October 17, June 3, April 5, 1863, and March 1, 1864, in the Mitchell Papers. See also letters and documents concerning a Court of Inquiry for two officers in the Mobile squadron, Wirt Family Papers.

respected for his courage and aggressiveness. In contrast to officers at other stations in the Confederacy, the officers in Mobile were apparently quite confident about what Buchanan would be able to do—right up to the battle of Mobile Bay. Most complaints concerned his strict observance of regulations, particularly about the wearing of uniforms. Shortly after taking command of the station, Buchanan issued an order requiring all officers to wear "at all times when on duty" the prescribed uniform. Elsewhere in the Confederacy, even in Richmond, the regulation requiring the wearing of the grey uniform was not strictly enforced. Many officers who had been in the old navy simply changed the buttons on their blue coats. Buchanan, however, was indignant when, as he wrote to Mitchell, one officer "reported to me for duty in a *black coat,* said he had no uniform and *had* never had one since he received his appointment." Lieutenant Gift's admiration for the admiral dimmed somewhat over the uniform incident. "A week or more since the remnant of the crew of the *Arkansas* arrived here," he wrote, "Admiral Buchanan . . . [informed] the officers that he had no use for them, as they had no uniforms! . . . I have heard it said that with some ladies a sleek coat . . . with brass buttons has a wonderful effect, but I was not prepared to believe that with a man who claimed to be a warrior of age (there is no doubt of that). . . . from this, I deduct that a fashionable tailor can do more to make a good officer in the estimation of old Buchanan than the great creating Prince of Heaven."[29] Gift was not altogether fair, for some of the *Arkansas*'s crew were retained, but most of them were transferred to Charleston.

Despite Old Buck's penchant for regulations and discipline and despite the discomforts and ill health that were always present while serving on ironclads in a semitropical area, life was generally pleasant for the officers of the Mobile Squadron. Mobile had a population of approximately 25,000 and was one of the most cosmopolitan cities in the Confederacy. William Howard Russell, the famous correspondent of the London *Times,* noted in his diary, "The city . . . abounds in oyster saloons, drinking houses, lager-beer and wine-shops, and gambling and dancing places . . . the most foreign-looking city I have yet seen in the States."[30] Naval duty was such that officers and men could take advantage of the many diversions in the city. The wooden

29. Gift to Ellen, August 2, 1863, Gift Papers; see also Simms to Jones, March 4, 20, 1864, Area file, Confederate Subject and Area File, National Archives Record Group 45.

30. Russell, *My Diary,* 108. Other wartime descriptions of Mobile can be found in De Leon, *Four Years,* 71–73; FitzGerald Ross, *Cities and Camps of the Confederate States.* ed. Richard Harwell (Urbana, 1958), 193–194; Arthur Freemantle, *The Free-mantle Diary.* ed. Walter Lord, 103–104.

vessels of the squadron rotated at guarding the passes to the bay—a tour down the bay lasting for two weeks to a month. When in harbor they usually anchored near the center of the city—opposite the post office and Battle House Hotel. Gift described a typical day at anchor in the harbor:

We are in four watches, which gives me two days on duty and two days off. On my liberty days I go on shore at half past nine and find some friends and acquaintances with whom I consume the time until 2:00 P.M. I then return on board to dinner (and by the way we live very well) and remain until after quarters at 4 and then go ashore until tea time. It seems precisely like living a very short distance from the city.

The war had little effect on social activities in the city. The genteel custom of calling upon certain prominent families in the city was still observed, and naval officers frequented the homes of Augusta Evans, Madame Le Vert, and others. The navy reciprocated by holding ship-board balls and dinners, and by taking moonlight cruises down the bay. The old admiral himself did not disdain such affairs; a journalist describing a river boat excursion which included the governor of Alabama, General Maury, and Buchanan, wrote, "A very good band of music from one of the regiments of the garrison played, and dancing was soon got up in the splendid saloon. . . . Admiral Buchanan, who was looking on, joined in this, and naturally by doing so created a great deal of confusion and merriment, at which he was in high glee."[31]

Social duties were a tonic for the monotonous but normal wartime duty of waiting. Occasionally, some excitement would be generated when a blockade-runner would slip into the bay. The Confederate steamers would then fire a few shells to discourage the blockaders from venturing too close. This respite was only temporary, however, and by 1864 blockade-running had slowed down to a trickle. The cordon had slowly tightened as more vessels joined the Union force off the bay. Early in 1864, Farragut returned from a long leave, and shortly afterward rumor reached Mobile that Union monitors were on the way. It was clear that the long-expected attack was near at hand.

On February 16, 1864, the *Tennessee* was placed in commission. Considered by many, including Alfred T. Mahan, to be the most powerful ironclad built from the keel up within the Confederacy, she was slightly more than two hundred feet in over-all length with a rather broad beam of forty-

31. Ross, *Cities and Camps,* 196. For social activities in Mobile, see Gift to Ellen, June 13, August 2, 1863; Grimball to mother, October 10, 25, 1862, Grimball Collection; George C. Waterman, "Notable Naval Events of the War," *Confederate Veteran,* VII (1899), 450; Mary Waring, *Miss Waring's Journal: 1863 and 1865.* ed. Thad Holt Jr., 4.

eight feet. Her six-gun battery of Brooke rifles and an improved ram provided a respectable armament, while she was protected by four inches of armor plate on her sides and stern and six on the forward side of the shield. These strong points, however, were more than offset by serious weaknesses. Her power plant was frail because of a system of "gears" designed to adapt her riverboat machinery to screw propulsion. Like all Confederate ironclads, she was slow, making approximately six miles per hour when fully loaded. An arrangement to lower heavy iron shutters over the ports after the guns were fired and withdrawn to load proved to be faulty: a well-placed shot would jam the shutter closed. The most serious weakness was that the tiller chains to the rudder head were exposed in open channels on the stern deck. The *Tennessee*'s commanding officer, James Johnston, was aware of these defects, but they were not corrected before the battle.[32]

The problem that concerned Johnston and Buchanan most after commissioning was crossing Dog River Bar into the lower bay—a formidable task as the bar had only nine feet of water at high tide and the *Tennessee*'s draft was thirteen feet even before provisions, stores, ammunition, and coal were taken on board. Wooden caissons or "camels" were built to float her over, but the first ones failed. The unwieldy warship was towed up the tortuous Mobile River into the Spanish River, a round-about route used because of her deep draft; after grounding several times, she arrived off the bar. Workmen then began fitting the caissons in place. They were filled with water, lowered and lashed to the ironclad's bottom with heavy chains, and finally the water was pumped out. Unfortunately, this raised the ponderous vessel less than two feet. Somewhat discouraged, Buchanan declared to Mitchell, "I am doing all I can to get the *Tennessee* over the bar. . . . What folly to build vessels up our rivers which cannot cross the bars at the mouths. . . . [The *Tennessee*] will have to go nearly twenty miles down the Bay before she will be in water sufficient to float her. . . . Her guns only brought her down four inches and I would not have put them in her, but for the difficulty of putting them in; besides I wanted to be prepared for the enemy from the time she started. . . ."[33]

---

32. *Official Records, Navies,* Ser. I, XXI, 909; *Ibid.,* 871. Why the *Tennessee* was not armed with a spar torpedo is puzzling. By the summer of 1864 these weapons had become standard on most Confederate ironclads. Farragut assumed that she had one. On August 13, one week after the battle of Mobile Bay, an officer was ordered to Mobile to supervise the fitting of spar torpedoes on vessels of the squadron. Lee to Davis, August 13, 1864, Area file, Confederate Subject and Area File, National Archives Record Group 45.

33. March 11, 1864.

The admiral's apprehensions at being attacked while on the bar were shared by other Confederate authorities. President Davis sent one of his aides to report on the situation, and after a strong appeal from the aide Buchanan reluctantly agreed to send the *Huntsville, Tuscaloosa,* and *Baltic* to reinforce the wooden gunboats guarding the lower passes. He did not like the idea of placing the two floating batteries, too slow even to stem the tide, into a position where it would be extremely difficult to recover them if necessary. Military commanders were understandably impatient with his caution. Colonel Jeremy Gilmer, who had little admiration for the sister service, remarked, "naval men find so many difficulties in the way of taking their heavy ships over the shoals of Mobile Bay that I get discouraged and almost despair at times of getting any assistance from them."[34]

There was some justification for the uneasiness that prevailed among the Confederates; Farragut, who was well-informed of the ironclad's progress, wanted to attack before the *Tennessee* reached the lower bay. His appeals for troops and at least one ironclad were unsuccessful, primarily because of the needs of Banks' Red River expedition. He did deceive the Confederates into believing an attack was imminent by firing at Fort Powell on Shell Island during the last two weeks in February.

Buchanan was relieved that the bombardment on Shell Island did not lead to an attempt by Union naval forces to enter the bay, for the *Tennessee* was still above the bar, awaiting the completion of six caissons of a new and larger type. By the end of March they were nearly finished when a fire broke out in the yard and destroyed them; the fire was probably caused by a workman who carelessly dropped a candle in some cotton used for caulking. Buchanan's misfortunes were not over. A week after the fire he received word that a large sidewheel ironclad similar to the *Nashville,* under construction at Selma, was damaged beyond repair on her launching. Even the *Nashville,* nearly ready for her trial runs, was disappointing to the admiral; "too weak," he told Mitchell.

By the middle of May the six new caissons were completed and attached to the *Tennessee*'s hull. When they were pumped out, there was barely enough water under her bottom to float her over the bar. On May 18, the ironclad was taken in tow by a steamboat, and with her own propeller working at the same time passed safely into the lower bay. For four days she swung at anchor just outside the bar while carpenters removed the caissons and the crew loaded on provisions, coal, and ammunition.

34. To wife, February 29, 1864, Jeremy F. Gilmer Papers (Southern Historical Collection, University of North Carolina Library, Chapel Hill).

On May 22 the admiral hoisted his flag on the *Tennessee* and ordered his squadron to prepare for action. Buchanan would have preferred waiting for the *Nashville* before challenging Farragut, but he was apparently under considerable pressure to act immediately. Davis had been urging him "to strike the enemy before he establishes himself on the Bay with his land forces."[35] The public as usual had an exaggerated opinion of the ram's ability. Buchanan wrote unhappily to Mitchell, "Everybody has taken it into their heads that *one* ship can whip a dozen and if the trial is *not made,* we who are in her are damned for life, consequently the *trial* must be made. So goes the world." His only chance was surprise—to attack the blockaders before they were aware that the *Tennessee* was in the bay. Shortly after sundown all hands were mustered on the quarterdeck where the admiral's fighting order was read to them—"received with three cheers," recorded one of the ship's engineers in his journal. The attack was delayed, however, because of rough weather. Buchanan planned to try again the following night, but the *Tennessee* was found aground when her anchor was raised. The following morning she floated free with the tide, but the flag officer had decided against an immediate attack.[36] In fact, Buchanan had given up any idea of offensive action. One can understand why the commandant of Fort Morgan found the admiral "humble and thoughtful" after this.

Mallory originally had sent his most aggressive senior officer to Mobile not only to raise the blockade off that city, but also to co-operate in a combined effort to regain New Orleans and the lower Mississippi River.[37] Several plans were suggested which included, at one time or another, the co-operation of armorclads being built in Europe, as well as the armies of first Beauregard, later Joseph E. Johnston, and finally Kirby Smith. Any plan to attack New Orleans hinged upon the availability of a powerful force of ironclads, and by

35. To Buchanan, February 19, 1864, *Jefferson Davis,* VI, 181–182.

36. Journal of Engineer John C. O'Connell in C. Carter Smith Jr. (ed.), *Two Naval Journals: 1864: At the Battle of Mobile Bay,* 1–3; Sidney A. Smith and C. Carter Smith, Jr. (eds.), *Mobile 1861–1865,* 28–29; *Official Records, Navies,* I, XXI, 935.

37. Johnston said in an article that Buchanan planned to attack Fort Pickens and Pensacola, but in none of Buchanan's correspondence to Mallory or Mitchell does he mention this, whereas New Orleans is mentioned several times. Johnston, "The Ram *Tennessee* at Mobile Bay," *Battles and Leaders,* IV, 402. For correspondence concerning an attack upon New Orleans see *Official Records,* Ser. I, XXXIV, pt. 2, 846, *Ibid.,* XVIII, pt. 2, 598; Hill to McPherson, December 18, 1863, Area file, Confederate Subject and Area File, National Archives Record Group 45; Buchanan to Mallory, April 6, 1863, Buchanan Letterbook; Gift to Ellen, June 20, 1863, Gift Papers; Buchanan to Mitchell, June 22, 1863, Mitchell Papers.

the late spring of 1864 it was crystal clear that such a force would not be ready in the foreseeable future. The three vessels under construction on the Tombigbee were without armor, and no armor was available; the *Tuscaloosa* and *Huntsville* were unseaworthy; the *Nashville* was nearly ready, but she was weak because of her exposed wheels, slow speed, and inadequate armor. In order to provide her with a limited amount of armor (bow and forward part of the shield), plate had to be taken from the decrepit *Baltic*. The old converted cotton lighter and first ironclad in the bay was so wormeaten that she was no longer seaworthy: "rotten as punk, and . . . about as fit to go into action as a mud scow," her commanding officer described her. In brief, Buchanan's ironclad squadron for offensive operations consisted of one ship —the *Tennessee*. He might have been able to raise the blockade, at least temporarily, with his one ironclad if surprise could have been achieved, but when this failed, he could only wait, hoping that his squadron would be strengthened before Farragut attacked.

Farragut was also waiting—waiting for the monitors that Welles had promised in January. Six months would pass before the first of these, the *Manhattan,* arrived off Mobile. In the meantime the wooden vessels in the fleet continued the routine but important duty of guarding the entrances to the bay. The smaller vessels were permitted to cruise about during the day but were required to anchor inshore at night. For the heavier vessels there was no such respite; week after week, month after month, they lay in a semi-circle off the pass in the tedium of drill, picket-boat duty, and the increasing lookout for a night attack, broken only by the monthly arrival of the beef boat from New York with mail and fresh provisions, and by an occasional trip outside to the "red snapper bank" for fresh fish. From March of 1864 on, Farragut was worried about the possibility of a surprise attack by the Confederate ironclads. Every night half of the crew of each ship remained at battle stations, the battery was cast loose, and all preparations were made for action.[38]

In July, word was received that a second ironclad, the *Tecumseh,* was en route to join Farragut's force and that two river monitors, the *Winnebago* and *Chickasaw,* had reached New Orleans. With the knowledge that these vessels would soon reach him, the Union admiral began preparations for the

38. Oliver A. Batcheller, "The Battle of Mobile Bay," *Magazine of History,* XIV (1911), 217–230; Horatio L. Wait, "The blockading service," in *Papers read before the Illinois Commandery of the Loyal Legion of the United States,,* II, 233; P. Drayton to H. Hamilton, May 2, June 4, July 14, March 2, 1864, Percival Drayton, "Naval Letters from Captain Percival Drayton 1861–65," *New York Public Library Bulletin,* X (1906), 577–625, 639–681.

attack. He planned to use the same tactics that had proved so successful at Port Hudson—each large wooden ship would have a smaller gunboat secured to her disengaged side, while the monitors would move past the forts in a separate column.

On July 12 the order "to strip for the conflict" was given; vessels were sent in succession to Pensacola to top off with coal and ammunition and to land all surplus spars, sails, and unnecessary chains. Major General Gordon Granger, assigned to command the army units in the operation, arrived off Mobile on August 1 followed the succeeding day by 2,400 troops. On August 3 the various commanders assembled on the *Hartford* for final instructions. Throughout the day the ships were readied for action. One young officer, flushed with the anticipation of coming battle, wrote in his diary, "this has been the most exciting day on the blockade. . . . sand bags have been piled up around the machinery, guns shifted to the starboard side, shot and shell rooms and magazines placed in readiness."[39] Anchor chains were ranged along the exposed side of the larger vessels to protect their machinery. These preparations continued after sunset while heavy rains accompanied by fierce lightning covered the area.

During the night Farragut postponed the attack because the *Tecumseh* had not arrived from Pensacola. The landing of troops on Dauphin Island in order to invest Fort Gaines was not canceled, however. Under the protection of six small gunboats, fifteen hundred soldiers reached the island and began the fifteen-mile march to the fort. The six gunboats then proceeded to bombard Fort Powell at Grant's Pass. In the afternoon, while another squall was blowing in, the *Tecumseh* arrived. The attack would be made the following morning.

August 5 dawned beautiful and cloudless, with ideal conditions for the attacking force.[40] An early-morning flood tide would carry damaged vessels

39. J. C. Gregg Diary, National Archives Record Group 45; see also the Journal of Pvt. Charles Brother, USMC on the U.S.S. Hartford, in C. Carter Smith Jr. (ed.), *Two Naval Journals: 1864: at the Battle of Mobile Bay*, 43.

40. In addition to the books and articles already mentioned in this chapter, the principal accounts used in describing this battle are Lewis, *Farragut;* Potter and Nimitz (eds.), *Sea Power: A Naval History;* Charles E. Clark, *My Fifty Years in the Navy;* Bern Anderson, *By Sea and by River: The Naval History of the Civil War;* Foxhall A. Parker, *The Battle of Mobile Bay;* Parker, "The Battle of Mobile Bay," in *Naval Actions and History, 1799–1898. Papers of the Military Historical Society of Massachusetts,* XII; Paul Henry Kendricken, *Memoirs of Paul Henry Kendricken* (Privately printed, 1910), 241–44; John C. Kenney, "Farragut at Mobile Bay," *Battles and Leaders,* IV, 379–400; Diggins, "Recollections of the cruise of the *U.S.S. Hartford;*" William M. Philbrick Journal, National Archives Record Group 45; "The Battle of Mobile Bay,"

past the fort and into the bay, and a breeze was blowing out of the southwest which would carry the smoke of battle toward Fort Morgan. At 5:30 A.M. the fleet got under way in two columns; the main column consisted of seven large ships, each with a gunboat lashed to her port side. To starboard of these vessels a second parallel column was formed, with the *Tecumseh* in the lead,

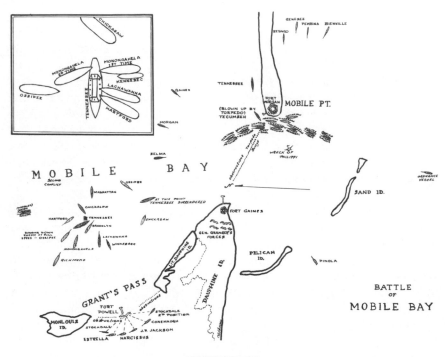

FIGURE 12

followed by the *Manhattan, Winnebago,* and *Chickasaw.* Farragut had relinquished the lead position in the main column to the *Brooklyn*—the only vessel with bow chase guns and a minesweeping device on her bow. The *Brooklyn,* with the *Octorara* lashed to her side, was followed in order by the *Hartford* and *Metacomet,* the *Richmond* and *Port Royal,* the *Lackawanna*

Mobile *Register,* August 5, 1908; A. D. Wharton, "Battle of Mobile Bay," the Nashville *Daily American,* September 13, 1877; James D. Johnston, "Fight in Mobile Bay," *Southern Historical Society Papers,* IX (1881), 324–348; Daniel B. Conrad, "Capture of the C.S. Ram *Tennessee* in Mobile Bay August, 1864," *Southern Historical Society Papers,* XIX (1890), 72–82.

and *Seminole,* the *Monongahela* and *Kennebec,* the *Ossipee* and *Itasca,* and the *Oneida* and *Galena.* On that clear day the fleet moving slowly toward the bay could be seen by thousands, including Confederate soldiers on the ramparts at Fort Morgan and blue jackets perched in the rigging of the gunboats shelling Fort Powell. The sight was most impressive. One officer on the *Ossipee* later recalled, "All our ships had their largest flags floating from peak, staff, and every masthead. From my position on the forecastle, I counted nearly sixty. It was a beautiful and inspiring sight."[41]

At 6:30 the battle began when the *Tecumseh* fired a 15-inch shell in the direction of Fort Morgan. The fort's guns replied, and by 7:00 the engagement had become general—each vessel firing as she came within effective range. Although her broadside was facing westward away from the fort, the little *Itasca* lashed to the side of the *Ossipee* also fired her guns several times. When her commanding officer, Lieutenant George Brown, was asked why, he replied that he wanted to add to the smoke.

After firing twice at the fort, the *Tecumseh* turned toward the Confederate ironclad *Tennessee,* which was moving slowly into the bend in the channel just clear of the mine field. Crossing the main column about 300 yards in front of the *Brooklyn,* Commander T. A. M. Craven maneuvered his monitor on a collision course with the enemy ironclad. Farragut's general orders required the vessels to pass "inside the buoys" next to Fort Morgan. This would keep them clear of the mine field, but the *Tecumseh* steamed outside of the buoys and penetrated the field. At approximately 7.30 she struck a mine, reeled to port, and went down within two minutes, bow first. Her propeller was still turning as she plunged to the bottom taking ninety-three of her crew including Commander Craven, with her. When the monitor went down, she was less than two hundred yards from the *Tennessee.*

The crew of the Confederate ironclad, along with the rest of Buchanan's squadron, had been at breakfast when the Federal fleet started for the bay. It was probably with relief that they manned their battle stations. Because the attack had been expected hourly, the *Tennessee, Gaines, Selma,* and *Morgan* had remained on station just north of Fort Morgan for over two months. Provisions and stores were brought out by lighter, and with a few exceptions the officers and men were unable to return to Mobile. Morale was not improved by the sticky, humid air which made living conditions on board the vessels, particularly the ironclad, all but intolerable.

As the squadron got under way, Buchanan signaled to his commanders to follow the motions of the flagship. They then stood in line abreast for the

41. Clark, *My Fifty Years,* 96.

approaching enemy ships with the *Tennessee* slightly to port and out in front. Although the admiral had evidently planned to ignore the monitors and steam directly for the more vulnerable wooden vessels, the *Tecumseh's* movements nearly prevented this. As the monitor approached, Johnston ordered his gunners not to fire "until the vessels are in actual contact." When the *Tecumseh* went down, the *Tennessee* turned again toward the main column.

Meanwhile, a lookout on the *Brooklyn* sighted suspicious objects in the water ahead. Her captain immediately backed his engines to avoid them. Earlier, Farragut had climbed into the *Hartford's* rigging for better visibility, where he was lashed to the after shroud by a piece of lead line fastened around him, and upon seeing his lead ship apparently backing down, he ordered the flagship to pass her and take the lead. As the *Hartford* passed on the port side of the *Brooklyn,* the flagship's captain informed Farragut that there was a "heavy line of torpedoes ahead." The admiral is supposed to have then shouted "Damn the torpedoes!" or something to that effect, and the *Hartford* followed by the rest of the column steamed directly across the minefield and into the bay. As most authorities rightly imply, this was the decisive moment in the battle, for the admiral's courageous decision to ignore the mines—a calculated risk, for he had earlier suspected that if there were any, they were inactive from long immersion—prevented the development of a chaotic situation which might have caused the attack to fail.

Upon taking the lead the *Hartford* found herself endangered by the approaching *Tennessee,* intent upon ramming. The lumbering ironclad was no match for the much faster Union vessel which easily maneuvered around her. The *Tennessee* also tried unsuccessfully to strike the *Brooklyn* (which had rejoined the line after the flagship), and then engaged each of the large ships as they passed. The *Monongehela,* fourth in the column, attempted to ram the Confederate ironclad amidship, but the *Tennessee's* helmsman swung her hard a-starboard and the collision occurred at an angle. The two vessels momentarily hung side by side with the gunboat *Kennebec* sandwiched between them. The *Tennessee's* small boat was torn from its davits by the gunboat's cutwater, while the Confederate vessel pumped two shells from her broadside guns into the *Kennebec's* lower deck. A number of men were killed and wounded, but damage was negligible. The *Tennessee* then continued down the column firing broadsides into the Union vessels. The *Oneida*—last in the column—was seriously damaged; a shot from the *Morgan* exploded her starboard boiler, and a broadside from the ironclad's guns carried away much of her lower rigging and severely wounded her captain. The Confederate ram then came to under Fort Morgan's guns.

In the meantime Buchanan's three small gunboats were contributing their light but deadly firepower to the struggle. The *Hartford* was hard hit, particularly by the *Selma,* which poured a raking fire into her. A marine on the flagship wrote that her cockpit looked like a slaughterhouse. Later twenty-one bodies were sewed up in hammocks for burial. A shell also exploded in the *Metacomet* causing a fire. The *Morgan* and *Gaines* exchanged shots with the Federal ships as they came within range. The Union fire was accurate, particularly against the *Gaines.* A shot burst near her wheel, destroying it, cutting the wheel ropes and killing the helmsman; a shot from the *Richmond* penetrated at the water line and caused serious flooding. When the *Selma* and *Morgan* hauled off and steamed up the bay (this was immediately after the Union vessels safely passed the fort), Farragut ordered his smaller gunboats to cast loose and give chase. The *Metacomet* and *Port Royal* followed the *Selma* and *Morgan* while the remaining vessels concentrated on the *Gaines.* With seventeen shots through her hull, the *Gaines* headed for Fort Morgan. Her commanding officer, Lieutenant John W. Bennett, hoped to beach his ship, but she sank about 400 yards off the fort. The *Selma* fought valiantly under the command of her white-haired captain, P. U. "Pat" Murphy, but had to surrender to the *Metacomet.* Murphy went on board the Union vessel to offer his sword and found an old friend, Lieutenant Commander J. E. Jouett, in command. Jouett later recalled that when the Confederate officer reached the quarterdeck, he said to him, "Pat, don't make a damn fool of yourself. I have had a bottle on ice for the last half hour."[42]

The *Morgan* was the only Confederate vessel to escape. After taking refuge at Fort Morgan, she fled to Mobile during the night.

Buchanan was not through. Shortly before 9:00 A.M., the *Tennessee* steamed for the Union fleet, assembled about four miles northwest of Fort Morgan. Farragut, mildly surprised at this, said, "I did not think Old Buck was such a fool." The Union flag officer assumed that Buchanan would wait until night and either attack then or attempt to slip back up the bay and over the bar if possible. The Confederate commander had no intention of retiring over the bar again, if for no other reason than that Farragut (he believed) would certainly not allow him time to do so. A night attack would have reduced considerably the odds against the slow ironclad, but "Old Buck" knew that Farragut would not sit back and wait for nightfall before doing something about the *Tennessee.* Buchanan could only hope for surprise by immediately attacking them while they were (he hoped) recovering from run-

42. James M. Morgan and John P. Marquand (eds.), *Prince and Boatswain,* 102–105.

ning the fort. Then, after doing what damage he could, the Confederate flag officer would beach the *Tennessee* near Fort Morgan and use her as a stationary battery. In this manner the *Tennessee* would be sacrificed, a course Buchanan had been prepared to take with his entire fleet if necessary.[43]

As the ram approached, signals flew from the flagship, ordering the monitors and larger vessels to attack. The *Monongahela* was the first vessel to slip her cable and head for the Confederate ironclad. The *Lackawanna* followed in her wake. Each rammed into the *Tennessee* but received far greater damage than inflicted. The *Hartford,* with Farragut once again perched in the rigging, was the third ship to crash into the ironclad, but while circling for another try, she in turn was rammed by the *Lackawanna.*

Meanwhile the monitors had finally entered the melee. "The *Mononga-hela* was hardly clear of us," wrote one of the *Tennessee*'s officers,

when a hideous monster came creeping up on our port side, whose slowly revolving turret revealed the cavernous depths of a mammoth gun. "Stand clear of the Port Side!" I shouted. A moment after, a thundering report shook us all, while a blast of dense sulphurous smoke covered our port holes, and 440 pounds of iron, impelled by 60 pounds of powder, admitted daylight through our side, where, before it struck us, there had been over two feet of solid wood, covered with five inches of solid iron.[44] That shot, from the *Manhattan*'s 15-inch gun, was the only one during the battle to penetrate the *Tennessee*'s armor.

The *Chickasaw* maneuvered into a position astern of the ram and pounded her mercilessly. Shots from the monitor's two 11-inch guns jammed port shutters, cut the exposed wheel chains and relieving tackle, and wounded and killed several men, including Buchanan, who once again was hit in the leg. The *Tennessee* rapidly became helpless, almost dead in the water with her smokestack gone, gun deck filled with suffocating fumes and heat, steering destroyed, guns unable to fire because of jammed port covers, and ammunition nearly exhausted. At 10:00 A.M. Johnston, with Buchanan's permission, surrendered.

The outcome of the battle can only be described as a foregone conclusion, considering the odds. Nevertheless, Farragut paid a high price for

43. Buchanan was quite critical of the *Morgan's* commanding officer when he discovered that she had not gone down fighting, but had escaped back to Mobile. Jones to McLaughlin, August 11, 1864, Catesby ap R. Jones letterbooks, National Archives Record Group 45; Scharf, *Confederate States Navy,* 566–567.

44. Quoted in Parker, "The Battle of Mobile Bay," 236. From a letter to Parker by A. D. Wharton, whose account of the battle published in the Nashville *Daily American,* September 13, 1877, is slightly different.

his victory: 145 killed and 170 wounded, counting those lost in the *Tecumseh*. His wooden ships were heavily damaged, although the only one lost was a supply vessel disabled by a shot from Fort Morgan as she attempted to follow the fleet into the bay. Buchanan lost twelve killed, twenty wounded, and the crews of the *Tennessee* and *Selma* captured. The wounded prisoners were transported to Pensacola the day after the battle. When the news reached Mobile of the admiral's captivity, an officer wrote, "I rather think [Old Buck] gritted his teeth and cursed a little."

13

Destruction

WITH THE loss of the *Tennessee,* the *Selma,* and the *Gaines,* the Confederate naval force at Mobile was reduced to four ships—the floating batteries *Huntsville* and *Tuscaloosa,* the partially-clad *Nashville,* and the *Morgan.* The old *Baltic* was decommissioned, and the three ships being built on the Tombigbee River were still without armor and unlikely to be completed in the near future, for the iron shortage was acute throughout the Confederacy. Unclad vessels were on the stocks or in the water awaiting armor at Charleston, Savannah, Columbus (Georgia), Richmond, and at several points in North Carolina. The Navy Department must have been optimistic that iron would become available, for ironclads continued to be laid down in the fall of 1864 and the winter of 1865. In Wilmington and Richmond, double-turreted monitor types were started, while an improved *"Albemarle"* was ordered from Gilbert Elliott. With assurance from Governor Vance that railroad iron would be provided for armor, Elliott promised that the vessel would be ready for service by 1865.[1] Until the new ironclad was operational, the *Albemarle* would remain in the Roanoke River defending Plymouth.

Commander James Cooke had been pleased with the *Albemarle*'s performance in the successful attack in April 1864 on Plymouth, North Carolina, and although she was damaged and forced to retire a few weeks later in an engagement against Union vessels in Albemarle Sound, he believed that with the addition of a second armored vessel, he could regain control of the Sounds. During June and early July of 1864 he kept Union forces in the Sounds in a continuous state of alarm by steaming down to the river's mouth every few days, remaining for several hours and returning to Plymouth. These excursions were interrupted in July when Cooke became ill and had to be relieved by John Newland Maffitt of North Carolina, late commander of the Confederate raider *Florida.*

1. For correspondence concerning this vessel see Elliott to Vance, May 11, 1864; Cooke to Vance, May 18, 1864; Pinckney to Vance, May 31, 1864; Whitford to Pinckney, June 3, 1864; Pinckney to Elliott, July 2, 1864; all in the Vance Papers. See also Minor to wife, May 14, 1864, Minor Papers; *Official Records, Navies,* Ser. I, X, 659.

Maffitt was without question a most capable captain, and his career while commanding the *Florida* was brilliant. But the attributes of a successful raider-commander—audacity and imagination—were detrimental to the captain of a shoal-water ironclad, destined to play a defensive role for several months. The two brief months that Maffitt commanded the *Albemarle* were not pleasant for him. Duty on board an ironclad frequently had a depressing effect on Confederate naval officers who had served on cruisers. Raphael Semmes, for example, upon assuming command of the James River Squadron in 1865, recorded in his diary the dejection he felt after viewing his "gloomy, candle-lighted" quarters on board the flagship *Virginia*.

Maffitt was depressed not only by the confinement of an ironclad but also by the defensive strategy that shackled him. Upon accepting command he immediately decided to attack the enemy fleet in the Sounds. When the local military commander at Plymouth heard of this, he strongly protested: "In the opinion of Commodore Pinckney and Captain Cooke . . . she will in all probability be captured or destroyed if she goes out. . . . the loss of the iron-clad involves, in all probability, the loss of Plymouth and Washington. . . ."[2] The dispute that followed reached Davis's cabinet, and although Mallory stoutly defended Maffitt ("while her loss must not be lightly hazarded, the question of when to attack the enemy must be left to the judgment of the naval officer in command."), no attack was made. In September, Maffitt requested a change of command.[3]

Although the *Albemarle* did not venture out of the Roanoke again after May, she not only remained a constant threat to control of the Sounds, but before Plymouth and the surrounding area could be retaken she would have to be destroyed or captured. Various plans were examined and rejected until Admiral S. P. Lee decided to send a small boat up the river one night to sink her with a torpedo or capture her. The department approved, and Lieutenant William Barker Cushing was chosen to lead the expedition. Cushing, whom Admiral David D. Porter later compared with the dashing cavalryman George A. Custer, was a delicate-looking young man who already had a reputation for reckless bravery in the navy. On a murky night late in October, Cushing and a volunteer crew in a small launch armed with a spar torpedo steamed up the Roanoke in search of the ram. Shortly after 10:00 P.M. as the boat approached Plymouth, the dark silhouette of the *Albemarle* moored to the bank could be seen. Cushing had maneuvered his boat to within fifty yards of the *Albemarle* when he spotted a log boom surrounding the vessel.

2. *Official Records*, Ser. I, XL, pt. 3, 751–753.
3. *Official Records, Navies*, Ser. I, X, 718–720; Maffitt, *Maffitt*, 336–338.

He then veered off, circled, and headed directly for the ram at full speed. Under heavy rifle fire from the ship and from the river bank, the launch struck the boom, slid over it, and came to a stop with her bow hanging over. Then Cushing coolly lowered the torpedo below the vessel's armor and exploded it. Within minutes the *Albemarle* was resting on the bottom in eight feet of water. Cushing and one man got away by swimming, two were killed, and the remainder were captured. As predicted, the loss of the *Albemarle* led to the recapture of Plymouth and the evacuation of the area by the Confederates.[4]

The *Albemarle* had the unwanted distinction of being the only Confederate ironclad destroyed by an enemy weapon. Of the twenty-two armored vessels completed and more than thirty laid down but not finished, four were captured and the rest (other than the *Albemarle*) were destroyed by the Confederates to prevent capture. This, more than anything else, explains the unpopularity of the navy throughout most of the war. Even the naval personnel were affected by this. A master's mate on the *Savannah* predicted, "if we are attacked we will follow the course of the other iron clads and either blow up or get captured."[5]

He was right, of course; the *Savannah* and most of the remaining Confederate ironclads were blown up during the last six months of the war. Four major naval squadrons, each including ironclad units, were still intact and potentially dangerous to the combined Union forces along the southern coast in the fall of 1864. Located at Savannah, Charleston, Mobile, and on the James River, they had played a significant role in checking efforts to occupy these seaports and the capital. Ironically, the fatal thrust that obliterated them came not from the sea but from the land. A major factor in this was Sherman's famous campaign through Georgia and the Carolinas.

Two weeks after Cushing's exploit at Plymouth, Sherman cut his railroad communication and with 62,000 veterans began his "march to the sea." Moving in four parallel columns, carrying pontoon bridges in sections

4. The best biography of Cushing is Ralph J. Roske and Charles Van Doren, *Lincoln's Commando: The Biography of Commander W. B. Cushing, U.S.N.;* see particular pages 193–245. See also *Official Records, Navies,* Ser. I, X, 624; and James Cooke's brief article on the *Albemarle's* destruction in *Battles and Leaders,* IV, 641–642. Cushing's official report is in *Official Records, Navies,* Ser. I, X, 611–613, and an article by him in *Battles and Leaders,* IV, 634–642. See also Lee to Senator Doolittle, February 20, 1865, in *Southern Historical Association Publications,* IX (1905), 115–116; and Porter to Wilson, n. d., quoted in the *North American Review,* CXLXI (1891), 296–303.

5. Richard Harwell (ed.), *A Confederate Marine,* 25; see also Gorgas, *Diary,* 110.

to ford the numerous streams, they met little opposition. The few thousand regulars and militia under Beauregard were scattered, and no attempt was made to concentrate them until it became clear that Savannah was the objective. By then it was too late. Although Jefferson Davis predicted in a speech at Macon that the Federal troops would be hurled back, not all believed in the power of words and proclamations. On November 29, Tattnall (in command of the Savannah naval station) began preparations to remove all stores and vessels under construction and to destroy the shipyard. Flag Officer Hunter, in command of vessels afloat, sent a requisition for haversacks and canteens.[6]

The Savannah squadron was composed of the floating battery *Georgia,* the ironclad ram *Savannah* (completed shortly after the *Atlanta* was captured), the wooden gunboats *Macon, Sampson,* and *Isondiga,* and the tenders *Firefly* and *Resolute.* The *Georgia*'s motive power was so inadequate that she could not move under her own power. For that reason the "nondescript marine monster," as a northern correspondent called her, was moored in a log crib near Elba Island where she could, by warping, bring a broadside to bear on either channel of the Savannah River.[7] For more than three years the navy as well as anxious Savannahians looked toward the sea for the expected attack, but, except for the capture of Fort Pulaski and reconnaissance activities along the coast, nothing happened. The squadron was "rusting in idleness," one officer told his wife, and a marine attached to the *Savannah* reported, "this station is so dull that all officers are getting orders."

As Sherman's columns approached the city, General William J. Hardee, in command of Savannah's defenses, asked Hunter to provide gunboats to protect vital bridges and patrol the rivers. The flag officer promptly responded by sending the *Macon* to guard the Savannah & Charleston Railroad bridge over the Savannah River, and the *Isondiga* to the bridge near Causton's Bluff. Hardee also wanted the two ironclads up the river as far as possible, but the *Savannah's* draft was too great to go above the city, and the lack of suitable towing vessels and heavy weather prevented the *Georgia's* relocation.[8] On December 10, the *Macon's* captain was ordered to destroy

6. *Official Records,* Ser. I, XLIX, 906; Hunter to Tattnall, November 29, 1864, William W. Hunter Papers (Howard-Tilton Memorial Library, Tulane University, New Orleans, Louisiana); Tattnall to Hunter, November 29, 1864, Savannah Squadron Papers.

7. Nordoff, "Two Weeks at Port Royal," 115–116.

8. Hunter to Gwathney, December 7, 1864, Hunter Papers; *Official Records, Navies,* Ser. I, 473–474.

the railroad bridge over the Savannah and to fall back to the right flank of the defense perimeter established around the threatened city. A belt of fortifications thirteen miles in length, manned by approximately 10,000 troops under General Hardee, ran from the Savannah River to the Little Ogeechee.

On December 12, as the *Macon, Sampson,* and *Resolute* were returning down the Savannah, they ran into an ambush. Federal batteries on bluffs overlooking the river opened fire on the small wooden steamers. The two gunboats were able to turn about and "with a barrel of bacon in the furnaces," steam back upstream out of danger; the tender *Resolute,* however, was disabled, forced aground, and captured.[9] Hardee lost the use of these vessels and the services of their commander. The ships were cut off from the city and its defenders, and Hunter, who was on the *Sampson,* was never able to join the remainder of his squadron.

On December 13, Sherman's troops took Fort McAllister, an isolated bastion on the Great Ogeechee River, and that night communications were opened with the blockading fleet. Hardee telegraphed Davis, "Unless assured that force sufficient to keep open my communication can be sent to me, I shall be compelled to evacuate Savannah." When the President was unable to reassure him, the decision was made to abandon the city.[10]

There was one avenue of escape. A bridge had been under construction across the Savannah River to link Savannah with South Carolina. But only the segment that ran from the city to Hutchinson's Island in the middle of the river was completed. A road had been built across the island to connect with the proposed link to the South Carolina shore, but this last portion was still unfinished, and the crossing had to be made by ferry. In order to expedite the evacuation, Hardee decided to build a pontoon bridge to replace the ferry. Fortunately, Sherman made no attempt to stop it; he apparently was reluctant to risk a large body of troops beyond the river where they might be cut off.[11]

On December 18, Beauregard arrived in Savannah to confer with

9. Scharf, *Confederate States Navy,* 652. Scharf was a midshipman on the *Sampson.*

10. Nathaniel C. Hughes, Jr., *General William J. Hardee: Old Reliable* (Baton Rouge, 1965), 262–263; Davis to Hardee, December 17, 1864, *Jefferson Davis,* VI, 421.

11. Two recent authorities agree that the presence of the Confederate gunboats in the river was an important factor in Sherman's decision, although only the *Isondiga* could navigate the river. She was used to provide protection for the pontoon bridge under construction. Hughes, *Hardee,* 265; see also Lawrence, *A Present for Mr. Lincoln,* 194.

Hardee and Commander T. W. Brent, captain of the *Savannah* and temporary commander of the squadron. One of the decisions made concerned the fate of the naval vessels. The *Isondiga* and *Firefly* would proceed up the river to join Hunter near Augusta; the *Georgia* would be scuttled; the *Savannah* would cover the withdrawal, wait two days to protect the rear of the army and stores at Screven's Ferry, and then try to break through the blockade and slip into Charleston.[12]

Two days after this conference the evacuation began. Throughout the day hundreds of civilians carrying what possessions they could in carriages and carts mingled with squeaking army wagons as they rumbled over the pontoon bridge. Nearby, the *Savannah* and *Isondiga* waited with guns ready to provide covering fire if Union troops unexpectedly appeared and attempted to hinder the exodus.[13] During the night as Hardee's weary troops started withdrawing from the lines, the final chapter for the Confederate navy at Savannah began. The unfinished ironclad *Milledgeville* was anchored in the river and set ablaze, and the large armored ram still on the stocks was fired. The *Georgia,* with her guns spiked, was sunk near the obstructions. Just before dawn the *Isondiga* was set afire and then exploded. Only the *Savannah* remained.

According to the arrangement made with Beauregard on December 18, Brent was to take his vessel to Charleston after protecting the rear of the army. The Navy Department was not aware of this decision, although the government did know that Savannah could not hold out. Mallory, sensitive to the incessant criticism hurled at the navy and himself, sent by special messenger what amounted to a plea not to surrender: "Under any circumstances, it is better for the vessels, for the Navy, for a cause and country, that these vessels should fall in the conflict of battle . . . than that they should be tamely surrendered to the enemy or destroyed by their own officers. If fall they must, let them show neither the weakness of submission nor of self-destruction, but inflict a blow that will relieve defeat from discredit."[14] The secretary's eloquent appeal did not reach Savannah in time. Brent, however, did make a half-hearted effort to escape; an attempt was made to remove the torpedoes in the Wilmington River in order that the ironclad might steam out by way of Wassaw Sound, but they were too deeply embedded in the

12. *Official Records, Navies,* Ser. I, XVI, 482; Hardee to Hunter, December 19, 1864, Savannah Squadron Papers.

13. One writer says that the *Savannah* steamed up the river and bombarded the flank of the Union lines, but this is doubtful because of her deep draft. Hughes, *Hardee,* 267.

14. *Official Records, Navies,* Ser. I, XVI, 481.

mud.[15] Brent was no Farragut, and rather than risk crossing the mine field, he decided to destroy the *Savannah*.[16]

Early in the morning on the 21st, Federal troops entered the city and raised the stars and stripes over Fort Jackson. Shortly after this, a battery of Union field guns reached the river bluff, unlimbered, and opened fire on the Confederate ironclad, anchored near Screven's Ferry. She replied, and until sunset occasional shots were exchanged with little damage to either side. According to a member of the *Savannah*'s crew, the artillery fire was extremely accurate—nearly every shot struck her sides and one, which did not explode, plunged down her smokestack. That night the *Savannah*'s crew abandoned ship and set her on fire. They then joined the rear guard of Hardee's army.

At approximately 11:30 P.M., as the tired seamen were making camp several miles from the river, the ironclad blew up. The explosion was seen, heard, and felt for miles. "It lit the heavens for miles," one of her crew wrote. "We could see to pick up a pin where we were and the noise was awful." Windows as far away as Hilton Head rattled, and the concussion was felt throughout the city.[17] Some of the crew could feel sentimental even about an uncomfortable ironclad. One young marine wrote, "You have no idea what a sad blow it was to me. Thinks I, there goes my pleasant quarters, my good clothes, my good warm overcoat, and I am forever cut off from Savannah and the hope of making myself agreeable to the Savannah girls. . . . But I thought of my canteen which I had been provident enough to fill with whiskey, and taking a good swig, I felt the generous fluid to course through every vein and fill me with fresh strength and spirit. . . ."[18]

The officers and men of the Savannah squadron, except those with Hunter at Augusta, walked to Hardeesville, caught the train to Charleston, and joined the squadron there. Sherman allowed them only a brief respite, however; on February 1, 1865, his army turned north through South Carolina. The drama that followed was a repetition of what had happened in Savannah. Hardee was in command of the city's defenses under Beauregard

15. The Savannah River could not be used because of the obstructions.

16. *Official Records, Navies,* Ser. I, XVI, 483, 485; Hardee to Beauregard, P. G. T. Beauregard Papers (Duke University Library, Durham, North Carolina); Tucker to Tombs, December 21, 1864, copy in *Confederate Veteran* Magazine File.

17. Robert Watson Diary (Typescript in Cornell University Library, Ithaca, New York); David P. Conyngham, *Sherman's March Through the South* (New York: 1865), 292.

18. Harwell, *A Confederate Marine,* 127–128.

and a conference was held on February 14, where the decision was made that Charleston would have to be evacuated.

The Charleston squadron at that time consisted of several wooden vessels, the flagship *Charleston* (completed in September 1863), *Chicora, Palmetto State,* and *Columbia.* The latter was a recently-completed, powerful vessel armored with six-inch plate. Unfortunately, she ran aground two weeks before the evacuation, broke her back, and remained stranded until repaired by the Union navy. This squadron was probably the most efficient in Confederate naval service; at least it had a relatively high percentage of seamen over conscripts, who were, according to the commanding officer of the *Palmetto State,* well trained and disciplined.[19] The Charleston ironclads apparently had less mechanical trouble than did their counterparts elsewhere. Even so, the squadron received its share of condemnation.

Beauregard, who was unhappy about what he called the "unseaworthy qualities" of the ironclads, blamed the loss of Morris Island on the absence of naval support. He also continued to urge that attacks be made on *New Ironsides* and the monitors, but the virtual uselessness of the Confederate vessels for offensive action caused Flag Officer Tucker wisely to resist the pressure. Instead, the *Palmetto State, Chicora,* and *Charleston* were used to reinforce the harbor defense. Each night one or more of them anchored in the channel between Forts Moultrie and Sumter. Armed with torpedoes and heavy cannon, they discouraged the Federal fleet from making a serious attack after the April 1863 engagement.[20] Even with the end in sight and self-destruction of his ships imminent, Tucker refused a request by President Davis to attack the blockading forces: "I have consulted with General Hardee and Commanding officers of the Squadron and it is decided impractical to make the attack as proposed by you. I have but two ironclads and they are with defective steam power."[21]

The destruction of the ironclads occurred on February 18. The night before, the Confederates destroyed the shipyards, including several experimental torpedo boats, an ironclad on the stocks, and another one recently

19. Rochelle to Scharf, January 12, 1887, in the James H. Rochelle folder, BZ File.

20. For offensive operations Tucker relied on torpedo craft called "Davids" as well as the submarine *Hunley.* A number of Davids were nearly ready for operation when Charleston was surrendered.

21. *Official Records,* Ser. I, XLVII, pt. 2, 1022; Davis to Tucker, January 15, 1865, *Jefferson Davis,* VI, 448–449. See also Rochelle, *Tucker,* 48; Bradlee, *A Forgotten Chapter,* 24; Roman, *Beauregard,* II, 98; Dahlgren, *Memoirs,* 586–587.

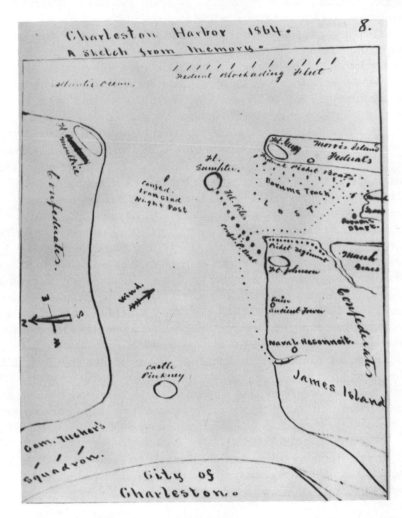

FIGURE 13

Map of Operations in Charleston Harbor drawn by Lieutenant Charles Borum, CSN.

launched. In the middle of the morning the three ironclads in the harbor—one by one—were blown up. "The explosions were terrific," the Charleston *Daily Courier* reported. "Pieces of the iron plate, red hot, fell on the wharves and set them on fire. . . . Tremendous clouds of smoke went up forming beautiful wreaths." Union forces were actually moving in to occupy the city when the detonations took place. An officer on one of the Federal warships recalled: "[it was] one of the grandest sights I can remember . . . apparently the whole upper works and deck were blown upwards into the air, where they appeared to float for an instant, then fall in the wild rice in the shallow water of the harbor."[22]

On George Washington's birthday—three days after Charleston surrendered—Wilmington fell to Federal troops advancing up the Cape Fear River from Fort Fisher. With the destruction of the navy there (no ironclads except one on the stocks), the only remaining Confederate warship in North Carolina was the *Neuse* in the Neuse River near Kinston. She had been operational since the early fall of 1864 but had remained stranded and helpless because of the strongly defended obstructions at the mouth of the Neuse and the fact that troops were not available to co-operate with her.

Early in March, Sherman's army crossed into North Carolina, at the same time that a Union force under General Jacob D. Cox was advancing from Wilmington in the direction of Goldsboro. On March 9, General Bragg ordered the evacuation of Kinston. The *Neuse* was to cover the army's retreat and "if practicable, before sacrificing, [she was] to move down the river by way of diversion, and make the loss . . . as costly to the enemy as possible." This was impossible because of the lack of coal and provisions; after shelling Union cavalry for a short period, the crew spiked the guns, set her on fire, and abandoned ship. She was supposed to blow up when the fire reached her magazine, but a loaded gun discharged, blowing a hole in her below the water line, and within a few minutes she sank in shallow water.

The morale of the southern people, like that of the army, had held up well until the summer of 1863 (the summer of Gettysburg and Vicksburg), fluctuated for the next year, and rapidly deteriorated after the fall of 1864. This defeatism inevitably affected the navy. A sailor, who ended up at Wilmington after he lost one ship at Savannah and another at Charleston, described in his diary the declining morale of his officers. On January 27 he wrote, "Officers are drunk and drilling us for their amusements. If these things continue much longer I shall certainly desert." Two days later he noted, "officers fiddling, dancing and drinking whiskey all day and nearly all night."[23] Although this sailor did not desert as he threatened, hundreds of

22. Robert Brand, "Reminiscences of the blockade off Charleston, S.C.," in *Papers read before the Wisconsin Commandery of the Loyal Legion of the United States*, II, 31.
23. Watson Diary.

his fellow seamen did in those last weeks. Semmes mentions in his diary that "boat loads" defected from the James River Squadron. The admiral took command of this squadron in the middle of February 1865 and found it "as much demoralized as the army." He added, "great discontent and restlessness prevails . . . constant applications . . . coming in for leave of absence."[24]

Inactivity contributed to the decline in morale. During the six weeks that Semmes commanded the ships in the James River, the squadron remained anchored at Richmond or near the obstructions below the city. Except for picket duty with small boats and launches, no hostile contact was made with the enemy.

On April 2, while Jefferson Davis was in his pew at St. Paul's Episcopal Church, he received a note from General Lee that Richmond must be abandoned. Late that afternoon, Semmes was having dinner on the *Virginia* when a messenger arrived from the Navy Department. "Not knowing the importance of the matter I delayed him until I finished dinner," he later wrote. The message ordered the destruction of his squadron. Before nightfall Mallory's orders were read to his assembled captains, who then hurriedly returned to their vessels, got under way, and proceeded to Drewry's Bluff.

The three ironclads in the squadron, *Virginia II, Richmond,* and *Fredericksburg,* were anchored, and after the crews took to the boats, the torch was applied. The remaining vessels—all wooden gunboats—picked up the crews and steamed back to the doomed capital. The gunboats had not gone far "before an explosion, like the shock of an earthquake, took place, and the air was filled with missiles," wrote Semmes in his *Memoirs.* "It was the blowing up of the *Virginia,* the late flag-ship. The spectacle was grand beyond description. Her shell rooms had been full of loaded shells. The explosion of the magazine threw all these shells, with their fuses lighted into the air. The fuses were of different lengths, and as the shells exploded by twos and threes, and by the dozens, the pyrotechnic effect was very fine."[25] The crews of the James River Squadron joined sailors from Drewry's Bluff, Richmond, and other stations and squadrons in Lee's last march. They surrendered after being cut off on April 6.

On that cheerless April day when Richmond was lost to the Confed-

24. Raphael Semmes Diary, 1865 (Duke University Library, Durham, North Carolina); Semmes, *Memoirs,* 803–804.
25. *Ibid.,* 811–812. See also A. O. Wright, "Destruction of the Fleet," *Record of the Confederate Navy,* I (1925), 8–10.

eracy, a force of Union cavalry under General James H. Wilson occupied Selma, Alabama, after a brief fight. The extensive naval works, including the gun foundry, had already been destroyed by the retreating Confederates. Wilson's raiders continued across the state, reaching the Chattahoochee River in the vicinity of Columbus, Georgia, about the middle of April. The Columbus Naval Iron Works, where machinery for ironclads and gunboats was manufactured, was partially destroyed, along with the ironclad *Jackson* built there.

The *Jackson* (originally the *Muscogee*) was laid down in the fall of 1862. Her design was unusual—a short hull with a casemate covering the entire length, powered by a center wheel. By the beginning of 1864 she was ready to be launched, but efforts to float her failed—her draft was too deep even during flood waters. She was then completely rebuilt; her hull was lengthened, casemate shortened, and a new power plant installed (including two propellers in place of the wheel). Another year passed, and she was nearly finished when Wilson's force advancing on the city resulted in her destruction. She was fired and set adrift to sink.[26]

Mobile fell while Wilson was on the way from Selma to Columbus. After the naval victory in Mobile Bay, followed by the capture of Forts Gaines and Morgan, nearly six months elapsed before Federal forces began to advance on the city of Mobile. Adequate troops had not been available, and the Federals felt no pressure to occupy the city, since control of the bay already effectively sealed the port from blockade-runners. The defeat of Hood's army by Thomas before Nashville in the middle of December freed a sufficient number of troops for such a movement, however, and on January 18, 1865, Grant ordered General E. R. S. Canby to take the city. Canby organized his force of about 45,000 men into two columns; one under General Frederick Steele would advance by way of Pensacola, and the other under Canby would move from Dauphin Island by way of the eastern shore of the bay.

Confederate military forces in the Mobile area consisted of approximately 10,000 men under General Dabney H. Maury. Nearly 5,000 manned

26. For the *Jackson's* construction see miscellaneous letters in the Gift Papers; Jones Papers, National Archives Record Group 45; Columbus *Inquirer,* December 21, 1863, January 1, March 16, 1864; Columbus *Daily Sun,* December 23, 1864; Gift to Governor John Milton of Florida, May 4, 1863, John Milton Letterbooks (Florida Hisorical Society Collection, University of South Florida, Tampa); Milton to Seddon, May 10, 1863, Milton Letterbooks; Yulee to Milton, May 23, 1863, Milton Letterbooks. For her destruction see *Official Records,* Ser. I, XLIX, pt. 2, 383; James H. Wilson, *Under the Old Flag,* II, 265.

two forts located to block Canby's two columns. Spanish Fort, directly across the bay from Mobile, consisted of three redoubts connected by rifle pits and backed up by artillery; Fort Blakely was three miles north of Spanish Fort at the junction of the Appalachee and Tensaw rivers. The city's defense also included the naval squadron under Flag Officer Ebenezer Farrand.

On March 27, Spanish Fort was besieged by the Union force from Dauphin Island; four days later Steele's mud-spattered troops reached Blakely. For nearly two weeks the two forts held out under heavy rifle and artillery fire. Naval support from the Confederate ironclads and gunboats was very effective, particularly against the bluecoats investing Blakely. The ships gave some fire support to Spanish Fort, but the vessels could not operate in the bay, and river obstructions prevented their moving into close range. The *Nashville* and *Huntsville* were able to navigate the Tensaw River to a position halfway between the forts. From there they shelled Union troops on the left flank of Spanish Fort and on the right flank of Blakely. Steele's troops were severely mauled by fire from the gunboats' batteries. He later wrote in his report, "The enemy's gunboats *Huntsville, Nashville,* and *Morgan,* took position in Tensaw River opposite Hawkin's right, and, with occasional intervals, kept up a constant fire night and day, which was very harassing and destructive. . . ."[27] Canby could do very little about the Confederate vessels; Union ships were unable to enter the river, and artillery fire, although accurate, caused little damage. Nevertheless, Spanish Fort fell on April 8; Blakely fell the following day. Supporting fire was noticeably absent the last two days because the vessels were nearly out of ammunition and a large percentage of the remaining shells were defective.

The capture of the two forts cleared the way to Mobile. Shortly before noon on April 12, Mayor R. H. Slough drove to the city limits in his carriage and yielded the city to advancing Federal troops. The Mobile Squadron was not surrendered, however. After sinking the *Huntsville* and *Tuscaloosa* in

27. *Official Records,* Ser. I, XLIX, pt. 1, 283. There is no mention of the *Tuscaloosa* in the reports concerning the operations around the two forts, and we can only assume that she was not operational at the time. The *Baltic* was decommissioned. See also the detailed report of Captain Bennett of the *Nashville* in *Official Records,* Ser. I, XLIX, pt. 2, 319–322; Smith, *Mobile 1861–65,* 40–42; Dabney N. Maury, "Defense of Mobile in 1865," *Southern Historical Society Papers,* III (1877), 1–13; Richard Irwin, "Land Operations Against Mobile," *Battles and Leaders,* IV, 410–411; Liddell to Gibson, April 6, 1865, Department of East Gulf Records, National Archives Record Group 109; Jennie M. Walker, *Life of Captain Joseph Fry: The Cuban Martyr,* 179–180; Waring, *Journal,* 9–13; C. C. Andrews, *History of the Campaign of Mobile including the Cooperative Operations of General Wilson's Cavalry in Alabama,* 167–168.

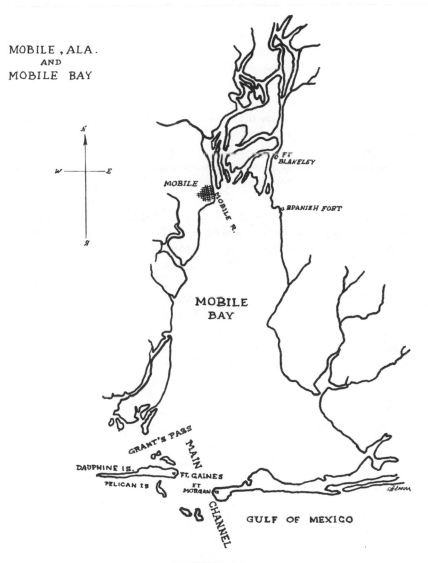

FIGURE 14

the Spanish River because they were unable to stem the current, Farrand took the remainder of his small force up the Alabama River and into the Tombigbee. They went up as far as Nanna Hubba Bluffs, and there they awaited developments. Commodore Henry K. Thatcher, who had replaced Farragut in command of the West Gulf Blockading Squadron, sent up a couple of monitors to watch the Confederate vessels but made no attempt to attack them. Finally, on May 8, nearly a month after Appomattox, Farrand surrendered to the Union naval officer.[28]

The Confederate home-water navy was down but not quite out. One lonely ironclad remained of the many that had been built during the preceding four years. This was the ironclad *Missouri* marooned up the Red River at Alexandria, Louisiana. The ironclad had remained at Shreveport until the waters in the river began to rise early in 1865. At the end of March, the vessel had enough water under her keel to steam down the river. Lieutenant Jonathan Carter, her commanding officer, wrote enthusiastically to General Simon B. Buckner, "I will . . . be pleased to welcome you on the deck of the *Missouri* when we arrive at Grand Encore. . . . I hope to be a valuable [addition] . . . to your forces defending the valley."[29] On April 8, the ironclad reached the rapids above Alexandria and anchored in position to co-operate with forts located on both sides of the river. There she remained —waiting. April passed, with the news of General Lee's surrender. May passed, and the last Confederate forces east of the Mississippi laid down their arms. Finally on June 3, Carter surrendered his vessel to a Union naval officer and accepted parole for his officers and men. Although the *Missouri* never fired a shot in anger against an enemy, she did have the distinction of being the last Confederate ironclad (perhaps vessel) to surrender in home waters.

28. The *Nashville, Baltic, Morgan,* and the steamers *Black Diamond* and *Southern Republic* were surrendered. Waterman, "Notable Events of the Civil War," IX, 25–26; Richard Taylor, *Destruction and Reconstruction,* 225–226; Thatcher to Welles, West Gulf Coast Blockading Squadron Letterbook, National Archives Record Group 45; Bennett to Littlepage, May 31, 1899, Bennett folder, BZ File.

29. Carter to Buckner, March 30, 1865, Carter Correspondence Book, National Archives Record Group 45.

14

Conclusion

IN A letter written two years after the end of the war, Mallory assessed the brief career of the Confederate navy:

I am satisfied that, with the means at our control and in view of the overwhelming force of the enemy at the outset of the struggle, our little navy accomplished more than could have been looked or hoped for; and if I have ever felt any surprise connected with its operations, it was that we accomplished so much. Our Navy alone kept those of the United States from reaching Richmond by the James river, and from reaching Savannah and Charleston; and yet, not ten men in ten thousand of the country, knew or appreciated these facts. . . .[1]

The former naval secretary's judgment of public opinion was only too true; not only did most Southerners—and probably most Northerners—consider the Confederate naval effort a failure, but most historians as well. This was particularly true of the ironclad program.

Most historians base this on the two assumptions that the program was designed to break the Union blockade and that relatively few of the vessels reached operational status.[2] It is true that the five initial ironclads were built in order to raise the blockade, but from the summer of 1862 until the end of the conflict construction concentrated on ironclads for river and harbor defense.

It is also true that only a limited number of these ironplated vessels was ever completed. Approximately fifty ironclads were laid down or contracted for within the Confederacy, and twenty-two of these were commissioned and placed in operation.[3] From the beginning, efforts to build warships

1. Mallory to Rochelle, May 21, 1867, James H. Rochelle Papers (Duke University Library, Durham, North Carolina).

2. Baxter, *Ironclad Warship,* 237; Durkin, *Mallory,* 155; Anderson, *By Sea and by River,* 300–301.

3. The ships commissioned were the *Albemarle, Arkansas, Atlanta, Baltic, Chicora, Charleston, Fredericksburg, Georgia, Huntsville, Manassas, Missouri, Nashville, Neuse, North Carolina, Palmetto State, Raleigh, Richmond, Savannah, Tennessee, Tuscaloosa, Virginia,* and *Virginia II.* The *Columbia* and *Jackson* which were completed but not placed in operation should perhaps be included here.

within the Confederacy were characterized by frustration. Raw materials essential for ironclad construction were usually available, but they could not be utilized because of a lack of transportation and because of the absence of adequate facilities to convert the materials into finished products. A chronic shortage of skilled labor seriously hampered naval building, although the problem was primarily the result of mishandling the available manpower. But when all factors are considered, the one that stands out is time. Materials needed to complete vessels were delayed because facilities were destroyed or had to be moved in the face of advancing enemy forces. Time and time again uncompleted ironclads were destroyed to prevent their being captured.

The year 1862 proved to be significant in the Confederate shipbuilding program. Although five ironclads were laid down or were being converted in 1861, it was the first *Virginia*'s performance in Hampton Roads and the *Arkansas*'s success against Union naval forces on the Mississippi that resulted in the Confederate government's decision to concentrate on ironclad construction for river and harbor defense. From the summer of 1862 until the end of the war, this remained a major objective of Confederate naval policy.

Since the end of the American Civil War, writers have emphasized the "makeshift" or "homemade" qualities of the Confederate vessels, particularly the ironclads. It has been suggested that Southern officers were realistic enough to see that their "makeshift" warships were no match for the vessels of their opponents, and that this created a sense of futility in attempting to accomplish an almost hopeless task.[4] Undoubtedly the makeshift conditions for shipbuilding in the South gave the ironclads a crude appearance, but as warships they were potentially formidable. Even Union officers generally agreed with this. Their greatest defects were mechanical: they lacked speed, were difficult to handle, and were frequently inoperable—all the result of inadequate and unreliable machinery. They were, however, adequately armored and armed. All in all, they were serviceable vessels and contributed to the Confederate war effort.

Just how much they contributed to the war effort—dominated generally by the strategy of defense—is difficult to determine. The presence of the first *Virginia* and later the James River Squadron prevented Union naval forces from gaining control of important stretches of the James River, a factor which played no small part in the Peninsular Campaign. The *Albemarle* threatened Union control of the North Carolina Sounds, and in the combined operations

4. Anderson, *By Sea and by River,* 301–302.

against Plymouth in the spring of 1864 she played an important role in the Confederate victory.

In February 1865, Mallory wrote to the chairman of the Senate Naval Affairs Committee,

> though the enemy has for two years had a formidable fleet of heavy ships . . . [including] seven Monitors, off the port of Charleston, with ability in speed and power at all times of night to pass the batteries, obstructions and forts, and to go to the wharves of the city, it was never attempted. Our three ironclads— moveable forts—with formidable batteries . . . were ever present in the harbor with steam up, ready for action. . . . But for them the enemy would have taken [the city]. . . . The same view may [be had] with reference to Savannah and Richmond, where the presence of our iron clads, prevented the enemy's approaches by rivers, and it is equally applicable at Mobile. . . .[5]

The secretary was at least partially correct; the presence of armored vessels did contribute to the reluctance on the part of Union naval officers to assault these ports by frontal attacks.

Throughout the war Union naval commanders had accurate information about the Confederate ironclads—when they would be completed, their performance, their batteries, and so on. At the same time, they overestimated the potential power of these vessels. This exaggeration created or at least contributed to a sometimes unwarranted fear described by contemporary naval officers as "ram fever." It was found in all blockading squadrons and generally affected all commanders, although David D. Porter wrote, "I don't understand the ram fever. I never had it."[6]

Welles claimed that Rear Admiral Goldsborough resigned his command of the North Atlantic Blockading Squadron because of "dread of the new *Merrimac* [*Richmond*] at Richmond. . . ." Captain Charles Wilkes during his brief tenure as commodore of the James River Flotilla was almost constantly expecting an ironclad attack and kept his small force in a state of continuous alarm.[7]

One consequence of this "fever" was the constant demand for monitors by squadron commanders. They shuddered to think what would happen if Confederate ironclads got loose among their wooden blockaders—"paper ships," Du Pont sarcastically called them. During the fall and early winter

5. to Brown, February 18, 1865, organization of the Confederate navy department file, Confederate Subject and Area File, National Archives Record Group 45.
6. to Radford, February 7, 1865, Area 7 file, National Archives Record Group 45.
7. Welles, *Diary,* I, 142; Jefferies, "Civil War Career of Charles Wilkes," 327.

of 1862–63, Du Pont wrote letter after letter to the Navy Department urging that ironclads be sent to reinforce his wooden vessels, and when they were not sent, he complained bitterly to his wife that "Fox . . . while keeping the iron clads all summer . . . to watch *Merrimack No. 2 [Richmond]*, has always pooh poohed those here." He was, of course, relieved when the *New Iron-sides* and two monitors arrived in January, although he wrote confidently, "I never worried . . . but I did feel bad that I could not be in Stono [River] and Ossibaw [Sound] myself at the same moment." One of Du Pont's officers, Commander Charles Steedman of the *Powhatan,* related to his wife an incident of "ram fever" on May 10, 1863:

I was as usual hurried off unexpectedly from Port Royal not allowing me a few hours to finish the necessary repairs on the engines. We have to thank that ass [Commander J. J.] Almy who came down with a cock and bull story about the appearance of Iron clads and Rams off Charleston, all of which had no existence except in his morbid state of mind. . . . I blame the Admiral . . . for permitting himself to be stampeded by men like Almy.[8]

Rear Admiral Dahlgren was not immune to the ailment. Early in June 1863, he recorded these comments in his diary: "I have no more than five monitors to count upon. The Rebels have four—one brand new. So I concluded to call up the *Pawnee* from St. John's. . . ." On June 5 he wrote, "The *Ironsides* was a large object in the view, and her absence is quickly noticed. The Rebels have four iron clads in the harbor. . . . Will they come out?" On December 27, 1864, he joined Sherman for a tour of captured Savannah when he had to return unexpectedly to his squadron. "When just near the General's quarters," he related in his diary, "there was a great rush for me with a dispatch from Charleston from Captain Scott (senior officer there), who hears that the Rebel iron-clads are to come out. . . . I returned at once. . . ."[9] A Master's Mate wrote in his journal, "when I arrived on board [the *Paul Jones*], I found there had been a ram fever. . . . Twice it was reported to the Captain that a rebel steamer accompanied by a ram or turtle back was seen coming down the Stono. . . ."[10]

8. Du Pont to wife, January 18, 1863, Journal Letters; Charles Steedman to wife, May 10, 1863, Charles Steedman Letters (Duke University Library, Durham, North Carolina).

9. Dahlgren, *Memoirs,* 456–457, 489.

10. Journal of George R. Durand, June 8, 1864, (New York Historical Society, New York City). For other examples of "Ram fever," see *Fox Correspondence,* I, 341–342; Philbrick Journal, September 10, 18, 1863, National Archives Record Group 45; Drayton to Hamilton, May 2, 1864, "Naval Letters of . . . Drayton," 654–655; Lewis, *Farragut,* I, 221.

Although "ram fever" was undoubtedly a factor in reducing the offensive spirit of Union naval officers, the danger from heavy cannon and torpedoes was more significant because of the actual damage inflicted.

As "fleets in being," Confederate ironclads also tied down Union vessels as well as large numbers of troops that could have been used elsewhere. Farragut's attack on Mobile was delayed more than a year because the monitors ordered to reinforce his squadron for the operation were held at Charleston; they were supposed to proceed to join him after the attack on the city in April 1863 but did not, primarily because of the presence of Confederate armored vessels there and at Savannah. In fact, he never did receive the monitors originally ordered to him.

Of the five seaports—Savannah, Charleston, Wilmington, Mobile, and Galveston—taken in the last six months of the war, two were taken by land forces from the rear, and two indirectly as a result of pressure from the rear. In all of the cities but one, Galveston, the Confederate navy had ironclads as part of the harbor defense. If time had allowed, the Confederate ironclads might have made a more significant contribution to the Southern war effort. As it was, they certainly achieved some success in the over-all strategy of defense.

Bibliographic Essay

Confederate naval history has not been adequately covered by serious students of the Civil War, apparently because it is believed that relevant manuscript material is nonexistent. The assumption that there is a lack of manuscripts is based primarily on the fact that the archives of the Confederate Navy Department were destroyed at the end of the war. When the *Official Records of the Union and Confederate Navies in the War of the Rebellion* were published, this belief was furthered because of the paucity of Confederate documents included. This has resulted in unfortunately little monographic work on this aspect of Civil War history, but in fact there is a great deal of manuscript material available.

The most important single source is in the National Archives in Washington, D.C. Two branches, the War Records and the Legal and Fiscal Records, house this material. Within the War Records Branch, two sections, the Navy and the Old Army, hold Confederate records.

Record Group 45 (Naval Records Collection of the Office of Naval Records and Library) includes Confederate naval documents. Until recently a majority of them were integrated with records (official and unofficial) of the United States Navy in various categories. These documents have now been separated, however, and form a category known as "the Confederate Subject and Area File." Apart from this file, Confederate material in Record Group 45 includes watch, quarter, and station bills; pay rolls; and collections of several Confederate naval officers.

Union naval documents including the Area files (particularly areas five, six, and seven, incorporating generally the eastern and southern coasts of the United States) were consulted. The Stephen C. Rowan and Henry K. Davenport letterbooks, J. C. Gregg diary, William M. Philbrick and Isaac De Graff journals, *Beaumont* diary, and *Weehawken* log, were especially useful.

For the chapter on "characteristics," the drawings and blueprints of Confederate vessels located in Record Group 19 (Bureau of Ships) proved most helpful.

Record Group 109 (War Department Collection of Confederate Records) is located in the Old Army Section. Scattered throughout this mass of documentary material (more than 5,000 cubic feet of records) are hundreds of letters concerning naval matters. Unfortunately, with few exceptions (the vessel file is one), the naval documents are not separately identified and are difficult to find.

For a complete breakdown of the various categories of documents in this record group see the *Preliminary Inventory (Number 101) to the War Department Collection of Confederate Records* (Washington, D. C.: The National Archives, 1957).

Additional Confederate naval material is found in Record Group 365, located in the Legal and Fiscal Branch. This group includes some records of the Confederate Department of the Treasury. Other records of the Treasury Department are located in the Confederate Subject and Area File, Record Group 45. Although the number of records relating to the navy is small, they are important. Included are copies of contracts for the construction of vessels, and other fiscal records concerning naval matters.

When the records which make up Record Group 45 were transferred from the Department of the Navy to the National Archives, some records remained in the custody of the Navy Department. Included are records concerning naval personnel, Confederate as well as United States. Classified under the heading "ZB File," they are housed in the National Archives Building.

The practice of military and naval officers keeping possession of the records of their commands was fortunately followed in the Confederate service. The result is that even though most of the "official archives" of the Navy Department were destroyed, copies of many of the records are available in various depositories. Probably the most important of these depositories are the Virginia Historical Society in Richmond, the library of the University of North Carolina, and the library of Duke University.

By far the most valuable manuscript collections in the Virginia Historical Society are those of John K. Mitchell and the two Minor brothers, Robert and George. The Mitchell papers are both official and unofficial and include his letterbooks while in command of the James River Squadron as well as incoming correspondence while he was in charge of the Bureau of Orders and Detail. Although the records concerning the James River Squadron have been largely reproduced in the *Official Records, Navies,* those to him as Chief of the Bureau have been generally neglected by historians. Nevertheless, they are most enlightening—particularly those from Buchanan and the other station and squadron commanders.

The Minor manuscripts (catalogued under Robert Minor and Minor Family) are voluminous. The collections include letters from a number of fellow naval officers to the brothers, numerous letters from Robert Minor to his wife, copies of letters and reports from Robert Minor to Mallory, and a diary of Robert Minor. The Minor papers constitute an extremely important, and neglected, source for Confederate naval history.

Other collections in the Virginia Historical Society that were useful include the papers of Robert E. Lee and of Charles T. Mason, the latter the engineer in charge of clearing a passage through the obstructions at Drewry's Bluff.

The Southern Historical Collection at the University of North Carolina contains a large number of manuscript holdings concerning Confederate naval history. Those examined and used include the James Albright Diary, Franklin Buchanan Letterbooks, 1861–63 (typescript), William Calder Papers, Francis T. Chew Journal, John H. Comstock Papers, French Forrest Papers (microfilm), Ellen Shackleford Gift Papers, Jeremy F. Gilmer Papers, William A. Graham Papers, Charles I. Graves Papers, Meta Grimball Diary, Henry Hamilton Papers, William A. Hoke Papers, McKay-Stiles Papers, Stephen R. Mallory Diary (typescript), William F. Martin Papers, George A. Mercer Diaries, William P. Miles Papers, Henry Phelon Papers, James Ryder Randall Papers, Dadney M. Scales Diary, Peter Evans Smith Papers, Ruffin Thomson Papers, William V. and James H. Tomb Papers, and the Wirt Family Papers.

Duke University has records of both Union and Confederate naval officers. The Union naval officers' records include the Franklin E. Smith Papers, Charles Steedman Papers, and Louis M. Goldsborough Papers. In the Goldsborough Papers are a number of letters from the flag officer to his wife while he was in command of the North Atlantic Blockading Squadron. His attitudes and actions concerning the *Virginia* are clearly outlined in this correspondence. Collections of Confederate naval officers used are the Francis W. Dawson Papers, John B. Grimball Papers, James H. Rochelle Papers, and a Diary of Raphael Semmes while in command of the James River Squadron in 1865.

Also examined at Duke were the P. G. T. Beauregard Papers, *Confederate Veteran* Magazine File, Confederate States of America Army Archives, miscellaneous officer and soldier letters, George Davis Papers, Jefferson Davis Papers, J. D. B. De Bow Papers, Charles Ellis Papers, Duncan McLaurin Papers, Francis W. Pickens Papers, and the Daniel Ruggles Papers.

From the summer of 1863 until 1865 the commander of the Savannah Squadron was William W. Hunter. Various parts of his official correspondence are at Tulane University, University of Texas, and Emory University. At Emory his papers are catalogued under the title, Savannah Squadron Papers. The Willink Brothers Papers housed at Emory also concern the Savannah Squadron, while the John Roy Diary at Tulane provided some information on the construction of ironclads in New Orleans.

The old *Century* magazine files are in the New York Public Library. A number of letters from Confederate naval officers (as well as other participants on both sides) concerning the series of articles published on the war in the 1880s are in the files. Bartholomew Diggins, "Recollections of the war cruise of the *USS Hartford*, January to December, 1862–1864," and the Percival Drayton Papers were also examined in the library. The Gustavus V. Fox Papers in the New York Historical Society provided insight into the attitudes of Union naval officers towards the Confederate ironclads. James S. Barnes, "My Egotistography," the Journal of George R. Durand while on board the steamer *Paul Jones* on blockade duty off Charleston, and the Henry A. Wise Letterbooks, all in the Society, were useful.

Other manuscript collections utilized are the Richard H. Bacot Papers, the Letterbooks and Correspondence of Governor Zebulon B. Vance, and the North Carolina Adjutant Department Letterbooks, 1861–65, in the Department of Archives and History, Raleigh, North Carolina: the Richard H. Bacot Papers, George H. Bier Papers, and the Mary A. Snowden Papers in the South Caroliniana Library, University of South Carolina, Columbia; the Roland Chambers Diaries, Department of Archives, Louisiana State University; the J. Thomas Scharf Papers, Maryland Historical Society, Baltimore; the John C. Rietti Papers, Daniel Ruggles Papers, and the Mississippi Governor's Papers, 1861–65, in the Department of Archives and History, Jackson, Mississippi; the Charles Ellet Papers, University of Michigan Library, Ann Arbor; the Henry M. Doak Memoirs, and Charles T. Sevier Memoirs in the Tennessee State Library and Archives, Nashville; D. W. Graply Diary, Historical Society of Pennsylvania, Philadelphia; Charles C. Jones Papers in the University of Georgia Library, Athens: Colin J. McRae Papers, the *Baltic* Construction Papers, and the Governor John G. Shorter Papers in the Department of Archives and History, Montgomery, Alabama; Shelby Iron Works Collection, University of Alabama Library, University; the Stephen R. Mallory Papers, University of Florida Library, Gainesville; and the Governor John Milton Letterbooks, Florida Historical Society Collection, University of South Florida, Tampa.

Also examined was the Diary of the *Flag* in the Mariners' Museum, Newport News, Virginia; a folder of manuscripts, "the Drewry's Bluff folder," in the Confederate Museum, Richmond; John Rodgers Papers, Matthew F. Maury Papers, and D. D. Porter Papers, Naval Historical Foundation, Manuscript Division, Library of Congress. The Jones Family Papers are also found in the Manuscripts Division of the Library of Congress; Edward C. Anderson Journal in possession of Mrs. Florence Crane Schwalb, Savannah, Georgia.

The Robert Watson Diary is the only contemporary account written by an enlisted man in the Confederate Navy that has been found. A typescript of this diary is in the Cornell University Library, Ithaca, New York. Part of it has been published in *Kinfolks, A Genealogical and Biographical Record*, ed. William C. Hardlee (3 vols., New Orleans, 1935).

A most valuable collection of papers for appreciating the effect of the ironclads on officers in the South Atlantic Blockading Squadron are the journal letters of Samuel F. Du Pont to his wife, September 1862 to July 1863. The Du Pont papers are located in the Eleutherian Mills Historical Library, Wilmington, Delaware. Typed copies were lent to the author by Rear Admiral John D. Hayes, USN (Ret.), Annapolis, Maryland, who has edited the papers for publication. The papers have since been published and are listed alphabetically in the bibliography that follows.

Bibliography

Acts of the Second Called Session, 1861, and of the First Regular Session General Assembly of Alabama Held in the City of Montgomery. Montgomery: Montgomery Advertiser Book & Job Company, 1862.

Adams, Francis C. *High Old Salts.* Washington, D.C.; Privately printed, 1876.

Alger, F. S. "Congress and the *Merrimac*," *New England Magazine*, XIX (February 1899), 687–693.

Almy, John J. "Incidents of the Blockade," in *War Papers of the Military Order of Loyal Legion, Washington Commandery.* Washington, D.C.: Washington, D.C. Commandery, 1892.

Ammen, Daniel. *The Atlantic Coast.* New York: Charles Scribner's sons, 1883.
———. *The Old Navy and the New.* Philadelphia: J. B. Lippincott Company, 1891.

Anderson, Bern. *By Sea and by River: The Naval History of the Civil War.* New York: Alfred A. Knopf, 1962.
———. "The Naval Strategy of the Civil War," *Military Affairs*, XXVI (Spring, 1962), 11–21.

Andrews, Charles C. *History of the Campaign of Mobile including the Cooperative Operations of General Wilson's Cavalry in Alabama.* New York: D. Van Nostrand & Company, 1867.

Andrews, Matthew P. *The Women of the South in War Time.* Baltimore: The Norman, Remington Company, 1920.

Baldwin, H. D. "Farragut in Mobile Bay, Recollections of One Who Took Part in the Battle," *Scribner's Monthly*, XIII (February, 1877), 542.

Barrett, John F. *The Civil War in North Carolina.* Chapel Hill: University of North Carolina Press, 1963.

Barthell, Edward E. Jr. *The Mystery of the Merrimack.* Muskegon, Michigan: Dana Printing Company, 1959.

Batcheller, Oliver A. "The Battle of Mobile Bay," *Magazine of History*, XIV (December 1911), 217–230.

Batton, John M. *Random Thoughts.* Pittsburgh: Privately printed, 1896.

Baxter, James P., III. *The Introduction of the Ironclad Warship.* Cambridge: Harvard University Press, 1933.

Bearss, Edwin C. *Rebel Victory at Vicksburg.* Vicksburg: Vicksburg Centennial Commemoration Commission, 1963.

————. "The Battle of Baton Rouge," *Louisiana Historical Quarterly,* XXXXV (Winter, 1962), 77–128.

————. "The Fiasco at Head of Passes," *Louisiana Historical Quarterly,* XXXXVI (Fall, 1963), 301–311.

Beauregard, P. G. T. "Defense of Charleston, South Carolina," *North American Review,* CXLVI (May, 1886), 419–450.

Belknap, George E. "Reminiscences of the Siege of Charleston," in *Naval Actions and History, 1799–1898. Papers of the Military Historical Society of Massachusetts.* Vol. XII. Boston: Griffith-Stillings Press, 1902.

Besse, S. B. *C. S. Ironclad Virginia, with data and References for a Scale Model.* Newport News: The Mariners' Museum, 1937.

Bill, Alfred H. *The Beleagured City: Richmond 1861–1865.* New York: Alfred A. Knopf, 1946.

Black, Robert C. *The Railroads of the Confederacy.* Chapel Hill: University of North Carolina Press, 1952.

Boyer, Samuel P. *Naval Surgeon: Blockading the South,* ed. Elinor Barnes and James A. Barnes, Bloomington, Indiana: Indiana University Press, 1963.

Bradlee, Francis B. *A Forgotten Chapter in Our Naval History: A Sketch of the Career of Duncan N. Ingraham.* Salem, Mass.: The Essex Institute, 1923.

Brand, Robert. "Reminiscences of the blockade off Charleston, S. C.," in *Papers read before the Wisconsin Commandery of the Loyal Legion of the United States.* Vol. II. Madison: Wisconsin Commandery, 1890.

Brooke, John Mercer. "The *Virginia* or *Merrimac:* Her Real Projector," *Southern Historical Society Papers,* XIX (January 1891), 3–34.

Brooke, George M. Jr. "John Mercer Brooke," 2 vols.; Chapel Hill: Unpublished Ph.D. dissertation, University of North Carolina, 1955.

Browne, Samuel T. "First Cruise of the *Montauk,*" in *Papers of the Soldiers and Sailors Historical Society of Rhode Island.* Providence: the Society, 1879.

Bruce, Kathleen. *Virginia Iron Manufacture in the Slave Era.* New York: The Century Company, 1931.

Bulloch, James D. *The Secret Service of the Confederate States in Europe.* 2 vols.; London: Richard Bentley & Sons, 1883.

Burgess, George W. "The ram *Arkansas* and the battle of Baton Rouge," *East and West Baton Rouge Historical Society Proceedings,* II, 34–37.

Butler, Benjamin. *Butler's Book.* Boston: A. M. Thayer & Company, 1882.

————. *Private and Official Correspondence of General Benjamin F. Butler during the Period of the Civil War.* 5 vols.; Norwood, Mass., Privately Issued, 1917.

Butler, Edward D. "Personal experiences in the navy, 1862–65," in *Papers read before the Maine Commandery of the Loyal Legion of the United States.* Vol. II. Augusta: Maine Commandery, 1899.

Bryan, T. Conn. *Confederate Georgia.* Athens: University of Georgia Press, 1953.

Canfield, Eugene B. *Notes on Naval Ordnance of the American Civil War, 1861–1865.* Washington, D.C.: The American Ordnance Association, 1960.

Capers, Gerald M. Jr. *The Biography of a River Town.* Chapel Hill: University of North Carolina Press, 1939.

Castlen, Harriet. *Hope Bids Me Onward.* Savannah: Chatham Printing Company, 1945.

Catton, Bruce. "When the *Monitor* Met the *Merrimac*," *New York Times Magazine* (March 4, 1962).

Cauthen, Charles C. *South Carolina Goes to War, 1860–1865.* Chapel Hill: University of North Carolina Press, 1950.

Chandler, Walter. "The Memphis Navy Yard," *West Tennessee Historical Papers* I (1947), 68–72.

Charleston, South Carolina: The Centennial of Incorporation, 1883. Charleston: The News and Courier Book Press, 1884.

Charleston *Courier*, 1861–65.

Charleston *Mercury*, 1862–64.

Chesnut, Mary B. *A Diary from Dixie.* Boston: Houghton Mifflin Company, 1949.

Civil War Naval Chronology, 1861–1865. 6 vols.; Washington, D.C.: Government Printing Office, 1961–1966.

Clark, Charles E. *My Fifty Years in the Navy.* Boston: Little, Brown, and Company, 1917.

Clark, Walter, ed. *North Carolina Regiments, 1861–1865.* 5 vols.; Goldsboro, North Carolina: Nash Brothers, Printers, 1901.

Clayton, William F. *A Narrative of the Confederate States Navy.* Weldon, North Carolina: Harrell's Printing House, 1910.

Cline, William R. "The Ironclad Ram *Virginia*," *Southern Historical Society Papers*, XXXII (December 1904), 243–249.

Columbus (Georgia) *Inquirer*. 1861–64.

Columbus (Georgia) *Sun*. 1861–64.

Coleman, Silas B. "A July Morning with the Rebel Ram *Arkansas*." *A Paper Prepared and Read before the Michigan Commandery of the Military Order of the Loyal Legion of the United States.* Detroit: The Michigan Commandery, 1890.

Conrad, Daniel B. "Capture of the C. S. Ram *Tennessee* in Mobile Bay, August 1864," *Southern Historical Society Papers*, XIX (November 1890), 72–82.

Conyngham, David P. *Sherman's March Through the South.* New York: Sheldon & Company, 1865.

Coulter, E. Merton. *The Confederate States of America, 1861–1865.* Vol. VII of *A History of the South.* ed. by W. H. Stephenson and E. Merton Coulter. 8 vols.; Baton Rouge: Louisiana State University Press, 1950–1951.

Cowley, Charles. *Leaves from a Lawyer's Life Afloat and Ashore.* Boston: Lee & Chepard, 1879.

Crandall, W. D. and I. D. Newell. *History of the Ram Fleet and the Mississippi Marine Brigade.* St. Louis: Privately printed, 1907.

Dahlgren, Madeleine V. *Memoir of John A. Dahlgren.* Boston: J. R. Osgood & Company, 1882.

Daly, Robert W., ed. *Aboard the USS Monitor: 1862: The Letters of Acting Paymaster William Frederick Keeler, U.S. Navy to his Wife, Anna.* Annapolis: United States Naval Institute, 1964.

————. *How the Merrimac Won.* New York: Crowell, 1957.

Davis, Charles H. Jr. *Life of Charles Henry Davis Rear Admiral 1807–1877.* New York: Houghton, Mifflin and Company, 1899.

Davis, Charles S. *Colin J. McRae: Confederate Financial Agent.* Tuscaloosa, Alabama: Confederate Publishing Company, 1961.

Davis, Robert. *History of the Rebel Steam Ram Atlanta with an Interesting Account of the Engagement which Resulted in Her Capture.* Philadelphia: by the author, 1863.

Dawson, Sarah. *A Confederate Girl's Diary.* Boston: Houghton-Mifflin Company, 1913.

DeLeon, Thomas C. *Four Years in Rebel Capitals.* Mobile: Gossip Printing Company, 1892.

————. *Belles, Beaux and Brains of the 60's.* New York: G. W. Dillingham Company, 1909.

Demaree, Albert L. "Our Navy's Worst Headache The *Merrimack*," United States *Naval Institute Proceedings,* LXXVIII (March 1962), 66–83.

Dew, Charles B. *Ironmaker to the Confederacy: Joseph R. Anderson and the Tredegar Iron Works.* New Haven: Yale University Press, 1966.

Dewey, George. *Autobiography of George Dewey, Admiral of the Navy.* New York: Charles Scribner's Sons, 1916.

Dictionary of American Fighting Ships. Washington, D.C.: Government Printing Office, 1963, Vol. II.

Drayton, Percival. "Naval Letters from Captain Percival Drayton, 1861–65," *New York Public Library Bulletin,* X (November-December 1906), 587–625.

Dufour, Charles L. *The Night the War Was Lost.* Garden City: Doubleday, 1960.

————. "The Night the War was Lost: the Fall of New Orleans; Causes, Consequences, Culpabilities," *Louisiana Historical Quarterly,* XXXIV (Spring, 1961), 157–176.

Durkin, Joseph T. *Stephen R. Mallory: Confederate Navy Chief.* Chapel Hill: University of North Carolina Press, 1954.

Eaton, Clement. *A History of the Southern Confederacy.* New York: The Macmillan Company, 1954.

Eggleston, John R. "Captain Eggleston's Narrative of the Battle of the *Merrimac*," *Southern Historical Society Papers,* XLI (September 1916), 166–178.

————. "The Navy of the Confederate States," *Confederate Veteran,* XV (October 1917), 449–459.

Evans, Cerinda W. "A Biographical Sketch of Robert Baker Pegram, 1811–1894, Lieutenant, U.S. Navy, Captain, C.S. Navy" (typed copy; The Mariner's Museum, Newport News, Virginia).

Evans, Clement A. *Confederate Military History.* 12 vols.; Atlanta: Confederate Publishing Company, 1899.

Federal Circuit and District Court Reports. Case No. 619. St. Paul, Minnesota: 1894.

Flatau, L. S. "A Great Naval Battle," *Confederate Veteran* (XXV (October 1917) 458–459.

Fornell, Earl W. "Mobile During the Blockade," *Alabama Historical Quarterly* XXIII (Spring 1961), 29–43.

————. "Confederate Seaport Strategy," *Civil War History,* II (December 1956), 61–68.

Foute, R. C. "Echoes from Hampton Roads," *Southern Historical Society Papers* XIX (January 1891), 246–251.

Franklin, S. R. *Memories of a Rear Admiral.* New York: Harper & Brothers, 1892.

Freeman, Douglas S., ed. *A Calendar of Confederate Papers.* Richmond: The Confederate Memorial Library, 1908.

Gift, George W. "The Story of the *Arkansas,*" *Southern Historical Society Papers,* XII (January-May 1884), 48–54, 115–119, 163–170, 205–212.

Girard, Charles. *A Visit to the Confederate States of America.* ed. W. Stanley Hoole. Tuscaloosa, Alabama: Confederate Publishing Company, 1962.

Gleaves, Albert. *Life and Letters of Rear Admiral Stephen B. Luce.* New York: G. P. Putnam's Sons, 1925.

Gosnell, A. Allen. *Guns on the Western Waters: The Story of River Gunboats in the Civil War.* Baton Rouge: Louisiana State University Press, 1949.

Grant, Richard S., "Captain William Sharp of Norfolk, Virginia, U.S.N.-C.S.N.," *Virginia Magazine of History and Biography,* XLVII (January 1949), 44–54.

Grant, Ulysses, S. *Personal Memoirs.* 2 vols. New York: Charles L. Webster & Company, 1885–1886.

Hackett, Frank W. *Deck and Field.* Washington, D.C.: W. H. Lowdermilk & Company, 1909.

Harwell, Richard, ed. *A Confederate Marine.* Tuscaloosa, Alabama: Confederate Publishing Company, 1963.

Hayes, John D. "Sea Power in the Civil War," *United States Naval Institute Proceedings,* LXXVII (November 1961), 60–69.

————. "Captain Fox—He is the Navy Department," *United States Naval Institute Proceedings.* LXXXI (September 1965), 64–71.

————, ed. *Samuel Francis Du Pont: A Selection From His Civil War Letters.* 3 vols.; Ithaca; Cornell University Press, 1969.

Heslin, James I., ed. "Two New Yorkers in the Union Navy: Narrative Based on Letters of the Collins Brothers," *New York Historical Society Quarterly,* XLIII (April 1959), 161–201.

Hill, Frederick S. *Twenty Years at Sea.* New York: Houghton, Mifflin & Company, 1893.

Hinds County *Gazette* (Raymond, Mississippi), December 9, 1874.

Holden, Edgar. "The *Sassacus* and the *Albemarle*," *Magazine of History,* V (May 1907), 266–274.

Hopley, Catherine C. *Life in the South.* 2 vols.; London: Chapman and Hall, 1863.

House, Boyce. "Confederate Naval Hero Puts the Flag Back in Place," *Tennessee Historical Quarterly,* XIX (June 1960), 172–175.

Hughes, Nathaniel C. Jr. *General William J. Hardee: Old Reliable.* Baton Rouge: Louisiana State University Press, 1965.

Hunter, Lewis C. *Steamboats on the Western Rivers.* Cambridge: Harvard University Press, 1949.

Hutchinson, William F. "The Bay Fight, a Sketch of the Battle of Mobile Bay, August 5, 1864," in *Papers of the Soldiers and Sailors Historical Society of Rhode Island.* Providence: the Society, 1879.

Jeffries, William W. "The Civil War Career of Charles Wilkes," *Journal of Southern History,* XI (August 1945), 324–348.

Johnson, Allen and Dumas Malone, eds. *The Dictionary of American Biography* 22 vols.; New York: Charles Scribner's Sons, 1928–1937.

Johnson, John. *The Defense of Charleston Harbor including Forts Sumter and the adjacent Islands 1863–1865.* Charleston: Walker, Evans & Cogswell Company, 1890.

Johnston, James D. "Fight in Mobile Bay," *Southern Historical Society Papers,* IX (December 1881), 471–476.

Johnson, Robert U. and Clarence C. Buel, eds. *Battles and Leaders of the Civil War.* 4 vols.; New York: The Century Company, 1884–1888.

Jones, Archer. *Confederate Strategy from Shiloh to Vicksburg.* Baton Rouge: Louisiana State University Press, 1961.

Jones, Catesby ap R. "Services of the *Virginia*," *Southern Historical Society Papers,* XI (January 1883), 65–75.

Jones, Charles C. Jr. *The Life and Services of Commodore Josiah Tattnall.* Savannah: Morning News Steam Printing House, 1878.

Jones, John B. *A Rebel War Clerk's Diary at the Confederate States Capital.* Philadelphia: J. B. Lippincott & Company, 1866.

Jones, Samuel. *The Siege of Charleston and Operations off the South Atlantic Coast.* New York: The Neale Publishing Company, 1911.

Jones, T. Catesby. "The Iron-Clad *Virginia*," *Virginia Magazine of History and Biography*, XLIX (October 1941), 297–303.

Jones, Virgil C. *The Civil War at Sea*. 3 vols.; New York: Holt, Rinehart, and Winston, 1960–1962.

Journal of the Congress of the Confederate States of America, 1861–65. 7 vols.; Washington, D.C.: Government Printing Office, 1904.

Journal of the Convention of the People of South Carolina, held in 1860, 61, and 1862 together with the Ordinances, Reports, Resolutions, etc. Columbia: R. W. Gibbs, Printer, 1863.

Kean, Robert C. *Inside the Confederate Government*. ed. Edward Younger. New York: Oxford University Press, 1957.

Kell, John M. *Recollections of a Naval Life*. Washington, D.C.: The Neale Company, 1900.

Kendall, John S. "Recollections of a Confederate Officer," *Louisiana Historical Quarterly*, XXIX (October 1946), 1041–1240.

———. *History of New Orleans*. 3 vols.; Chicago: The Lewis Publishing Company, 1922.

Kendricken, Paul H. *Memoirs of Paul Henry Kendricken*. Boston: Privately printed, 1910.

Kimmel, Stanley. *Mr. Davis's Richmond*. New York: Coward-McCann, Inc., 1958.

Knox, Dudley W. "River Navies in the Civil War," *Military Affairs*, VIII (Spring, 1954), 29–32.

Kollock, Susan M., ed. "Kollock Letters," *Georgia Historical Quarterly*, XXXIV (September 1950), 241–243, 36–62.

Labree, Ben., ed. *Camp Fires of the Confederacy*. Louisville: Courier-Journal Press, 1899.

Lawrence, Alexander A. *A Present for Mr. Lincoln, the Story of Savannah from Secession to Sherman*. Macon: Ardivan Press, 1961.

Laws of the State of Mississippi passed at a Regular session of the Mississippi Legislature held in the city of Jackson, November and December, 1861. Jackson: Cooper and Kimball, Printers, 1862.

Lewis, Charles L. *David Glasgow Farragut*. 2 vols.; Annapolis: United States Naval Institute, 1941–1943.

———. *Admiral Franklin Buchanan*. Baltimore: The Norman, Remington Company, 1929.

Longstreet, James. *From Manassas to Appomattox*. Philadelphia: J. B. Lippincott & Company, 1895.

Lonn, Ella. *Foreigners in the Confederate Army and Navy*. Chapel Hill: University of North Carolina Press, 1940.

MacClean, Malcolm. "The Short Cruise of the *C.S.S. Atlanta*, "*Georgia Historical Quarterly*, XL (June 1956), 130–143.

McClinton, Oliver W. "The Career of the Confederate States Ram *Arkansas*," *Arkansas Historical Quarterly,* VII (Winter, 1948), 329–333.

Maffitt, Emma. *The Life and Services of John Newland Maffitt.* New York: The Neale Publishing Company, 1906.

Maffitt, Emma M. "The Confederate Navy," *Confederate Veteran,* XXV (April–July 1917), 157–158, 217–218, 264–265, 315–316.

Maguire, John F. *The Irish in America.* London: E. & F. Spon, 1868.

Mahan, Alfred. T. *The Gulf and Inland Waters.* New York: Charles Scribner's Sons, 1883.

Martin, John L. "A Great Naval Battle," *Confederate Veteran,* XLI (March 1923), 93.

Maury, Dabney N. "Defense of Mobile in 1865," *Southern Historical Society Papers,* III (January-June 1877), 1–13.

Melvin, Philip. "Stephen Russell Mallory, Naval Statesman," *Journal of Southern History,* X (May 1944), 137–160.

Merrill, James M. *The Rebel Shore: The Story of Union Sea Power in the Civil War.* Boston: Little, Brown & Company, 1957.

———. "Confederate Shipbuilding in New Orleans," *Journal of Southern History,* XXVII (February 1962), 87–93.

Merriam, Henry C. "The Capture of Mobile." in *Papers read before the Maine Commandery of the Loyal Legion of the United States.* Vol. II. Augusta: Maine Commandery, 1899.

Milligan, John D. *Gunboats Down the Mississippi.* Annapolis: United States Naval Institute, 1965.

Mobile *Register.* August 5, 1908.

Mobile *Advertiser and Register.* 1861–64.

Montgomery (Alabama) *Advertiser.* 1862–63.

Moore, Frank., ed. *Rebellion Record, A Diary of American Events.* 12 vols ; New York: G. P. Putnam & Company, 1864–1868.

Morgan, James M. and John P. Marquand., eds. *Prince and Boatswain.* Greenfield, Massachusetts: A. Hall & Company, 1915.

———. "The Pioneer Ironclad," *United States Naval Institute Proceedings,* LXXIII (October 1917), 2275–2280.

———. *Recollections of a Rebel Reefer.* Boston: Houghton Mifflin Company, 1917.

Morgan, William H. *Personal Reminiscences of the War of 1861–65.* Lynchburg, Virginia: J. P. Bell Company, Inc., 1911.

Nash, Howard P. Jr. "A Civil War Legend Examined," *The American Neptune* XXIII (July 1963), 197–203.

Moseley, Cynthia E. "The Naval Career of Henry Kennedy Stevens as Revealed in His Letters, 1839–1863." Chapel Hill: Unpublished M.A. Thesis, University of North Carolina, 1951.

Nashville *Daily American,* September 13, 1877.

Neill, John H. Jr. "Shipbuilding in Confederate New Orleans." New Orleans: Unpublished M.A. Thesis, Tulane University, 1940.

New Orleans *Picayune*. 1861–62.

New Orleans *True Delta*. 1861–62.

Newton, Virginius. *Merrimac or Virginia*. Richmond: William Ellis Jones, 1907.

———. "The *Merrimac* or *Virginia*," *Southern Historical Society Papers*, XX (January 1892), 1–26.

Nichols, Roy. "Fighting in North Carolina Waters," *North Carolina Historical Review*, XL (Winter, 1963), 79–82.

Nordoff, Charles. "Two Weeks at Port Royal," *Harper's New Monthly Magazine* XXVII (June 1863), 116.

Official Records of the Union and Confederate Navies in the War of the Rebellion. 31 vols. Washington, D.C.: Government Printing Office, 1894–1927.

Paine, Albert B., ed. *A Sailor of Fortune: Personal Memories of Captain B. S. Osborn*. New York: Doubleday, 1906.

Parker, Foxhall A. "The Battle of Mobile Bay," in *Naval Actions and History, 1799–1898. Papers of the Military Historical Society of Massachusetts*. Vol. XII. Boston: Griffith-Stillings Press, 1902.

———. *The Battle of Mobile Bay*. Boston: A. Williams & Company, 1878.

Parks, William M. "Building a Warship in the Southern Confederacy," *United States Naval Institute Proceedings*, LXIX (August 1923), 1299–1307.

Patrick, Rembert W. *Jefferson Davis and His Cabinet*. Baton Rouge: Louisiana State University Press, 1944.

Perry, Milton F. *Infernal Machines: The Story of Confederate Submarine and Mine Warfare*. Baton Rouge: Louisiana State University Press, 1965.

Porter, John W. H. *A Record of Events in Norfolk County, Virginia*. Portsmouth, Virginia: W. A. Fisher, 1892.

Porter, David D. "A Famous Naval Exploit," *North American Review*, CXLIX (September 1891), 296–303.

———. *Incidents and Anecdotes of the Civil War*. New York: D. Appleton & Company, 1885.

Potter, E. B. and Chester W. Nimitz, eds. *Sea Power: A Naval History*. Englewood Cliffs, New Jersey: Prentice-Hall, Inc., 1960.

Pratt, Fletcher. *Civil War on Western Waters*. New York: Henry Holt Company, 1956.

Pratt, Julius W. "Naval Operations on the Virginia Rivers in the Civil War," *United States Naval Institute Proceedings*, LXXI (February 1919), 185–195.

"Proceedings of the Confederate Congress," *Southern Historical Society Papers* XLIV–LII (1923–1959).

Quad, M. *Field, Fort and Stream*. Detroit: Detroit Free Publishing Company, 1885.

Ramsay, H. Aston. "Wonderful Career of the *Merrimac*," *Confederate Veteran* XXV (July 1907), 310–313.

―――. J. L. Worden, and S. D. Greene. *The Monitor and the Merrimac*. New York: Harper and Brothers, 1912.

Ramsdall, Charles W., ed. *Laws and Joint Resolutions of the Confederate Congress*. Durham: Duke University Press, 1941.

Read, Charles W. "Reminiscences of the Confederate States Navy," *Southern Historical Society Papers*, I (May 1876), 331–413.

Register of Officers of the Confederate States Navy, 1861–65. Washington, D.C.: Government Printing Office, 1931.

Report of Evidence Taken Before a Joint Special Committee of Both Houses of the Confederate Congress, To Investigate the Affairs of the Navy Department. Richmond: G. P. Evans and Company, 1863.

Report of the Chief of the Department of the Military of South Carolina to His Excellency the Governor. Columbia: C. P. Pelham, Printer, 1862.

Reports and Resolutions of the General Assembly of the State of South Carolina, 1861–65. Columbia: C. P. Pelham, Printer, 1866.

Richmond *Dispatch*. 1861–64.

Richmond *Examiner*. 1861–65.

Richmond *Whig*. 1861–63.

Roberts, Walter. *Semmes of the Alabama*. Indianapolis: The Bobbs-Merrill Company, 1938.

Robinson, William M. Jr. *The Confederate Privateers*. New Haven: Yale University Press, 1928.

Rochelle, James H. *Life of Rear Admiral John Randolph Tucker*. Washington, D.C.: The Neale Publishing Company, 1903.

Roman, Alfred. *The Military Operations of General Beauregard in the War Between the States, 1861 to 1865*. 2 vols.; New York: Harper & Brothers, 1884.

Ropp, Theodore. "Anaconda Anyone," *Military Affairs*, XXVII (Summer, 1963), 71–76.

Rose, F. P. "The Confederate Ram *Arkansas*," *Arkansas Historical Quarterly*, XII (Winter, 1953), 333–339.

Roske, Ralph J. and Charles Van Doren. *Lincoln's Commando: The Biography of Commander W. B. Cushing, U.S.N*. New York: Harper, 1957.

Ross, FitzGerald. *Cities and Camps of the Confederate States*, ed. Richard Harwell. Urbana: University of Illinois Press, 1958.

Rowland, Dunbar., ed. *Jefferson Davis, Constitutionalist: His Letters, Papers and Speeches*. 10 vols.; Jackson, Mississippi: Little & Ives Company, 1923.

Russell, William H. *My Diary North and South*, ed. Fletcher Pratt. New York: Harper & Brothers, 1954.

Sandersville *Central Georgian*. March 9, 1862.

Savannah *Republican.* 1861–64.

Savannah *Morning News.* 1861–64.

Scharf, J. Thomas. *History of the Confederate States Navy.* New York: Rogers & Sherwood, 1887.

Scheliha, Victor Ernst Von. *A Treatise on Coast Defense.* London: E. & F. Spon, 1868.

Selfridge, Thomas O. Jr. *Memoirs of Thomas O. Selfridge Jr.: Rear Admiral, U.S.N.* New York: G. P. Putnam's Sons, 1924.

Semmes, Raphael. *Memoirs of Service Afloat during the War Between the States.* New York: J. P. Kennedy & Sons, 1869.

Sinclair, Arthur. "How the *Merrimac* Fought the *Monitor,*" *Hearst's Magazine* (December 1913), 884–894.

Smith, C. Carter, ed. *Two Naval Journals: 1864: At the Battle of Mobile Bay.* Mobile: Graphic Inc., 1964.

———— and Sidney A. *Mobile 1861–1865.* Mobile: Graphic Inc., 1964.

Smith, William M. "The Siege and Capture of Plymouth," in *Personal Recollections of the War of the Rebellion. Addresses Delivered before the New York Commandery of the Loyal Legion of the United States.* Vol. I. New York: New York Commandery, 1891.

Soley, James R. *The Blockade and the Cruisers.* New York: Charles Scribner's Sons, 1890.

South Carolina Convention Documents 1860–1862; Reports of the Special Committee of Twenty one on the communications of His Excellency Governor Pickens together with the Reports of the Heads of the Departments and other papers. Columbia: C. P. Pelham, Printer, 1862.

Sprunt, James. *Chronicles of the Cape Fear River 1660–1916.* Raleigh: North Carolina, Edwards & Broughton Printing Company, 1916.

Statutes at Large of the Provisional Congress of the Confederate States of America. Richmond: R. M. Smith, Printer, 1864.

Stephen, Walter W. "The Brooke Guns from Selma," *Alabama Historical Quarterly,* XX (Fall, 1958), 462–475.

Still, William N. Jr. *Confederate Shipbuilding.* Athens: University of Georgia Press, 1969.

————. "Selma and the Confederate States Navy," *Alabama Review,* XIV (January 1962), 19–37.

————. "Confederate Naval Strategy: the Ironclad," *Journal of Southern History,* XXVII (August 1961), 330–343.

————. "The Confederate Ironclad *Missouri,*" *Louisiana Studies,* IV (Summer, 1965), 101–110.

————. "The Career of the Confederate Ironclad *Neuse,*" *North Carolina Historical Review,* XLIII (January 1966), 1–13.

————. "Confederate Naval Policy and the Ironclad," *Civil War History,* IX (June 1963), 145–156.

———. "Facilities for the Construction of War Vessels in the Confederacy," *Journal of Southern History,* XXXI (August 1965), 285–304.

Sulivane, Clement L. "The *Arkansas* at Vicksburg in 1862," *Confederate Veteran,* XXV(November 1917), 496–497.

Taylor, Richard. *Destruction and Reconstruction.* New York: D. Appleton and Company, 1900.

The Greyjackets. Richmond: Jones Brothers and Company, 1867.

The War of the Rebellion: A Compilation of the Official Records of the Union and Confederate Armies. 130 vols.; Washington, D.C.: Government Printing Office, 1880–1901.

Thompson, R. M., and R. Wainwright, eds. *Confidential Correspondence of Gustavus Vasa Fox, Assistant Secretary of the Navy 1861–1865;* 2 vols. New York: Naval History Society, 1918–1919.

Tindall, William. "True Story of the *Virginia," Virginia Magazine of History and Biography,* XXXI (January, April 1923), 1–38, 89–145.

Trexler, Harrison A. "The Confederate Navy Department and the Fall of New Orleans," *Southwest Review,* XIX (Autumn 1933), 88–102.

———. *The Confederate Ironclad Virginia (Merrimac).* Chicago: University of Chicago Press, 1938.

Vail, I. E. *Three Years on the Blockade.* New York: The Abbey Press, 1902.

Vandiver, Frank E., ed. *The Civil War Diary of General Josiah Gorgas.* University, Alabama: University of Alabama Press, 1947.

———. Rebel Brass: *The Confederate Command System.* Baton Rouge: Louisiana State University Press, 1956.

Waddell, James I. *C.S.S. Shenandoah: The Memoirs of Lieutenant Commanding James Waddell,* ed. James D. Horan. New York: Crown Publishers, 1960.

Wait, Horatio L. "The blockading service," in *Papers read before the Illinois Commandery of the Loyal Legion of the United States.* Vol. II. Chicago: Illinois Commandery, 1885.

Walke, Henry. *Naval Scenes and Reminiscences of the Civil War in the United States, on the Southern and Western Waters During the years 1861, 1862, and 1863.* New York: F. R. Reed and Company, 1877.

Walker, Jennie M. *Life of Captain Joseph Fry: the Cuban Martyr.* Hartford, Connecticut: The J. B. Burr Publishing Company, 1874.

Walker, Peter F. *Vicksburg: A People at War, 1860–1865.* Chapel Hill: University of North Carolina Press, 1960.

Wallace, J. W. *Cases Argued and Adjudged in the Supreme Court, 1863–1874.* 23 vols.; Washington, D.C.: 1864–76.

Waring, Mary. *Miss Waring's Journal: 1863 and 1865,* ed. Thad Holt, Jr. Mobile: Graphic Inc., 1964.

Waterman, George C. "Notable Events of the War," *Confederate Veteran,* VI (1898), 59–62, 170–173, 390–394; VII (1899), 16–21, 449–452, 490 492;

(1898), 59 62, 170–173, 390–394; VII (1899), 16–21, 449–452, 490–492; VIII (1900), 21–24, 53–55; IX (1901), 24–29.

Welles, Gideon. *Diary of Gideon Welles Secretary of the Navy Under Lincoln and Johnson,* ed. Howard K. Beale. 3 vols.; New York: W. W. Norton Company, 1960.

Werner, H. O. "The Fall of New Orleans, 1862," *United States Naval Institute Proceedings,* LXXVI (April 1962), 78–86.

West, Richard S. Jr. *Mr. Lincoln's Navy.* New York: Longmans, Green & Company, 1957.

————. *The Second Admiral: A Life of David Dixon Porter, 1819–1891.* New York: Coward-McCann, 1937.

————. *Gideon Welles, Lincoln's Navy Department.* New York: The Bobbs-Merrill Company, 1943.

White, Ellsberry V. *The First Iron Clad Naval Engagement in the World.* Portsmouth, Virginia: Privately Printed, 1906.

Whittle, William C. "Opening of the Lower Mississippi," *Southern Historical Society Papers,* XIII (December 1895), 560–572.

Wilkinson, John. *The Narrative of a Blockade-Runner.* New York: Sheldon & Company, 1877.

Williams, Francis L. *Matthew Fontaine Maury: Scientist of the Sea.* New Brunswick, New Jersey: Rutgers University Press, 1963.

Williams, T. Harry. *Beauregard: Napoleon in Gray.* Baton Rouge: Louisiana State University Press, 1954.

Williams, G. M. "The first Vicksburg expedition, and the Battle of Baton Rouge," in *Papers read before the Wisconsin Commandery of the Loyal Legion of the United States.* Vol. II. Madison: Wisconsin Commandery, 1890.

Wilmington *Journal,* 1861–65.

Wilmington *Weekly Journal.* 1863–65.

Wilson, Herbert W. *Ironclads in Action.* 2 vols.; London: L. Low Marston & Company, 1896.

Wilson, James H. *Under the Old Flag.* 2 vols.; New York: D. Appleton & Company, 1912..

Winters, John D. *The Civil War in Louisiana.* Baton Rouge: Louisiana State University Press, 1963.

Wright, A. O. "Destruction of the Fleet," *Record of the Confederate Navy,* I (January 1925), 8–10.

Yearns, Wilfred B. *The Confederate Congress.* Athens: University of Georgia Press, 1960.

Index

C.S.S.SAVANNAH.

Scale ⅜ in = 1ft.

Cross Section.